Penguin Handbooks

Greenhouse Gardening

Gardening with a greenhouse can widen your horticultural horizons considerably. With even a simple structure it is possible to by-pass the obstacles imposed by an unsuitable climate and grace your garden with early lettuces, passion-flowers or luscious red tomatoes

Ronald Menage has compiled a comprehensive handbook in *Greenhouse Gardening*, making use of the most up-to-date techniques and information. Among the new developments he describes are capillary watering, natural gas heating and electro-static shading, whilst traditional methods are fully covered as well. Advice on siting and erection, on equipment and fertilizers, and detailed chapters on individual plant species (flowers, vegetables or fruit), will help you set up and use your greenhouse, whether for exotic flowers or out-of-season vegetables.

Ronald Menage is one of the country's leading horticultural journalists, and an expert on greenhouse gardening. His book *Introduction to Greenhouse Gardening* won the 'Best Gardening Book of the Year' award from *Garden News* in 1964. He is also the author of *Greenhouse Manual, Introduction to Greenhouse Gardening, Gardening for Adventure, Growing Exotic Plants Indoors, Keeping House Plants Alive and Well* and *100 Gardening Questions and Answers*. He contributes regularly to all the major British gardening magazines, especially *Popular Gardening* and *Practical Gardening*. A former senior biochemist with a pharmaceutical company, he now lives and works near Wimborne Minster, Dorset, where he gardens and maintains a number of different experimental greenhouses and frames.

Ronald H. Menage

Greenhouse Gardening

Penguin Books

Penguin Books Ltd,
Harmondsworth, Middlesex, England
Penguin Books,
625 Madison Avenue, New York, New York 10022, U.S.A.
Penguin Books Australia Ltd,
Ringwood, Victoria, Australia
Penguin Books Canada Ltd,
41 Steelcase Road West, Markham, Ontario, Canada
Penguin Books (N.Z.) Ltd,
182–190 Wairau Road, Auckland 10, New Zealand

First published in Great Britain by Hamish Hamilton 1974
This revised edition published in Penguin Books 1977

Made and printed in Great Britain by
Richard Clay (The Chaucer Press) Ltd,
Bungay, Suffolk
Set in Monotype Plantin

Contents

Preface

This book is intended as an introduction to home greenhouse gardening, and as an attempt to provide practical guidance. I hope it will help beginners to start right. It should also give useful information to experienced growers, since every attempt has been made to keep the text up to date.

In most cases recommendations given are based on my own personal findings, and I have preferred to give these even when they differ from the conventional view. Some of the information about equipment and technique is published here for the first time.

Everything described in this book is available, and readers will, I hope, find the list of suppliers' addresses on page 237 helpful. There is a great deal of confusion these days about names – I have therefore tried to give those that are most commonly known.

I have tried to cover all the most popular and rewarding aspects of the home greenhouse in useful detail, rather than gloss over the vast possibilities. Once the basics are mastered, there is no limit to what you can grow and enjoy under glass.

R.H.M.

Acknowledgements

This book has benefited from the help of many nurseries, who supplied material for trial, and from the moral support of gardening friends. Special thanks are due to the nurserymen H. Woolman Ltd, the original sponsors of the book. I am also deeply grateful to Mr F. Whitsey, editor of *Popular Gardening*, whose kind approbation has for many years been enormously encouraging to my writing.

1 Introducing Greenhouse Gardening

ADVANTAGES AND BENEFITS

As soon as you acquire a greenhouse, a new and exciting world of gardening opens up. Any plant grown outside is subject to many hazards – extremes of weather alone can cause much disappointment. In the greenhouse you can have almost full control over the environment. You can govern temperature to a considerable extent and provide artificial warmth if necessary. You can decide how much water the plants should receive, and there is better control of feeding, since nutrients are not washed away by rain as they are in the open. The composition of feeds, fertilizers and nutrients can be balanced better to suit individual plant types. Weeds, pests and diseases are easier to avoid and control, and you can take full advantage of sterilized potting composts which make growing so much more reliable. Even light can be adjusted by the use of shading to give maximum light when it is needed and shade when the sunlight is too intense.

A greenhouse can be enjoyed the year round and the winter can be as colourful and interesting as the summer. It is a delightful place in which to work or potter in winter, especially for the retired, the not-so-young or the infirm. A greenhouse can be a place of beauty, and a conservatory for the display of decorative plants, to trap their scent and protect them from weather damage; or it can be used for more 'down-to-earth' and utilitarian purposes – growing fruits and vegetables, cut flowers for sale or home decoration, winter salads, flower show exhibits; for propagating garden plants, raising bedding plants and housing collections of specialist plants like chrysanthemums, orchids, carnations, alpines and the like. With a little warmth, plants from almost the world over can be grown – your scope is unlimited. Greenhouse gardening can be a never-ending adventure.

11

Greenhouse Gardening

Nowadays many people like to make the greenhouse part of the home. There is nothing new in this. The Victorians used to delight in very grand conservatories, elaborately built and filled with exotic plants. There they would entertain friends or take afternoon tea. The modern, more modest equivalent is the garden room or lean-to structure that can be set against the main house. The so-called prefabricated 'home extensions' are also usually well supplied with large windows and perhaps a roof letting in some light. These, too, make useful garden rooms where many house plants will thrive.

Only flat-dwellers can be ruled out as possible candidates for greenhouse gardening proper, although they can still use windows and have miniature window-sill greenhouses and plant cases. Small greenhouses are now available to suit the smallest garden. You don't have to have a garden – a greenhouse can be erected in a concrete yard or even on a flat roof or large balcony.

HOW THE GREENHOUSE WORKS

The Romans built greenhouses or plant houses of a kind, but the structure as we know it only became possible with the discovery of glass and the manufacture of glass sheet. The first building that could be truly described as a greenhouse was erected in the Apothecaries' Garden, Swan Walk, Chelsea, in the seventeenth century, and still exists today. The greenhouse was, therefore, a British invention. The greenhouse eventually became the hobby of the wealthy and in the Victorian era anyone of any distinction had a handsome conservatory or 'hot-house'. With the passing of the Victorians, greenhouse gardening declined and remained a possibility only for the more affluent classes. But since the end of the Second World War, there has been a dramatic change. More people have gardens of their own; they have more spare time and longer holidays. At last people are seeing the wisdom of guarding against the freakish pranks of our climate. There have also been advances in greenhouse design. It is no longer necessary to have one built, or to build your own. The market abounds with prefabricated designs to suit all purposes and situations. Mass production and bulk buying of materials have made possible price ranges to suit all pockets, and more recently plastic has reduced costs even further. However, at this stage we must learn a little about how the greenhouse functions, since glass and plastic have different properties.

At one time glass structures were known as 'sun traps', since they seemed to catch and intensify the sun's warmth in some way and hold it for long periods. This is because sunshine contains rays that we cannot see or appreciate directly, for example those that give us a sun tan. When some of these rays (not all) strike an object they may be transformed into heat energy and be radiated away again as warmth, or the object itself may be heated, warming the air around it. These short-wave rays (of the type easily convertible to heat) can penetrate glass easily; but the longer waves they are converted into cannot escape back through the glass so readily – hence the warmth-trapping effect. Most plastics are more transparent to the long waves and radiant heat. Consequently a plastic greenhouse may change its temperature quickly with the coming and going of sunshine. Even on sunless days, a certain amount of radiant energy from the sun gets through the clouds and this is often sufficient to be trapped and keep a glasshouse comfortably warm. In winter, when the air is bitterly cold outside, a glass greenhouse interior may be at summer temperature if the sun is shining.

COSTS – CAN YOU AFFORD TO BUY AND MAINTAIN A GREENHOUSE?

As I have already pointed out, greenhouse gardening is no longer the sole privilege of the wealthier classes. There are nowadays so many firms supplying a range of designs and sizes at very reasonable prices that it is generally best to select one of these. Often making your own greenhouse proves more expensive than buying a prefabricated type, though in certain cases it may be a good idea: for example, when building in an awkward position against a dwelling and a side wall, or between two houses where there is often a narrow passage. There are firms that make greenhouses and conservatories, garden rooms, etc., to the customer's requirements, but this is usually quite an expensive business. There is little reason why anyone should not be able to afford a small home greenhouse – it is certainly much cheaper than owning a television set!

The question of rates frequently arises. Again, rates need be no problem. You have to be careful if you are erecting a lean-to greenhouse, conservatory, or garden room, against a dwelling so that it becomes part of the house: in this case there may be a few building regulations to comply with, and nearly always there will be a *small* increase in your rates. Free-standing greenhouses in the garden, however, are often completely immune from rates, particularly if under 1,000 cubic feet capacity. Even so, it is always wise to consult your local authority because regulations differ from place to place. If you are renting a property it is also wise to consult the landlord before erecting any garden buildings.

Greenhouse running costs depend on what you intend to do with your greenhouse. There are numerous possibilities, and a glance through the following pages will reveal several of them in greater detail. In very few cases will greenhouse gardening be a drain on your finances. Often it will save you money and even bring a profit. This is particularly so if you grow your own bedding plants for the garden, house plants, cut flowers, and vegetables and fruits like lettuce, cucumbers, tomatoes and strawberries – all of which are quite easy to grow, and expensive to buy in the shops.

You can do more with a greenhouse if you can provide a little winter warmth, but this need not cost a great deal if you go about it in the right way. The subject of heating costs, saving fuel, and economical heating apparatus is dealt with in Chapter Three, which is entirely devoted to greenhouse heating.

Greenhouse plants are generally quite cheap if bought as young specimens or rooted cuttings. This is in fact the best way to buy, and you will get better results than by purchasing large, well-established plants; older plants are not so happy about sudden changes of environment. One of the most economical ways to build up a collection of popular and unusual plants is by growing from seed. Some of the rarer greenhouse bulbs and orchids may be quite expensive, and in these cases a full study should be made of the subject before risking much expenditure; when possible, try the cheaper varieties first. Some of the exotics that need constant warmth may also be costly, and again you should make sure that you can provide the conditions they require to keep them growing.

A greenhouse is usually supplied with basic essentials like staging. As you progress you will find that you can add refinements and equipment. Few of these are absolutely essential, and the most important are fortunately fairly cheap (see Chapter Four). Various gadgets and automatic aids can be added as your finances allow.

GREENHOUSE TYPES AND THE PLANTS YOU CAN GROW

Greenhouses are classified according to the temperatures maintained, as follows:

Unheated greenhouse	No heating at any time
Cold house	Not allowed to fall below freezing
Cool house	Minimum about 40/45°F (4/7°C)
Warm house	Minimum about 55°F (13°C)
Stove house (sometimes called 'hot-house')	Minimum about 65/75°F (18/24°C)

These classifications are not too rigid. Sometimes the 40/45°F house is described as a 'cold' greenhouse. The 55°F house called a warm house above may be described as an 'intermediate house'.

The most popular type of greenhouse is the type we describe here as the cool greenhouse. With a winter minimum of about 40°F (4°C) you can grow a vast range of plants from all over the world. Most of the plants from temperate zones will thrive, and many sub-tropical and tropical plants can be kept alive over winter, although they may not actually grow or prove decorative or useful then. The cool house is certainly the one to aim for if you are planning a general purpose greenhouse for growing all the favourite pot plants, for raising bedding plants and for garden propagation. For this reason this book is mainly concerned with cool house work, but plants needing only the protection of glass, and no artificial heat at all, are also dealt with, together with plants demanding only frost protection. At this point it is worth drawing some extra attention to the possibilities of the unheated and the cold greenhouse.

THE UNHEATED GREENHOUSE

The sole purpose of this greenhouse is to give protection from the excesses of nature – wind, cold and rain. It can be used to grow better anything that normally grows outdoors in this country. However, it should be realized that hardy plants often object to being coddled with extra warmth and humidity and perhaps poor ventilation; the function of the unheated greenhouse is to give weather protection only. It is ideal for all those plants that flower early and may be prone to weather damage, for example camellias, alpines, some of the more tender small shrubs, innumerable spring flowering bulbs, lilies, some succulents and cacti, ferns, fuchsias, hydrangeas, carnations, chrysanthemums, and many garden annuals and biennials grown in pots. In the last case, a remarkable standard of perfection can be achieved – often so high that common annuals become something quite exotic!

An unheated greenhouse can be provided with warmth at any time if convenient or necessary – say in early spring to start plants growing or for seed sowing and so forth. It can also be used to give winter protection from frost or excessive cold to the roots of the more tender garden plants grown in terrace pots, small tubs, and other ornamental containers. Sometimes roots can also be taken up from garden borders and stored in an unheated greenhouse whilst they are dormant over winter.

THE COLD GREENHOUSE
(not allowed to fall below freezing)

This type can be used for most of the purposes described for the unheated greenhouse, but often it is best to make use of the warmth for getting earlier flowers or crops and for protecting plants that are invariably killed or severely damaged by frost in the open. In those parts of the country where the winter is severe, all those plants that can be seen thriving outdoors only in the west and south will be very happy. The cold greenhouse is the best for growing many bulbs to perfection, and most of the spring flowering kinds will benefit by being *gently* forced, and will flower much earlier. A wide range of plants that are mistakenly thought to need the cool house can also be grown quite easily in the lower temperature of the cold greenhouse. These include such popular subjects as cinerarias, salpiglossis, calceolarias, and – believe it or not – the exotic bird-of-paradise flower, *Strelitzia regina* (usually classed as a warm house plant). There is much scope for further experiment here.

YOU CAN HAVE MORE THAN ONE TYPE OF GREENHOUSE

Although it is usually best to begin with one type of greenhouse, usually unheated, cold or cool, there is no reason why you should not go in for, say, all three types of greenhouse gardening at the same time. The best way to do this is to have a greenhouse divided into compartments, each maintained to give the right conditions for the plants. Of course, you can always add other greenhouses, separately sited, to your garden if you prefer. This subject is dealt with fully in the next chapter.

Those plants preferring a fair warmth can be economically grown in warmed frames inside a cold or cool greenhouse, provided they are reasonably low-growing and compact. See also pages 57 and 59.

2 The Structure

You will now see that there are many ways in which you can use a greenhouse. Before choosing a structure it is vital to be clear in your mind about what you want it for and what you propose to do. If you are taking up greenhouse gardening for the first time, or are still vague about the scope of the subject, it would be advisable to glance through the book and return later to the matter of choosing a greenhouse discussed in this chapter. The market now abounds with different designs, shapes, sizes and constructional materials, and since one might suit your purpose better than another, a detailed account of them is given here.

CHOOSING PLANTS TO SUIT A GREENHOUSE AND VICE VERSA

A common mistake made by beginners in greenhouse gardening is that they try to grow too many different kinds of plant under the same conditions. Thought must be given to how much warmth, light or shade, or humidity and ventilation, the plants require, and every attempt made to provide the best environment. Too often, for example, cacti (which like light and a dry atmosphere) are put with shade-loving plants preferring moist air; or you may see hardy plants, which only need protecting from frost, in a cool greenhouse where the temperature is unnecessarily high for them. More absurdly, plants that may eventually reach a considerable height are sometimes given a house with a very low roof, and large, high greenhouses used for nothing but low salad crops or the like, which could be more economically grown in frames.

With care and understanding a surprisingly wide range of different plants can be grown in the same greenhouse if proper consideration is given to where they are placed and how they are treated. More information on this will be found in Chapter 6. However, some greenhouse designs may be better suited to plant collections than others. Also, if you are only interested in growing, for example, grapes, orchids, carnations or alpine plants, you can get structures specially designed for them.

BASIC TYPES OF GREENHOUSE STRUCTURE

There are three basic types of greenhouse structure: the partially glazed (with a dwarf wall of timber, brick, concrete or some other material, and the framework on top); the totally glazed or glass to ground; and the lean-to (see Fig. 1). The lean-to can have a dwarf wall or it can be glass to ground. Formerly one often saw a sunken type, called a 'pit' by professional gardeners, which served

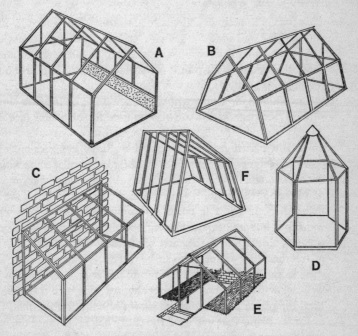

1 *Basic Modern Greenhouse Shapes*
A: plant house (this may be totally glazed or have a base wall on one or both sides). B: Dutch light shape. C: lean-to. D: round house. E: sunken house or 'pit'. F: high south wall.

much the same purpose as the wall type. However, as the pit is a framework over an excavation in the ground, less heat is lost and temperatures tend to be more constant. For this reason it was popular for propagation and for plants demanding warmth, but it is not ideal for the small, home garden. It is not easy to install and requires proficiency; drainage can be a problem on some sites; the soil dug out has to be put somewhere; and it may take a good deal of time and effort to erect. Even so, provided the excavation is well done, it is still possible to get a framework made to fit, assuming you are prepared to meet the extra expense this will entail – the door end will be below ground level and you will have to enter the greenhouse via a flight of steps.

The partially glazed greenhouse

This type is sometimes called a 'plant house'. It is generally fitted with staging and used for growing collections of pot plants; thus most of the work is done at waist level, which can be important for the not-so-young or for people with some infirmity. The area under the staging usually receives less light, which is an advantage if you are growing shade-loving plants. It should not be used for storing rubbish (see page 74). It can also be used for blanching (see page 204).

Partially glazed greenhouses may have brick, concrete or timber bases. Sometimes one finds bases of asbestos or similar compositions, but these retain less heat than a more substantial base wall, and one advantage of the partially glazed house is that heat losses are less than when the glass is taken to ground level. However, where warmth is important much depends on the site. On an open sunny site, any obstruction to the entry of the sun's radiation means a loss of free heat. In winter this can be a disadvantage; on clear days the sun can shoot up the temperature under glass even when it is well below freezing outside. Greenhouses with base walls are not ideal for plants that have to be grown initially from ground level or for tall plants that will need the entire height, because the lower regions may be considerably shaded by the side walls. Plenty of light is always worth having – you can always give shade if necessary.

The totally glazed or glass-to-ground greenhouse

This type is probably the most versatile of all and the best choice if a general purpose structure is required. It can be fitted with staging or not, as preferred. If staging is fitted there is usually sufficient light underneath to keep many plants happy. When shelving is fitted too, it is surprising how many plants can be successfully grown, because there is usually good overall penetration of light. As I have already said, it is easy enough to provide shade when necessary. A glass-to-ground house can, if necessary, be converted to a partially glazed house by filling in the lower panes with timber or plastic, or simply by replacing the glass. However, such treatment may well spoil the structure or its appearance. A glass-to-ground house is excellent for all tall plants and plants like tomatoes and chrysanthemums. Climbers can be accommodated, and there is plenty of scope for baskets and plants in hanging containers. Sometimes it is convenient to have staging only on one side, reserving the other for plants grown from ground level (see figure, page 72). A possible disadvantage of glass to ground, especially when there is a path alongside the greenhouse, is that one runs the risk of accidentally kicking the glass and striking it with wheelbarrows or the like.

The totally glazed greenhouse is also a good choice for many plants or crops to be grown on a semi-commercial scale or in quantity, such as winter salad crops and cut flowers. Although some of these can be grown just as successfully in frames, which are more economical to heat, if much personal attention and cultivation is needed it is more convenient and pleasant to work inside during the winter.

The lean-to greenhouse

The most popular form of the lean-to is the conservatory or garden room and home extension built against the dwelling and entered through a communicating door. A lean-to can also be built against a garden wall or against some garden building or garage. It is best for a lean-to to face south; there is then more scope because of the wider range of plants that can be grown with plenty of light available. However, even a north-facing lean-to can be useful for many shade-loving plants. In fact, many favourite greenhouse pot plants

21

enjoy the shade in such circumstances, and a north-facing lean-to can become quite a successful conservatory if you choose your plants carefully.

Lean-to structures can of course have base walls or be totally glazed according to preference. Most of the garden-room type lean-to buildings have base walls to give some privacy and reduce heat loss in winter. You may be interested to know that an all-glass lean-to is no good for sunbathing: the rays that give a tan are absorbed by the glass and converted to warmth!

A lean-to is very economical to heat. Often it will derive sufficient warmth from a dwelling to keep it frost free. A lean-to erected against a sunny garden wall may hold considerable warmth overnight. The wall stores the heat it receives during the day and gives it out at night.

For vines, climbers, wall shrubs and many fruits, the lean-to makes a splendid home; the plants can be trained against the rear wall or up into the roof (see also Chapter 12). It is also useful when you want to maintain fairly high temperatures all year round.

GREENHOUSE SHAPE AND OTHER STRUCTURAL DESIGNS

The conventional greenhouse shape with vertical sides and gabled roof should not be dismissed just for the sake of being different and modern. For many years it has been found satisfactory and it uses space to the best advantage. The pitch of the roof leads condensation to one side and sheds rain well. You will notice that some greenhouses have the sides sloping at an angle – called the Dutch light design. Such structures can be made up from standard frames, and Dutch lights can be used for protecting low-growing flowers and vegetables; but the advantage of a side with a slight slope is that there is less glass thickness for the sun's rays to travel through. However clear a glass may appear to be to the eye, some light is always absorbed. This can make a slight difference to some crops, though it is of concern mostly to the commercial grower interested in early produce. However, a greenhouse with an excessive side slope can be undesirable for the home garden. It may be difficult to work close to the sides and is certainly not advisable if you want much staging. Some greenhouses are given a slightly circular slope to the roof and sides by panes placed at suitable angles; this also permits maximum light. Fortunately most of them are also designed for use in the home garden, and they can generally be equipped with the usual staging if desired.

In recent years several designs have appeared that have obviously been made for appearance or novelty rather than any serious purpose. A bad fault is a roof that is too flat. This often leads to condensation drip which can be a nuisance in the conservatory or home extension type of structure; and in winter it can cause constantly moist conditions at the roots of plants, which may lead to rot.

A notable original design is the high south wall type (see Fig. 1). This must have the high side facing south, since it is angled to capture the maximum solar radiation in winter. It is particularly useful for light-loving tall subjects like tomatoes and chrysanthemums; grow these along the high south wall and use the staging on the north side for pot plants that prefer less light.

There are a number of circular or hexagonal greenhouses available. This shape is not really new, and was popular in Victorian times for ornamental conservatories. A round house can look very attractive as a garden feature and when filled with decorative plants. It does not use space so well, and if you are looking for a practical design for general-purpose growing it would be advisable to choose the more conventional square or rectangle. A useful design is that which combines glass to ground on one side with a dwarf wall or boarded base on the other.

Another practical design is the combination greenhouse which has a shed attached. The shed may be alongside, so that the greenhouse forms a lean-to, or it may be at one end. The shed can be used for potting and/or the storage of the usual garden tools. It should of course make an ideal potting compartment. It is best if the greenhouse can be entered from the shed, rather than the shed entered from the greenhouse. This means less opening of doors in winter, letting cold air into the greenhouse section. The lean-to type of shed/greenhouse should have the glass facing south, if possible, when sited.

Another recent appearance is the mini-greenhouse. This is little

23

more than a plant case, generally mounted on legs for convenience. It is best used for choice plants of the decorative kind, although it can make a useful propagator and it can be sited inside the greenhouse too. A plant case or mini-greenhouse inside can be heated to a high temperature economically, so that tropical plants can be grown in it – provided slow-growing or small subjects are chosen. Small orchids and plants like African violets do very well in heated plant cases. A plant case of recent design is a tall structure mounted on castors, which can be opened up rather like a screen to give easy access to the plants displayed on shelves. It is called by the makers 'the flower tower'.

Compartments and extensions

I have already stressed that it is important to give plants the environment they prefer with respect to temperature, humidity, ventilation and so on. So that this can be done for a wider range of plants under the same roof, it is useful to have the greenhouse divided by partitions – one or more – with communicating doors For example, a greenhouse divided into two compartments could have the first section, at the door end, devoted to plants needing little warmth or none at all, with the section at the far end used for more tender subjects. Similarly, one section can be well ventilated, if necessary, and the other maintained at a high humidity for those plants that like it. If you want several sections at different temperatures, the centre section or sections should be hottest and the outer sections coolest. This way heating is more economical because losses are reduced. It is far better and more convenient than having several separate greenhouses.

Most makers now provide designs that allow for the addition of partitions, which can be easily fitted at any time. If you make an extension to your greenhouse it may be worth constructing it as an extra compartment.

It is a common mistake for beginners to start off with a greenhouse that is rather small. Before long it is bursting at the seams with plants – and overcrowding often leads to trouble and disappointment. It is therefore wise to buy a greenhouse that can be extended, if and when the need arises, and to leave enough space for an extension when erecting it.

CONSTRUCTION MATERIALS

The warmth-trapping effect of glass structures has already been briefly dealt with (page 13), in comparing glass with plastic. There are some further differences which are of considerable importance and must be taken into account when buying a greenhouse.

Plastic greenhouses

It must be understood that none of the plastics is a substitute for glass. Plastics are by nature very much softer. They can be scratched and abraded much more easily. In some circumstances they may weather badly, particularly on windy sites where there is much wind-blown grit, sand or dust. Unfortunately, once this happens dirt seems to collect on the surface and become ingrained. It is difficult to clean off, and attempts to do so only make things worse.

Some plastics also change chemically with time and on exposure to sunlight over long periods. They usually become brittle and may crack and disintegrate.

A further disadvantage is that water does not wet a plastic surface and form a film as it does on glass. This often causes condensation to collect in droplets, which may drip constantly, especially if the roof is insufficiently sloped. The drips can be annoying to anyone working below, particularly in the home-extension type of lean-to, and harmful to plants, since they cause excessively wet conditions during the winter months when careful watering is essential. The effect is worse when corrugated plastic sheeting is used for a roof and the slope is only slight. Condensation then drips from the entire length of the corrugations.

In their present state of development, plastics are not really a wise choice for a permanent greenhouse, which is probably to be heated artificially. Only a few plastics of the more expensive type can be compared with glass for aesthetic appearance and clarity – clean, clear, sparkling glass is extremely pleasing. Some of the more flimsy plastics sag and buckle, and move about with the wind. They can look terrible and do anything but enhance the appearance of a garden when used in a structure.

25

In spite of these severe criticisms – which could well make plastic manufacturers my lifelong enemies! – plastics have a number of distinct advantages. They are lightweight and unbreakable, and are therefore excellent for temporary plant protection, emergency repair, and for use when glass is impractical owing to breakage risk. In the garden and the greenhouse, in fact, they have innumerable uses, which will be brought to the reader's attention later in this book. Used with common sense and understanding, they can be invaluable and may replace glass in many instances.

There are a number of different types of plastic, classified according to their chemical composition. Polythene is perhaps the best known and most frequently used. Ordinary polythene is not recommended for outdoor garden work. It soon deteriorates on exposure to sunlight and disintegrates. For making temporary greenhouse structures, use a special grade resistant to ultra-violet light. Even then, don't expect it to last more than about two to three years (much depends on the site).

Flexible but stronger plastics are available, such as acetate sheeting and PVC, often sold under trade names. Some are re-inforced with wire. These are of course longer lasting. For more permanent structures, rigid PVC sheets can be used, and these are usually corrugated for strength. One of the best grades for green-house construction is the ICI Novolux, which is guaranteed for a number of years against weathering. ICI issue plans and designs for several 'greenhouse-type' structures, which are attractive but have practical disadvantages for serious greenhouse work (see Greenhouse shape, page 22).

All plastics used as a replacement or in place of glass should be as clear, colourless and transparent as possible. Great care should be taken in cleaning so as not to scratch the surface. Only one shading paint – Coolglass, the electrostatic type described on page 52 – is suitable for application to plastic without fear of scratching on removal. Most plastics should not be brought into close contact with creosoted timber, since they may become dis-coloured or damaged.

A recent plastic, perhaps the nearest to glass in appearance and hardness, is Transpex. This is an acrylic plastic similar to that from which dentures are made. At present it is expensive, but it is a good choice when you require something unbreakable that resembles glass as closely as possible.

Greenhouse framework and glazing

Very recently there has been a great swing in favour of aluminium alloy framework. This material has valuable properties that make it ideal. It is rust-proof and rot-proof and it cannot warp. It is very resistant to oxidation and the effects of weather, and needs no painting, treatment or maintenance whatsoever. A good aluminium framework will last more than a lifetime with practically no attention. This high praise, however, applies only to modern aluminium alloys. Some of the early alloys were far from weather resistant, and later development was greatly influenced by research into alloys of aluminium resistant to seawater and suitable for marine use. Aluminium framework is relatively cheap, and it is possible to make very sophisticated glazing bars, permitting various simple forms of glazing, with clips alone. The various types of patent glazing produced by the manufacturers of aluminium houses all have the advantage of quick and easy glazing and simple removal of glass if necessary. Most aluminium houses are therefore easily taken down and can soon be put up again elsewhere if the need arises.

The Robinson greenhouse (see Appendix), has unique glazing strips instead of the usual clips. This eliminates the possibility of glass cracking through the uneven pressure of clips, gives closer contact of the overlaps, keeping out dirt and algae, and lends a neat streamlined appearance to the exterior of the glazing bars.

A new aluminium frame is shiny, but after a time the metallic sheen is lost due to a coating of protective aluminium oxide that forms through exposure to the air. More expensive frames are stove-enamelled, and this finish retains its attractive appearance indefinitely. An aluminium framework can be painted with a gloss paint if desired, but you should avoid this if possible.

Aluminium frames can look out of place in some surroundings. They seem to fit modern gardens laid out in a formal style, and they go well with modern architecture; but in informal settings, and near period buildings, they can appear an intrusion. In such cases mellow timber might blend better, although white-painted frames can also look pleasant.

Galvanized steel is also used for framework, although on comparing prices and properties it is difficult to see any advantage over aluminium. Galvanized steel needs painting regularly. If the zinc galvanized layer is damaged to expose the steel below, rust will start corrosion. Steel is also much heavier and less easy to work. Both aluminium and galvanized steel frames can now be bought with white or green plastic finishes (see Appendix). White-coated aluminium is particularly attractive, and is worth considering where the shiny or metallic appearance of the natural alloy looks out of place.

All metal frameworks are of course very strong (or should be). They will usually take the weight of hanging baskets or plant containers, and shelving, without fear of the roof collapsing. They can usually be assembled quickly and easily with a spanner and screwdriver, single-handed, even by very elderly or infirm people. Glazing can be easily done either with plastic strip and clips (simple patent glazing) or with a special non-hardening plastic putty. Ordinary linseed oil putty must never be used on metal frames. There are special compositions that never set hard, allowing the frame and glass to expand and contract with temperature so that the glass does not crack or break.

It is sometimes said that metal greenhouses are cold. This is doubtful. It is true that metal conducts heat better than timber, but in a metal greenhouse there is less area of frame and consequently more light, with greater benefit from the sun's warmth. In any greenhouse the area of frame compared with the area of glass is so small that the difference is negligible in any case. However, in the dwarf wall-type greenhouse, or plant house (page 19), metal panelling for the base walls should be strictly avoided unless they are well lagged. A metal base will become icy cold like refrigerator plates in winter, resulting in a fantastic heat loss.

All timber greenhouses need maintenance from time to time, often every year. This means painting or coating with one of the special timber dressings, to restore appearance and ensure preservation. Perhaps the most popular wood is so-called western red cedar, or similar 'cedar' types, which have an attractive appearance and blend almost anywhere. They are remarkably weather-resistant and have little tendency to warp or attract wood-destroying insects and fungi likely to cause rotting. Teak and oak are some other useful timbers. Cheap timbers and softwoods are best avoided unless you are prepared to spend considerable time each year in their restoration and preservation.

The glass used in greenhouses is 24-ounce sheet. It must be clear, colourless and of good quality. Opaque or coloured glass is not suitable.

WHAT TO LOOK FOR WHEN BUYING A GREENHOUSE

Only you will know how much you can spend, and how large a greenhouse you can accommodate. Attention has already been drawn to the advantages of extendibility and compartments. It may be an advantage to have a structure requiring little maintenance or none at all, depending on the time you can afford. The appearance of the surroundings may have to be taken into account. Check on the advantages and disadvantages of the different greenhouse types outlined on page 19, and do make sure you know what you want to do with your greenhouse.

In general, look for strength of structure and workmanship of high standard. Timber with knot holes and imperfections will not do. If you have a house with a boarded base in mind, make sure that it is substantial and not 'matchboarding'. Ordinary putty is best avoided if possible. There are excellent timber houses on the market having frames in which the glass is just slid in through grooves; an example is the Alton greenhouse (see Appendix). Believe it or not, this form of glazing does not let in the rain, and the glass can always be instantly slid out for maintenance or access to the roof, or even for extra ventilation. Pre-glazed sections are available too, but don't overlook the need for an adequate roof slope.

Good ventilation is always important. See that the house has adequate vents. A small house will need at least one top and one side vent (see also page 45). Doors and vents must fit properly when closed; draughts will push up fuel bills drastically in winter. Often a sliding door is useful. It can be used for extra air, like a ventilator, and will not slam – but such doors can sometimes be ill-fitting. Don't buy the first greenhouse you see. Write to a wide range of the firms who advertise and get their illustrated catalogues. If possible follow this up with a visit to their show-places. Greenhouses can also be inspected at many garden centres, and at the national shows at Chelsea and Southport. (See also Chapter 4 – vents, fittings, etc.)

The elderly or infirm, or those for some reason unable to erect a greenhouse, may be interested to know that the firm of Robinsons (see Appendix) provides an erection service. Since this eliminates Value Added Tax, it also constitutes a considerable financial saving.

The Robinsons range of greenhouses is also designed without elaborate foundations. Instead, there are ground anchors that can be bolted to the frame after erection. You only need to make a small hole for each anchor and to fill this with a small amount of liquid concrete. This avoids mixing and carrying large quantities of concrete and lifting heavy concrete foundation plinths. See also page 31.

SITING THE GREENHOUSE

If possible, choose an open site which gets all the sun available – unless you are only interested in shade-loving plants. The conventional rectangular greenhouse is best orientated east–west so that the best use can be made of winter sunlight. You may then only need to shade the south side in summer. It is wise to put the greenhouse as near the dwelling as possible. This allows convenient running of electricity and mains water to the greenhouse. It also means less walking about in the open for the gardener during rainy or snowy weather, and the greenhouse is more likely to get regular visits. Siting the greenhouse near the dwelling is particularly desirable if you have a hot water boiler that needs regular stoking with fuel from indoors.

Make sure the site is well drained. Hollow ground is best avoided since it can attract frost as well as water. On very exposed sites some form of windbreak on the side of the prevailing wind is desirable. This can be a belt of conifers (small ones), at a reasonable distance so as not to cast a shadow, or a wall or fence. Don't have trees anywhere near by. They cast shade, make the glass dirty, endanger it with the possibility of falling branches, and may harbour pests and diseases likely to attack greenhouse plants. Their roots may upset foundations too. As already mentioned, a potting shed near at hand is desirable. If the ideal site is not possible, don't be deterred from having a greenhouse. You will merely have to select plants that like the conditions you have to offer – there's always something that will grow anywhere.

ERECTION HINTS AND MAINTENANCE

Putting up a prefabricated greenhouse is simple and it can often be done without help in a weekend or so. Elaborate foundations are rarely necessary, but when a frame is to be erected on dwarf walls of brick or concrete some care must be taken. It is wise to get a professional bricklayer to carry out the work if you are not familiar with the job. Plans for the base are issued by the makers of the frame.

With most prefabricated greenhouses it is possible to obtain plinths of concrete to set them on. This gives an excellent firm foundation, easy to lay. The ground should of course be firm and properly levelled. Don't use freshly dug and cleared ground unless it is well firmed. The manufacturers always issue erection instructions and hints on the preparation of the site. If you need to make some form of concrete foundation, it is usually easily done by digging a shallow trench and filling with a very fluid mix of concrete that can find its own level. Concrete blocks or bricks can be set on top if necessary. All greenhouses with boarded base or glass-to-ground are best given a layer of brick or concrete to raise them just above ground level, thus preventing the glass from becoming splashed with mud from roof drip. If concrete plinths are supplied these will be adequate. It is also wise to make a path of concrete or paving slabs around the house, close to the glass, both to prevent splash and for easy access. The Robinsons greenhouses (see Appendix) have a low base of asbestos sheeting – claimed to be as heat insulating as 4-inch brickwork – that cuts out the danger of glass breakage by kicking. Their houses also have a special simple foundation arrangement (see page 30).

A prefabricated greenhouse is usually supplied with the glass cut to size. Should it be necessary to cut glass, place it on several layers of newspaper, mark the line of the cut with a wax pencil or ink pen, and score along the line with an ordinary steel wheel glass cutter available from any builders' merchant. Use a straight edge to guide the cutter. A characteristic harsh hissing sound is emitted if the cutter is scoring the glass effectively. Keep the cutter upright and press down firmly. Turn the glass over on the paper and then tap along the score mark with the 'hammer' part of the cutter. The glass will usually crack easily along the line and can be pulled apart. Narrow edges can be removed by levering off with the notches in the glass cutter handle. Score the glass as already described, then, with the score mark uppermost select a notch that just fits the glass and lever downwards. Rest the glass so that the edge is just over a flat surface to do this.

Most modern, quick-drying, hard gloss paints are suitable for greenhouses, but obviously the surface must be properly prepared. For sealing cracks and leaks, glazing tapes are useful, and there is a variety of widths and types on the market.

For cleaning glass a solution of the water softener Calgon can be used. Just brush on with a soft brush and rinse off with clean water. This chemical is relatively harmless to plants and most greenhouse framework. In obstinate cases, a bath stain remover can be used, but this must be applied with care and kept off the framework in most cases. It will generally clean off the most difficult grime, including lime deposits. It should not be allowed to contact plants. Use according to label instructions.

3 *Heating the Greenhouse*

Providing just enough warmth to keep out frost greatly increases the possibilities of the greenhouse, and a little more widens the scope still further. To heat a greenhouse need not be an expensive business provided the right equipment is used and every effort is made not to waste heat. In fact, this is rarely the case, and much of the equipment on the market could do with considerable improvement. Here an attempt will be made to suggest heating apparatus that will prove economical, and the correct way of using it will be explained as well as ways to avoid heat waste – and hence reduce fuel bills.

ASSESSING HEATING REQUIREMENTS

It is important to try to make a rough estimate of the amount of heat your greenhouse will require. When the exterior is at a lower temperature than the required minimum, heat will of course be gradually lost to the outside. A heater must replace this heat as it is lost and so maintain the desired temperature. It should not raise the temperature unnecessarily, since this will result in waste, but it should be able to supply heat in sufficient quantity to cope with the most severe winters. It should be appreciated that the greater the temperature gradient between the interior and the exterior, the faster heat will be lost.

The heat lost from a greenhouse can be calculated in terms of British thermal units per hour (BTU/hr). The heat yield of fuels and the heat output of heaters can also be assessed in terms of the same units. It follows that, if you know the amount of heat lost from your greenhouse at the coldest time of the year, you can choose a heater that will have sufficient output to make good the loss.

The heat lost will of course depend on the size of the greenhouse, the temperature you want to maintain, the lowest possible outside temperature for the area in which you live, and the materials of construction. Exact estimates are rarely possible, but the assessment is extremely useful and it will save installing heaters that are either totally inadequate or with outputs far in excess of what is necessary.

Since different materials of construction and the surface area they cover will affect the rate at which heat is lost, the calculation involves factors for glass, timber, brick and so on, and most ordinary gardeners find it somewhat tedious. It is always better to make a small overestimate, since if the recommendations given later are followed there is no need to run a heater at the maximum output all the time. For this reason it is convenient to assume the greenhouse is an all-glass structure – which means the maximum heat loss. For greenhouses with base walls and lean-to types, the figures will be lower than those given here; but the following table will be a good guide to the size of heater that should be installed, and you will certainly have no need to worry about problems during an exceptionally severe winter.

The table assumes a possible minimum temperature of approximately 12° frost (20°F or minus 7°C) and the figures should allow you to increase the temperature a few degrees if you wish (see also Conserving warmth, page 43).

Since electricity is an important greenhouse heater fuel, the rating in watts is given for convenience. All good paraffin heaters and hot water heaters fired by solid fuel or oil should have their BTU/hr output ratings stated by the manufacturers. If your greenhouse size does not exactly correspond with the dimensions given in the table, a rough match will do. You can also add your own figures. If, for example, you have a large greenhouse 10 feet by 30 feet long, you can add the BTU/hr rating given for 10 by 20 feet to that given for 10 by 10 feet. For a minimum temperature of 32°F (a frost-free greenhouse) you would therefore need 11,800

APPROXIMATE GREENHOUSE HEATER RATINGS

Green-house size (in feet)	Approximate temperature required							
	35°F (2°C)		40°F (4°C)		45°F (7°C)		50°F (10°C)	
	BTU/hr	Watts	BTU/hr	Watts	BTU/hr	Watts	BTU/hr	Watts
5 × 6	3,000	900	4,000	1,200	5,000	1,500	6,000	1,800
6 × 6	3,600	1,000	4,800	1,400	6,000	1,800	7,000	2,100
6 × 8	4,200	1,200	5,700	1,700	7,100	2,000	8,600	2,500
6 × 10	5,200	1,500	7,000	2,000	8,750	2,500	10,000	2,900
6 × 14	6,200	1,800	8,400	2,500	10,500	3,000	12,500	3,700
8 × 8	5,200	1,500	7,000	2,000	8,750	2,500	10,400	3,000
8 × 10	5,800	1,700	7,800	2,300	9,750	2,900	11,700	3,400
8 × 12	6,600	1,900	8,800	2,600	11,000	3,200	13,200	3,900
8 × 14	7,000	2,000	9,300	2,700	11,600	3,400	14,000	4,200
10 × 10	7,300	2,100	9,800	2,900	12,200	3,500	14,600	4,300
10 × 15	9,700	2,800	12,900	3,800	16,100	4,700	19,200	5,600
10 × 20	11,800	3,500	15,800	4,700	19,700	5,800	23,600	6,900

+ 7,300 = 19,100 BTU/hr, or about 5,600 watts if electricity is used. In a case like this two 3,000-watt electric heaters could be installed.

If we consider a small greenhouse, say 5 by 6 feet, and we again use electricity, we see that a 1,000 watt heater is more than adequate, though a more powerful heater, with an efficient thermostat, can be used without wastage; it will simply be switched on less frequently. However, for technical reasons it is less economic to have unnecessarily high ratings.

The importance of the thermostat

In case some readers are not familiar with the thermostat and its operation it may be worth explaining more fully. Of vital importance for economic greenhouse heating and for effective temperature control for the plants' well-being, a thermostat is any device that controls temperature by regulating the fuel supply to the heater. It usually works by certain metals expanding or contracting with temperature change; this movement controls the electrical contacts, the flow of fuel, or the flow of air to solid fuel, so that the speed with which it burns is regulated. In the case of electricity very accurate thermostatic control is possible; for this reason some other types of heater use electricity to operate motors or electromagnets, which govern the flow of oil, air or solid fuel.

Accurate and reliable thermostatic control is a feature to look for when buying a greenhouse heater; more information will be found under the various heater-type headings in the following pages. A thermostat will usually have a dial graduated in degrees and ranging from just above freezing to about 90°F (32°C). The indicator on the knob should be set to the temperature required. Sometimes the actual temperatures are not indicated, in which case the temperature must be set in the first place by reference to a thermometer. In all cases it is wise to check the temperature by referring to an accurate thermometer, and to then adjust the pointer setting if necessary. (See also page 49.)

COST OF GREENHOUSE HEATING

Nowadays it is impossible to assess heating costs accurately, since fuel prices change so rapidly. The price of fuel may also vary from place to place, and according to the quantity in which it is bought; bulk buying can cut costs dramatically. If, then, a particular fuel like anthracite or paraffin is used for domestic heating, it may be worth choosing a similar form of heating for the greenhouse.

If the BTU heat output of a fuel is known, it is possible to make a rough assessment of cost from its current price. This assumes you know the rating of your heater and the amount of heat needed in terms of BTU, which you can get from the table already given. The BTU heat output of various fuels is given opposite:

Paraffin:	157,000 BTU/gallon
Solid fuels:	12,000/14,000 BTU/lb
Electricity:	3,412 BTU/unit
Fuel oil:	165,000 BTU/gallon
Liquid propane or butane:	21,500 BTU/lb
Gas fuels:	100,000 BTU/therm

These output figures all assume efficient use of the fuel. Poor heating apparatus and thermostatic control, and bad installation, can waste at least half the possible output. Although the figures may seem to differ widely, there is not really an enormous difference in the price of fuels. At present solid fuel is the cheapest. Then come natural gas and paraffin close together. These are followed by bottled gas and electricity, also close, but the most expensive. I am referring, however, to the *basic cost* of the fuels – *the efficiency with which they can be used must be taken into account.* Electricity, for example, may seem expensive – but it can be used with practically no waste whatsoever, and there are other advantages (see page 39). The efficiency of a certain fuel may cancel out its apparently higher cost.

If you know the price of your fuel per gallon, pound, unit, or therm, and the amount of heat you require per hour for your greenhouse, it is only a matter of simple arithmetic to arrive at a rough cost. Don't forget that the heater will probably be out of use during the warmer months of the year. Also costs will vary depending on where you live in the country. In the colder north, heaters will be used more than in the south, and much will depend upon the severity of the winter.

VARIOUS FORMS OF GREENHOUSE HEATING

Paraffin-oil wick-type heaters

These are still the most widely used in Britain. Both here and in North America, in areas where electricity is reliable and reasonable, a good paraffin heater is handy in case of emergency, whatever other form of heating may be installed. Abnormally cold weather may also make an extra paraffin heater useful.

Unfortunately there are disadvantages, but some can be overcome. Firstly, a wick heater is difficult to control by thermostat. There are models available, but they need improvement. The main problem at present is to achieve a sufficiently low heat output at the 'off' or pilot-light stage. A flue is a desirable feature, since thermostatic models may produce fumes harmful to plants.

The ordinary oil heater, of course, needs frequent attention so that the wick can be adjusted as the weather fluctuates; otherwise a lot of paraffin may be wasted. It is not an ideal choice if you have to be away from your greenhouse for long periods.

Another important point is that when paraffin burns it produces about its own volume of water released as vapour, and much carbon dioxide. The carbon dioxide doesn't matter – it can be beneficial to plants – but the water vapour can be a nuisance. In winter it is best to keep the greenhouse atmosphere on the dry side, or at any rate not to encourage excessive humidity (see also page 77), so ventilation is necessary. Ventilation is also essential to let in air for combustion of the paraffin. If insufficient air gets to the burner, fumes will be given off. But ventilation means the entry of cold air, so that the full BTU output of the paraffin is not really used to greatest advantage.

Many people have trouble with paraffin heaters, but it is nearly always their own fault. We have already seen that care must be taken over adequate ventilation. The burner must also be kept clean and the wick trimmed according to the maker's recommendation – or again there will be fumes. Don't spill paraffin on the burner when filling so that it can be volatilized by the warmth of the heater, and never use crude paraffin – only the domestic grades are suitable. Crude paraffin, such as 'washings' from garages may contain sulphur compounds and other chemicals that burn to produce gases extremely poisonous to plants. Some plants are extremely sensitive to fumes from paraffin heaters – tomato seedlings, schizanthus and some orchids. Such plants will usually show browning or blackening of the leaf edges and yellowing of foliage. On orchids and thick-leaved plants this may not appear until they have been exposed to the fumes for some time.

When buying an oil heater it is especially important to see that you get one with an adequate BTU/hr heat output. Many oil heaters are far too small for the job they are expected to do.

It is not enough to know that a heater will burn for so many hours on so much paraffin: the heat it yields must be sufficient and you don't get this for nothing. For example, to keep a 6 by 10 foot greenhouse frost-free you will have to have an oil heater burning about a quarter of a pint of paraffin per hour, bearing in mind that the BTU output of paraffin is about 157,000 BTU/gallon (see tables on pages 35 and 36).

Do not use domestic oil heaters for the greenhouse; there are specially designed models. The blue-flame type is recommended.

Because the air supply to the burner is better the paraffin is more efficiently oxidized and there is less risk of fumes. Catalytic-type oil heaters have been known to give off fumes in some circumstances, but these again are mostly used for domestic heating. Greenhouse oil heaters often have pipes or ducts to spread the heat, and this is a good feature to look for; some may have hot water pipes as well as hot air ducts. Often a humidity trough intended to be filled with water is fitted, but this is usually not a good idea. As already pointed out, paraffin gives off a lot of water vapour in burning, and there is rarely any need to increase the humidity still further. Such troughs can, however, sometimes be used for vaporizing pesticides.

Other good design features to look for in oil heaters are the stainless steel lamp chimney, the oil level indicator and the separate oil tank connected to give automatic filling by means of a constant level device. In any case, an oil reservoir of fair size is desirable to reduce the chore of filling. Copper tanks are best since they are less likely to rust and spring leaks.

Other types of oil heater

An oil heater burning waste sump oil from garages is available (page 41). There is also a convector warm-air type, fitted with a flue, burning 35 sec diesel oil or 28 sec central heating paraffin. This can be very accurately controlled by electrically-operated thermostat. The 'low' to 'high' heat output ratio is 1:4 (see Appendix).

Electrical heating

Electricity has already proved itself to be perhaps the most efficient and effective greenhouse heating fuel. Modern technology has made it extremely reliable and there is rarely trouble from breakdown for long periods.

With world shortages of other fuels it seems that electricity will have to become the main fuel eventually, its source being atomic energy. Electrical heating may therefore be a wise investment for new installations. Moreover, electricity can be used in so many other ways that it is worth your while to lead a power cable to the greenhouse (see also Chapter 4, page 61). Advice notes on electrical installation are given by suppliers.

Undoubtedly the most efficient and convenient form of heater for the average home greenhouse is the fan heater. This, used in conjunction with an accurate thermostat, will control temperature to within one or two degrees and there is virtually no waste of heat or fuel. The plants also enjoy the air circulation that the fan gives, and healthy growing conditions prevail. Electrical heating does not contaminate the air with combustion products, and needs no attention at all for very long periods. The air circulation reduces trouble from fungoid diseases dramatically.

Some greenhouse fan heaters have a fan that is constantly running and a built-in thermostat that only switches on the heat when necessary. With this type the warmed air is therefore kept vigorously stirred after the thermostat switches off the heat. This is not an advantage, since the air whirling around the cold greenhouse sides will quickly lose its heat. Still air is a poor heat conductor, but set in motion the heat transfer is rapid. The best fan heater should consequently have a separate thermostat that controls both fan and heat, so that warm air is supplied as needed. When the fan is off the air remains relatively motionless – although there will still be some movement caused by convection. The arrangement gives the benefit of intermittent air circulation, but quick heat loss due to constant circulation is avoided.

Because there is no contamination of the air and no need for extra ventilation, a fan-heated greenhouse can be left practically sealed for several months during severe weather, which cuts waste further. Another important point is that the greenhouse can be lined with polythene to give a 'double glazing' effect (see page 43). With a lining it does not matter if a continuously running fan is used because the warm air cannot come into direct contact with the glass. In large greenhouses it is also possible to use a continuously running fan without fear of too much heat waste, since the greater volume of air will be circulated less quickly. I am assuming, of course, that the fan is an average size.

The usual rating for fan heaters is from about one to three kilowatts. A switch to adjust the heat is a desirable feature. More than one heater can be used if necessary. The fans are usually designed to need little lubrication and maintenance is negligible.

Convection heaters are sometimes used but seem to be uncommon. These consist of a cabinet with holes at the top and bottom. Heating wires inside warm the air which rises to flow out at the top. Cold air is drawn in at the bottom. Another popular electric heater is the tube. Heating tubes are used in a similar way to the old hot water pipes, but since they are hollow, and have only a heating wire inside, they hold little heat when switched off. Fan heaters and convection heaters share this excellent characteristic. It means that they all respond instantly to a thermostat and accurate temperature control is possible.

Ordinary domestic electric fires of any kind are not suitable for the greenhouse and may be very dangerous where there is water and moisture. The radiant heat given by some is damaging to plants.

When it is possible to choose your own thermostat, always select the rod type with variable temperature control. A thermostat should always be checked by reference to a thermometer regardless of whether it has the degrees marked or not. The scale is often inaccurate. Also check after a thermostat has been out of use for some time, before using the heating system again. (See also page 36.)

Hot-water-pipe heating

Hot-water pipes have been used for many years. In their modern form they are still useful, especially when you want to maintain high temperatures. For technical reasons they are more efficient and economical when operating at higher temperatures. Because of their great heat-holding capacity they respond slowly to thermostatic control, but at higher temperatures they react faster.

The water for the pipes can be heated with an immersion heater, but this is not recommended, since it can be very expensive. Generally, solid fuel or oil-fired burners are preferable. Natural gas could also be used and recently a model burning waste sump oil from garages has been introduced (see Appendix). There are a variety of boiler designs on the market; the modern ones are very easy to install and can be operating in a matter of hours. No major alterations to the greenhouse are necessary.

Modern solid fuel boilers are designed to reduce stoking, and the clearing of ash, to a minimum. Most have a reasonable thermostatic control, but obviously this cannot be so accurate as with more easily controlled fuels. Oil-fired boilers are of course semi-automatic and need little attention. Small installations use paraffin as fuel, but larger ones may use fuel oil, with an electric pump to supply the fuel to the boiler. Oil is usually better controlled thermostatically.

In all hot-water-pipe systems the maker's instructions regarding installation must be followed exactly. The pipes must rise gently from the boiler. Nowadays aluminium alloy pipes are preferable to heavy cast iron. Boilers are always rated in terms of heat output as BTU/hr (see table on page 35), but manufacturers will advise if given details of your greenhouse. The pipe length necessary to give out sufficient heat must be considered. An idea of the approximate pipe length needed can be obtained from the following table:

Greenhouse temperature	Length of 4-inch piping (in feet) for every 1,000 cubic feet
45–50°F (7–10°C)	36
50–55°F (10–13°C)	42
60–65°F (15·5–18·5°C)	50
70–75°F (21–24°C)	55
80°F (26°C)	60

It is no use having a large boiler if there is insufficient surface area of pipe to distribute and radiate the heat. Only the fuels recommended by the boiler maker must be used. The pipes are best filled with rainwater or, at first, with other soft water. They may have to be topped up from time to time via the expansion chamber situated at the far end of the pipe run. Large installations may have a mains constant-level system of the water-tank and ball-valve type.

Natural gas heating

Coal gas is not easily adapted for greenhouse heating because both coal gas and its combustion products are poisonous to plants. Natural gas is perfectly safe and on combustion it gives the same products as paraffin – carbon dioxide and water vapour. For natural gas heaters, the comments regarding ventilation and humidity made under Paraffin-oil wick-type heaters apply (page 37), assuming that the natural gas heater is allowed to pass its combustion products into the greenhouse atmosphere.

It is usually more convenient to use a piped natural gas supply. A special natural gas greenhouse heater is available. This is neat, portable to some degree and thermostatically controlled, but there could be a better arrangement for heat distribution. Bottled natural gas – propane or butane – can be used but tends to be expensive. Where gas cannot be piped these can, however, prove convenient. Propane is advisable when the storage bottle is to be kept outside the greenhouse; butane may not volatilize quickly enough in very cold weather. The larger the bottles or cylinders, the more economical these liquefied gases become.

Most amateurs with an average size greenhouse seem to prefer two 42 lb bottles of propane. An automatic changeover valve can be fitted to avoid interruption of the gas supply during replacement of a bottle. The bottles or cylinders do, of course, carry an initial hire charge.

CONSERVING GREENHOUSE WARMTH

Obviously ill-fitting doors and vents and broken glass will let in much unwanted cold air and shoot up fuel bills enormously. All such sources of draught must be dealt with. Many people have found that lining the greenhouse with polythene cuts fuel bills dramatically (a 40 per cent saving is theoretically possible). As mentioned above, electrically heated houses respond well to 'double glazing' of this sort. Use the thinnest polythene available. It must be as clear as possible. Remember that it is the static air trapped between the plastic and the glass that forms the insulation, not the polythene. Don't leave gaps; it should not be possible for air to flow freely between the plastic and glass. In timber houses the lining is easily put up with drawing pins; a half-inch to one-inch space between the glass and plastic is ideal. In metal houses it is usually necessary to fasten pieces of timber batten to the interior of the glazing bars. An adhesive like Evostick will do the trick if used when the surfaces are dry. The drawing pins can then be pressed into the wood. With some aluminium greenhouses that have an inner flange on the glazing bars it is often possible to fasten the polythene with clothes pegs. Special suckers are also available for making the job of lining easier. The edges of polythene sheet can be held together with a smear of glycerine.

Correct positioning of heaters will do much to avoid waste. No part of the greenhouse structure should be allowed to become heated to a temperature higher than necessary. Don't put heating tubes too near the glass. If possible spread them around the greenhouse to even out heat distribution. Unfortunately they are often sold mounted in banks. A fan heater should go in a central position at one end, and a convection heater in the middle of the greenhouse, slightly to one side. Oil heaters should also go slightly to one side to give better heat circulation. During a very severe winter or in an emergency, old blankets or sacking can be thrown over the roof at night to conserve heat, but do not forget to remove these coverings in the morning. Dirty glass will radiate heat more readily, so see that the glass is kept sparkling clean in winter. This will also let in as much of the sun's radiation as possible.

Unless dirt has got between the glass and polythene in a lined greenhouse, and provided the polythene is clear and that light entry is good, a lining can often be left up for the summer months. Much depends on how much light the plants you are growing require. Always line vents separately so that they can be opened.

Storage heaters

Some people have used storage heaters with an off-peak tariff for greenhouse heating. However, this type is difficult to control thermostatically. There may be too much heat at times and not enough when it is wanted. They are best used as background warmth with another heat source maintaining the maximum thermostatically.

Oil heaters with electric heaters

As with storage heaters, an accurately controllable electric heater can be used to keep the maximum level of heat with an economical paraffin heater for background warmth. This way the more expensive fuel has less work to do. However, be sure that if fan heating is used with paraffin lamps there is no current of air likely to upset combustion or interfere with a lamp's working.

4 Accessories and Fittings

As purchased, a greenhouse is usually supplied with the bare essentials only, and most interior and exterior fittings have to be added according to your growing requirements.

VENTILATION

A greenhouse should have one top ventilator and one side vent for every 6 to 8 feet of length, assuming a width of up to about 10 feet. For alpine plants, and many of the more hardy annuals and cut flowers, more ventilation is desirable (see pages 29, 68, 78). It is an advantage not to have the vents all on one side of the greenhouse so that they can be opened according to wind direction (see page 50). In rare cases ventilators are supplied as extras. Should this occur, do not be tempted to cut costs by doing without a ventilator or two. You don't have to open ventilators if it is not necessary, but it is wise to have them so that they can be used freely when the plants require plenty of air.

The conventional hinged ventilator with stay bar is still fitted to many greenhouses, but there are now louvred vents in some aluminium framed houses and sliding vents (patent) in Alton greenhouses that can be fitted as optional extras or alternatives in their timber range. Unfortunately some louvred vents do not close to give an airtight seal. This can lead to draughts in winter and should be checked when purchasing. The sliding vents on the Alton range are reasonably draught-free, and have the advantage of being fitted as bottom ventilation. This is in the glass-to-ground type of house only. Some other types of greenhouses are also designed to permit the vents to be fitted at staging level or at ground level. There is some controversy about which is best, but to keep the greenhouse cool when the weather is very warm the ground-level vents are preferable. The hot air tends to rise quickly and escape through the top ventilators, and this draws cool air in at ground level, thus giving a complete air change. However, it has been argued that cool air, being heavier than warm air, will fall to ground level on entering from a staging level vent.

STAGING

At one time staging was nearly always supplied as the conventional slatted type made up from timber battens. It is now possible to get metal frameworks supporting wire (or plastic) netting, sheet asbestos or some similar material. In winter a net or slatted staging is desirable so that air and warmth can circulate, particularly in

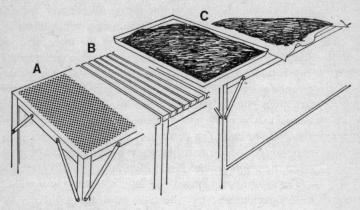

2   *Types of Staging*
A: wire or plastic mesh. B: slats. C: moisture-retaining material (spread over plastic or in trays).

greenhouses equipped with a fan heater. The more recently introduced net-type staging has given excellent growing conditions.

In summer, it is a good idea to cover such staging with plastic sheet or some similar material and spread this with any moisture-retaining substance such as grit, vermiculite or peat (see Fig. 2). This aids greenhouse humidity (see page 77; also Chapter 5, page 67). Some people prefer to make their own staging from brick or concrete, and this, being bulky, will hold considerable warmth. It is quite a good choice for greenhouses where plants demanding moderate warmth are being grown. A substantial staging will absorb warmth during the day, if the greenhouse is heated by the sun, and give it off during the night. Temperatures tend to fluctuate less. It will act in much the same way as a storage heater.

Never take any form of solid or covered staging right up to the greenhouse sides; always leave a gap of a few inches to prevent currents of cold air that may form in the vicinity of the glass from falling and circulating on the surface of the staging.

The whole greenhouse need not be fitted with staging. Sometimes

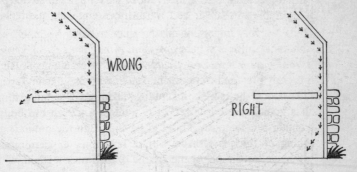

3 *The Wrong and the Right Way to Install Non-slated Staging Leave a gap at the back of the staging so that currents of cold air that descend from the glass do not circulate around the plants. The arrows indicate the direction of flow.*

it is convenient to leave free the side getting the most light, so that plants can be grown from ground level. This particularly applies to glass-to-ground houses and those with glass-to-ground on one side and a dwarf wall or boarded base on the other.

SHELVING

This is useful in the spring, when the greenhouse is often full of propagations from cuttings and plants being raised for bedding. It should not be put up so that shade is cast, to their detriment, on the plants below. In a bright, uncluttered greenhouse there is no point in putting plants on shelving high near the glass in the mistaken belief that they will get more light. Modern greenhouses with narrow glazing bars give almost as much light at staging level. In winter there is a possibility that plants high up on shelving will become chilled if there is little or no artificial warmth.

The many beautiful trailing plants you can grow in hanging containers can also be displayed from pots on shelving. Most greenhouses are designed to take shelving and the makers supply the necessary fittings. For safety these should always be used, since pots of moist compost can be extremely heavy.

THE GREENHOUSE FLOOR

This is a very important matter, since so many beginners seem to think that the floor is to be grown in. *If the ground soil of a greenhouse is used there is invariably trouble.* Today we recommend using only properly prepared composts in containers (see Chapter 7, page 90). The floor is therefore best kept for walking on or standing things on. If a greenhouse border effect is wanted, a trough can be used to contain the compost. This can be sunk into the ground, using a lining of thick polythene with a few holes or perforations for drainage, or the polythene can be draped over a frame of timber boards resting on the greenhouse floor. The depth of the trough or frame will depend on the plants being grown. Alternatively, such containers can be filled with peat and the plants in pots plunged in this. (See also page 72, especially Fig. 8, and Tomatoes, page 191.)

A greenhouse floor can be of concrete or similar material. The disadvantage of concrete, however, is that water can collect in puddles. It also holds little moisture over long periods, and is therefore unsatisfactory in summer because of its poor contribution to atmospheric humidity (see page 77). Generally it is simple and convenient to use the ground on which the greenhouse stands. This can be pressed firm and covered with shingle or gravel of the type used for drives and paths to give a clean, neat appearance. To make walking more comfortable, concrete paving slabs can be put down on top where required. A floor of this type will hold plenty of moisture and keep the greenhouse nicely humid in summer. In winter it should be allowed to dry out so as to keep the air drier. Any total weedkiller – sodium chlorate or any of the proprietary path weedkillers – can be watered into such a floor freely, but plants must of course always be stood on plastic or paving so that their roots cannot enter the treated ground.

A recently introduced product particularly suitable for greenhouse floors is Liquisafened Chlorate. You can use this freely in timber greenhouses without fear of the woodwork becoming highly inflammable if you splash – as may happen if you use ordinary sodium chlorate solutions.

POTS AND GROWING CONTAINERS

These are discussed in detail in Chapter 7. Generally plastic pots will be found more convenient nowadays, but it may be useful to have a few clay pots available for special purposes. Wooden seedtrays are not recommended (see page 228).

For hanging baskets the plastic-covered wire type is useful, but there are some designed for easier watering and to avoid drip. Many other containers for hanging and putting on walls can be found in the shops, but these should always be critically examined for practicability. In general it is best to avoid highly decorative containers of any kind, and also those in colours, likely to detract attention from the plants. Neutral colours, such as terra-cotta, green, and sometimes white and black, are the wisest choice.

THERMOMETERS

At least one accurate thermometer is vital to the successful running of any greenhouse. Undoubtedly the best choice is the maximum and minimum type. This has tiny indicators inside the glass capillary, which can be set with a magnet or, in the newest designs, by gravity. There are also dial types. The indicators will show the highest and the lowest temperatures that have been reached since you set them. For example, by setting the indicators in the evening you can see in the morning just how low and how high the temperature has been overnight. This is the only way to assess any heating system properly. It is also invaluable in summer to check whether overheating has occurred during an absence, and whether shading has been effective. It is wise to buy a good quality maximum and minimum thermometer. Cheap kinds are often made from metals that corrode in the greenhouse atmosphere, the graduations becoming illegible after a short time.

Other thermometers may be required for propagators or for checking soil or compost temperatures in pots, plunges and the like. Special soil thermometers are available.

It is hoped that temperatures will eventually be given in the Centigrade scale. This is extremely simple: the freezing point is 0° and the boiling point of water 100°. In this book both Centigrade and Fahrenheit are given. For measuring air temperature numerous dial-type thermometers, which are usually reasonably accurate, have come on to the market. For composts and liquids, glass thermometers with mercury, or spirit coloured red, are the most practical.

EXTERIOR FITTINGS

In some cases it is a good idea to make wire frames to go over doors or ventilators to keep out birds or domestic pets, and sometimes small children, who can do a lot of damage in a few minutes. Much depends on individual circumstances and the greenhouse situation; you must decide yourself whether it is worth going to the trouble.

Gutters can be bought to fit most greenhouses, or the ordinary domestic plastic guttering can be fitted if necessary. Guttering is useful to lead away water and prevent excessive saturation of the greenhouse floor due to seepage in winter. It also prevents mud splashing on glass-to-ground greenhouses. Unfortunately many people think that the collected rainwater should be used for their greenhouse plants. In fact, *to do this is likely to invite disaster*. Rainwater collected from a roof is likely to contain weed seeds, and innumerable pests and diseases. Often the matter is made worse by storing the water in open butts in which dead leaves and filth accumulate, all adding to the pest and disease build-up. Don't, then, use such water for irrigation in your greenhouse. There is no point in using carefully prepared and sterilized compost if you do (see also page 90).

When a greenhouse is sited some distance from the dwelling house it is often useful to fit a weather-vane. This is a great help in selecting the best ventilators to open, in seeing which is the lee-side and in noticing changes in wind direction. In some areas wind rushing through a greenhouse can create devastation: gales can even damage the structure if vents are opened directly facing the tempest. Modern weather-vanes are now available in aluminium alloy, in many attractive designs that will enhance the appearance of a greenhouse.

BLINDS

Shading when necessary is of the utmost importance – many beginners in greenhouse gardening fail dismally merely because they do not appreciate this fact. In winter the greenhouse benefits from all the sun it can get, but in summer the sun-trap effect can be too much of a good thing. An unshaded greenhouse in a sunny position in summer can become so hot that everything inside is ruined in a few hours – even tropical plants! Nearly all greenhouses will require shading at some time or other. (See also Chapter 6.)

The purpose of shading is to protect the plants, especially the shade lovers, from intense light and to keep the greenhouse cool. To keep down the temperature, the sun's rays must be stopped *before* they get inside the greenhouse. This means some form of exterior blind or a preparation, applied to the glass, that will reflect the heat rays *before* they get through. For many years either blinds were fitted to the greenhouse roof or a shading paint was applied to the glass. The former is somewhat expensive; blinds usually have to be made specially to fit a particular greenhouse. However, the advantage of blinds is that they can be removed easily when the weather changes. Blinds are available made from timber slats or bamboo, and possibly aluminium ones will soon appear on the market.

Blinds made from solid materials should of course let some light through – hence the slats. Owing to the change in the sun's position, the light passing through on a sunny day will gradually move over the plants so that exposure to the sun is not prolonged. Blinds made from fabric or plastic and in sheet form should be semi-transparent, and so should shading paints applied to the glass.

Blinds are best fitted on rails so that they do not come into close contact with the roof; in this way, heat absorbed from the sun is not directly transferred to the roof. A few inches of air space between the blinds and the roof is desirable. This allows air to circulate and dissipate heat absorbed by the blind.

It should be appreciated that blinds fitted to the interior of the greenhouse may protect the plants from injury caused by intense sunlight but will not keep down the temperature as well (see How the greenhouse works, page 12). But if you prefer this method, roller blinds made from various materials are available for interior fitting.

For many years green shading materials were applied to glass. This is in fact *quite wrong* and due to a complete misunderstanding of the principles involved in shading. *It is of no advantage to have any shading material, including blinds, coloured green.* The green pigment in plants actually absorbs energy – for photosynthesis. It is cool in a woodland glade because this energy is taken up by the foliage and what is not used is dissipated. When a green substance is applied to glass the situation is quite different. Energy will be absorbed and transferred directly to the glass. A green-shaded greenhouse can actually get hotter than an unshaded one!

Research in this country and in Holland has proved that the best colour is white. In fact this has been known for centuries by people in tropical countries, who avoid dark-coloured clothing and often whitewash their homes. In sunlight a dark surface becomes much hotter than a light-coloured one. Shading paints applied to the glass should therefore be *white*. In the past shading paints had to be applied and left for most of the summer because they were so difficult to remove; they were also often troublesome to prepare and apply.

ELECTROSTATIC SHADING PAINT

This has completely revolutionized greenhouse shading and is a fairly recent introduction. The material is called Coolglass. It is a liquid concentrate that can be diluted with water instantly to give any degree of shading required. It is an intense white and is formulated to reflect those rays that cause scorching of foliage and overheating of the greenhouse when the sun is powerful. The diluted concentrate can be brushed on to the glass or applied with a spray. The particles are so minute that there is no risk of sprayers becoming clogged.

The curious property of Coolglass is that, once applied and dry (it dries almost at once), it cannot be washed off even by torrential downpours. The particles remain attached to the glass presumably by an electrostatic attraction. Coolglass can, however, be removed immediately by wiping with a dry duster – just like wiping a blackboard. The shading can consequently be applied or removed in much the same way as a blind, according to changes in the weather, but its cost is negligible in comparison to the cost and installation of blinds. Another advantage is that the degree of shade can be varied and adjusted very easily. For example, a weak dilution can be applied early in the year, and this can be oversprayed, or removed and replaced, with a stronger concentration as the sun increases in intensity. It is non-poisonous and will not damage structures, but it should be applied with care to red cedar frames so as not to spoil the wood's appearance. It is best applied with a brush in this case.

Coolglass is the only shading safe for plastic, since it will not scratch the surface when you wipe it off. Some plastics may not wet very easily, but you can usually overcome this problem by adding a few drops of washing-up liquid to the diluted concentrate. Severely scratched or abraded plastic is best not treated with shading paint of any kind, since the paint may become ingrained and difficult to remove. Adhesion may be unsatisfactory on polythene.

Where the roof is not easily accessible, Coolglass can be applied with a brush or sponge tied to a stout cane or pole (see Fig. 9, page 79). It can be removed, similarly, by attaching a dry duster to a soft broom.

MISCELLANEOUS AIDS AND GADGETS

In all greenhouses potting has to be done at some time or other. If there is no potting shed with a bench, it is worth making a small portable potting bench that can be put on the staging or on some other support when required. The bench is merely a tray-shaped wooden board with three sides, made to fit conveniently on the size of staging you have (see Fig. 10, page 94). Compost can be mixed on this and pots filled without the danger of spilling, and scooping is also easier. In order to maintain hygienic conditions (see page 74), the surface of the tray is best covered with an easily cleaned material like Formica. An easily portable, lightweight and clean potting-bench tray can be made from sheet aluminium.

To keep compost clean and hygienic, a few plastic bins – small dustbins or buckets with lids – are useful. All compost materials should be kept in clean covered containers (see page 90). A soil sterilizer is essential if you are going to make your own composts – you can improvise one, but it is far better to buy a proper sterilizer. An electric type is the most convenient. Sizes to suit all requirements are available, and they are not expensive. It is much cheaper to make your own seed and potting composts if you have the time and materials (see page 93). Sterilizers to be used with gas rings or primus stoves are also obtainable. Detailed information on soil and compost sterilization is given in Chapter 7.

Humidity is often an important consideration, and is discussed on page 77. To help in seeing just how much moisture there is in the air, a direct reading hygrometer may be useful, especially for beginners. This is a small dial-like instrument costing little. As well as giving readings in per cent relative humidity, it should indicate 'wet', 'normal', and 'dry' air conditions for simplicity.

To assess watering requirements a moisture meter is also useful for beginners. This works on the principle of electrical conductivity. The instrument consists of a probe attached to a little meter, which gives readings like 'wet', 'moist', and 'dry'. The best form of the moisture meter is the JMA meter, which has a scale graduated in numbers. The meter is supplied with a book of guide tables giving optimum readings for a wide range of plants and cultural operations. It takes much of the guesswork out of watering and is especially recommended for beginners, who tend to be too heavy with the watering-can (see also page 74).

A recent space-age electronic device, also with probes, gives an audible indication of both moisture and fertilizer content of the soil (see Appendix).

Another gadget that is often useful is the frost forecast thermometer. This is actually a kind of psychrometer – another instrument for measuring humidity. If the instrument is properly placed and maintained, its scale gives a good warning of the likelihood of frost. This is especially useful if you have garden frames which you can protect by covering at night; it also allows you to adjust the greenhouse heating.

FRAMES AND CLOCHES AS GREENHOUSE ADJUNCTS

It is not possible to deal with frame and cloche gardening proper here. It is a specialized subject to which a whole book could be devoted. However, it should be realized that frames, in particular, can take over much greenhouse work. Many of the low-growing subjects and pot plants frequently given greenhouse space could just as well be grown in frames for much of the time. These include favourites like cinerarias, calceolarias and the like. Frames can be easily, and economically, heated with electric soil warming cables. Dormant plants can be kept in frames, and much propagation and seed sowing can be done in them. All this gives much more free space in the greenhouse, which could perhaps be put to better use for taller plants. It certainly allows the greenhouse to be used for more decorative plants or for the stages during which plants are most suitable for display. Cloches can also be used for protecting the more hardy plants before they are taken into the cold or unheated greenhouse for display, and for protecting bowls and pots of hardy bulbs.

Frame recommendations are given where appropriate in this book. Frame design and the constructional materials follow much the same lines as greenhouses and similar advantages and disadvantages apply. It is frequently useful to have shady frames, and for this reason the north side of a greenhouse is a convenient place to have frame space. Sometimes the frames can be placed or built in contact with the greenhouse side. This helps to conserve warmth. Sometimes frames can be heated from a greenhouse heating system, especially when hot water pipes are employed. Generally, however, electric soil-warming cables will be found most convenient. Suppliers of soil-warming cables will recommend suitable types, ratings, fittings, and air-warming cables for frames if given the dimensions and temperatures required. It is also possible to heat a frame with a small paraffin oil heater placed in a sunken pit in the frame. Care is needed with ventilation (see page 38). Oil heaters of the type used for placing under cars are not suitable since they are likely to give out fumes.

The ground covered by a frame should not be used for growing. It can be treated in the manner as suggested for greenhouse floors (page 48). It can also be covered with plastic sheeting so that pots can be placed on it, out of contact with the soil. Modern lightweight frames are also useful inside the greenhouse for use as propagators (see page 57) and for covering plunge beds (see below).

THE PLUNGING BED

This consists of a bed of moisture-retaining material such as well-weathered ashes, grit, or peat, outside the greenhouse in a sheltered place (see Fig. 4). When it is necessary to stand pot plants outside

4 *Plunge Bed*
A: cover to keep out rain and to prevent waterlogging. B: layer of grit or gravel to deter worm entry.

during summer the pots are immersed up to their rims in the plunging bed, which is kept thoroughly moist. Plastic pots should be plunged so that their rims are just below the surface, but if certain plants are to spend a fair time in the plunge during some stage of their culture, it is wise to choose clay pots for them. The clay is porous and will allow moisture through. Plunged pots are kept damp and cool throughout the day, whereas if they stood in the open, on the ground surface, they would soon become baked by the sun and the plants ruined. And plunged pots, of course, cannot blow over.

Another use for the plunging bed is the growing of bulbs, which often need plunging after potting to ensure development of a good root system. This is especially important when forcing (see page 139).

Whatever material is used for the plunge bed it can be kept in position by a rectangle of four boards. Alternatively a pit can be made in the ground if the drainage is good. The moisture-retaining material must be kept moist – not waterlogged. For this reason a frame often makes a convenient plunge bed or a cover for one.

PROPAGATING BENCHES AND ELECTRIC PROPAGATORS

The propagation of many greenhouse subjects from seed, cuttings, off-sets and so forth requires temperatures considerably higher than is needed for the mature plants. In some cases it is possible to take advantage of the natural warmth of summer for propagation; but summer in many areas is unreliable and, in any case, the temperatures required for some forms of propagation may be higher than we could expect to get naturally for any length of time.

For this reason some means of obtaining a localized higher temperature is essential, particularly in the case of the greenhouse gardener wishing to grow plants from seed early in the year.

To attain the higher temperatures for propagation it is necessary to construct a propagating bench or case. This merely consists of a section of the staging supplied with extra heat and covered with some moisture-retaining material, such as sand, peat, pearlite or vermiculite, and preferably enclosed by a glass frame to retain warmth and a moist atmosphere.

In greenhouses heated by hot water pipes the staging could be lowered in one place to be nearer the pipes, or supplementary oil or electric heating put underneath. In some pipe-heated houses it may be worth running some extra pipes under a section of the staging at one point. In houses heated by paraffin oil lamp it may be possible to place the lamp under the staging and to utilize the staging space directly overhead for propagation. Some electric heaters (not fan heaters), may be similarly adapted but large ones may be too forceful; in this case you will have to buy an extra smaller heater to warm the propagating area. Specially designed propagators for heating by paraffin, fitted with suitable burners, are available (see Appendix).

Where there is electricity, propagation is easy. Excellent electric

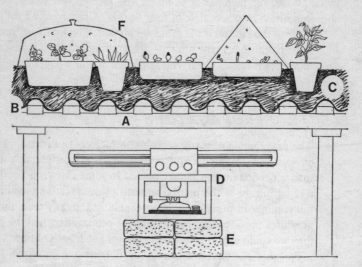

5 *Propagating Bench (Bottom Heat)*
A: staging. B: galvanized iron sheeting. C: moist peat. D: oil heater. E: bricks or similar objects to adjust height of the heater and hence temperature of the bench. F: glass cloches or tents to cover containers where higher temperature or humidity is necessary.

thermostatically-controlled propagators are available commercially. Alternatively, an area of the staging can be heated with a soil-warming cable.

With a soil-warming cable it is an easy matter to make your own excellent and effective propagating bench or case. In many cases it is preferable to buying a commercial propagator. A soil-warming cable is embedded in a layer of sand spread out on the bench; the sand is then covered with moist peat, and the pot and pans or boxes of cuttings, etc., immersed in the peat. A rod-type thermostat (see page 41) inserted in the peat layer is ideal for controlling the temperature (see Fig. 6). When you want to propagate a wide range of plants requiring different temperatures, this can often be done on the same warming bench by varying the depth of immersion of the pots or boxes in the peat. Glass laboratory thermometers are useful for checking temperatures.

A soil-warming cable bench can be covered with a glass frame or sheets of glass with advantage. Such an enclosure can be used for accommodating small tropical plants if desired. It can be used for all the usual methods of propagation too, and when a covering is

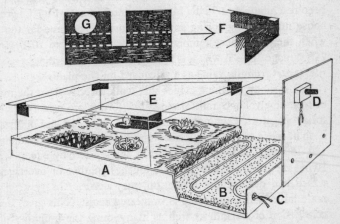

6 *Home-Constructed Propagator*
A: base of timber or asbestos sheeting. B: soil-warming cable on layer of sand. C: warming cable wired in circuit with thermostat (D) is a useful refinement. E: glass sheets to retain moisture. F: metal corner pieces to hold glass are cut as shown in (G) and bent along dotted lines (use sheet zinc or aluminium).

supplied the peat layer can often be dispensed with, the pots and containers being placed on the sand over the warming cables (which is more convenient). In this case the thermostat should be given the job of controlling the air temperature inside the propagator. More information on bench warming is given in Chapter 15 under Bedding plants, page 228.

In my experience a greenhouse propagating bench needs at

least 12 to 15 watts per square foot if it is to reach temperatures in the 70 to 80°F (21 to 27°C) range. Not all greenhouse plants need this temperature for propagation, but it is advisable to be able to reach it if necessary. As already explained, with an adjustable thermostat no heat is wasted even if the source of heat is overrated and capable of an excess. Unfortunately a number of commercial propagators do not reach a high enough temperature – this must be checked before purchase.

You should bear in mind that the temperature reached by a propagator or bench depends on the surrounding air temperature. For example, a non-thermostatically controlled propagator that has been reaching about 75°F (24°C) in winter in a 45°F (7°C) greenhouse may, during spring spells of sunshine, become far too hot when the greenhouse temperature rises to the 60 to 70°F (16 to 21°C) range. This is why it is always wise to fit a thermostat to save fuel (apart from its value as a safeguard for the plants).

You can buy warming cables that work directly from the mains or from low voltage transformers. The former are usually the best for propagators. Common ratings are 75, 120, 150 and 300 watts. Two or more can be used if necessary, but for a small greenhouse a 120–150 watt cable will heat a bench about 5 feet by 2 feet. When laying the cable see that no part touches another or overheating, which can damage the insulation, may occur. Always keep the material in which the cable is immersed moist. This gives better conduction of warmth as well as maintaining the humidity often important to propagation. Do not immerse electric warming cables in *dry* peat, or peat that is likely to dry out; because of the heat insulating properties of dry peat, the cable may seriously overheat.

WATER SUPPLY

Clean water is essential in the greenhouse (see page 76). A mains water tap in the greenhouse itself will be found most convenient. A watering lance can be attached for manual watering and automatic systems (see page 77). If the local water board approves, plumbing can be done simply with modern high pressure alkathene tubing. This will not burst on freezing, and can be fitted with connectors.

ELECTRICITY SUPPLY

This has become almost essential, since electricity can be put to so many uses, including lighting for dark evenings. Proper fittings must be used and expertly installed. Greenhouse supply lines and switchplugs, etc., are specially made (see Appendix).

5 *Automation in the Greenhouse*

With present-day technology it is possible to automate many of the greenhouse chores that can be a problem to those who have to be away all day – or even for several weeks. This means that business people, weekend gardeners, and those who enjoy long holidays, can still have a greenhouse without worrying that all their work will be ruined during their absence.

Nowadays automation has become so commonplace that often equipment can be purchased together with a greenhouse. For this reason this chapter has been put before the one on general routine. Beginners may prefer to read Chapter 6 first, and then return to this one when the requirements of watering, humidity and environmental control are understood.

TEMPERATURE

In artificially heated greenhouses temperature is partly controllable by thermostat. (This aspect of the subject is discussed in Chapter 3.) However, temperature depends on other factors, such as the amount of sunlight entering the greenhouse, ventilation, and the cooling effect of moisture evaporating from the greenhouse. You can therefore control the temperature by varying these other factors. Which to vary depends on the nature of the plants, and recommendations are given where appropriate in this book. See also the headings Ventilation and Automatic shading, this chapter, and Blinds, page 51.

A thermostat can of course be used to control various other forms of automation affecting temperature. Generally the rod type already described (page 41) is the best. However, there are other designs on the market. The moving air type is also accurate. It consists of a tiny fan blowing a *gentle* current of air over the thermostat control device, which gives greater accuracy in operation and a better sampling of air temperature. Unfortun-

62

ately, because of their large fan, constantly running fan heaters are sometimes not the best system (see page 40). For fan ventilation a special thermostat is necessary (see under Ventilation).

If possible it is always best to site a thermostat as though it were a plant – that is, at the same distance as the plants from the glass or in the coolest position in the greenhouse. With fan heaters and other electrical heaters, it is often recommended that the thermostat should be sited about one-third of the way along the greenhouse, one-third down from the roof ridge and about 7 inches from the glass. It should not be in a draught or near the source of heat. When used to operate ventilation or humidity in summer it should not be put in direct sunlight.

WATERING

Although comparatively recent, automatic watering has made rapid advances and there are now numerous systems on the market. A choice often has to be made to suit your particular requirements or the type of plants grown.

The capillary sand bench

This very successful method was first introduced by the National Institute of Agricultural Engineering. Its operation depends on the natural phenomenon of capillary attraction – water will rise against gravity through a porous substance. In this case sand is used, and this is kept constantly moist by a water supply. If pots are placed on the moist sand and pressed down so that the compost they contain comes into close contact with the sand, moisture will rise up in the compost. As the plants use up the water and deplete the moisture in the compost, it is replaced from the sand bench, which is in turn kept moist from the mains or a water reservoir.

The system depends on arranging a water supply that will maintain the sand in a moist condition. There is a variety of methods, the most common being a constant-level water supply, the water of which is fed to the sand bench by means of wicks. To operate the constant level one can either use the ball-valve, well known to plumbers, or a float valve refinement, usually made

63

especially for the purpose. Other possible methods of keeping the sand moist are described in this chapter.

It is easy enough to make your own capillary sand bench, and the NIAE set-up is illustrated in Fig. 7. A number of proprietary kits and apparatus is also available. Some of these have neat float valves and utilize narrow-bore high-pressure plastic tubing with

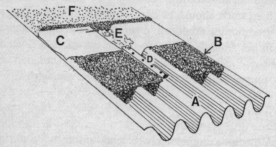

7 *Cut-Away Diagram Showing Stages in the Construction of the NIAE Automatic Capillary Watering Bench*
A: corrugated roofing asbestos (or plastic). B: corrugations filled with shingle (with the exception of the centre one). C: polythene sheeting spread over the levelled-off shingle and depressed into the centre corrugation. D: plastic pipe with holes drilled at intervals. E: glass fibre (as used for insulation) to prevent pipe holes becoming blocked with sand. F: layer of washed sand on which the pots are stood (the plastic water supply pipe is connected to one of the several constant level float valves on the market).

simple connections, so that plumbing becomes easy and elegant. The tubing is often little thicker than electric cable, so the capillary apparatus can be used for house plants in rooms.

Most of the proprietary capillary units are now in the form of plastic trays that can be connected together to extend the area of watering as needed. Recently a plastic-backed textile material or type of matting, that can be used in place of sand, has been introduced (see Appendix). This has so far given promising results and may well render sand obsolete in the future. The matting is lightweight and easy to use, and, if necessary, it is easier to sterilize than sand. It can be kept moist by trickle watering via a siphon system or by the photo-electric method described later. Vermiculite and similar mineral substances of a porous nature can also be used in place of sand. Some proprietary tray systems use these because of their light weight. Some of the smaller systems also use inverted bottle water reservoirs so that a mains connection is unnecessary, but their running time is of course very limited.

The pots used on a capillary sand bench, or on the newer matting, must not be crocked (see page 100). The compost in them must come into close contact with the porous base. The compost must be nicely moist when the pots are put on the capillary bench, or further moisture will not flow up into them. Plastic pots are advisable, although clay can be used. Clay may become slimy and coated with lime or algae in a short time.

Algae are often a nuisance, and can be checked by the use of Panasand, which is mixed with the sand used for the capillary bench. It will discourage algae and slime and also help to prevent plants from rooting through the drainage holes and into the sand. Panasand can be lightly sprinkled on capillary matting, if this is used, and it will have the same effect. The new product Algofen is extremely effective in keeping capillary matting free from slime and algae (see page 83).

Trickle irrigation

This can be manual, semi-automatic or completely automatic. It is basically an arrangement whereby water is conveyed to the plants via plastic tubing. Sometimes the delivery tubes are fitted with adjustable nozzles so that the quantity of water each plant receives can be controlled. This arrangement can be very convenient in frames even if the flow of water is controlled manually. However, an automatic water flow can be easily arranged. The simplest is a small cistern fitted with a siphon tube to which the trickle line or drip-feed line is attached. The cistern is filled by means of a valve with a sensitive control knob so that the rate of filling can be easily adjusted. This means that the frequency with which the water siphons over can be regulated to suit the plants' requirements. The disadvantage of this method is that a good deal of experiment may be needed to get the siphon frequency right, and there is no automatic correction if the weather conditions, and therefore the plants' requirements, change drastically. The flow of

65

water into a trickle irrigation pipeline can, however, be controlled in a fully automatic way by the use of the so-called 'electronic leaf' or by the very recently introduced photo-electric method. These are described below.

For a greenhouse with many pots scattered about on staging and shelving, the trickle or drip irrigation system may prove inconvenient because of the network of pipes that has to be led to each plant container. However, a system with a reduced number of outlet nozzles can be used to irrigate a capillary sand or mat bench and to distribute water over it uniformly.

The electronic leaf

These are also known by other names, depending on the makers; most consist essentially of a specially designed surface from which moisture is allowed to evaporate. When it reaches a certain stage of dryness it activates an electric circuit that controls an electro-magnetic (solenoid) water valve; the valve then allows water to flow into whatever system is used to distribute the water – generally trickle or mist jets. At the same time the surface is re-wetted and the cycle is repeated. The process is automatic because the rate of evaporation of water from the surface depends on the humidity of the atmosphere and other atmospheric conditions prevailing in the greenhouse. With most designs of 'electronic leaf', provision is made for personal control of the watering frequency and the amount of water delivered; the method is, therefore, very versatile. It is also used to control mist propagation (see page 226).

The photo-electric method

This is probably the best automatic control so far introduced. It depends on the fact that plants use water according to the amount of solar energy they receive. On bright days, when the temperature will generally be higher in the greenhouse, plants take up water for their growth and the higher rate of photosynthesis that then occurs. On dull days, and in the dark, very little water is needed since growth almost stops. In the photo-electric method the controlling device is a photo-electric cell with a special electronic circuit combined. The amount of light falling on the cell governs the frequency with which a solenoid water valve delivers water to the plants. Thus, on bright, warm days the water will be delivered very frequently, but as the light fails, or on dull days, the frequency will change accordingly, and in the dark no water will be delivered. Again there is provision for considerable personal control to suit a variety of conditions, and the method can be used for a capillary bench, trickle or drip irrigation, overhead sprinklers, or misting jets for watering or humidity control, or mist propagation. Unlike the 'electronic leaf', the photo-electric cell is unaffected by slime, algae or lime deposits from the water supply. It therefore gives reliable and accurate control over very long periods without any attention.

The tidal bench

This system waters pot plants by basal irrigation. The bench consists of a waterproof tray which can be made, if necessary, by draping plastic film over a frame of boards. At intervals that can be controlled by the electric methods already described, water is pumped into the tray, so that the bottoms of the pots are standing in an inch or so of water, and then pumped out so that the pots are left without water at their base. The frequency of pumping can be controlled to give a 'high tide' time, long enough for the compost in the pots to take up sufficient water but not long enough to cause waterlogging. Ordinarily, pot plants must not be allowed to stand in water for too long (see page 74). The water supply for a tidal bench comes from a constant-level tank, and the water pumped out of the bench is returned to avoid waste. Modifications of this system – where, for example, the water siphons out instead of being pumped out – can be made. This method of automatic watering is clean and relatively simple, and worth further experiment, especially where pot plants of similar size, in the same size pots, are being grown.

HUMIDITY CONTROL

Manually, this is done by 'damping down' (see page 77). The moisture in the greenhouse atmosphere will also be governed by the moisture in pots and on the staging, and by any method of automatic watering employed. With automatic watering the humidity may also look after itself. In some cases it may be necessary to improve humidity, or to control humidity but retain manual watering. A high humidity in summer will, in any case, substantially lower the need for manual watering (see page 74). The best way to get water into the atmosphere is by misting jets; those automatic watering systems that can be adapted to supply jets can also be used to improve humidity.

VENTILATION

Automatic ventilation is easy and effective. However, it is always advisable to combine automatic ventilation with automatic watering or humidity control. Where there is no way of getting moisture into the greenhouse atmosphere, automatic ventilation – or unattended manual ventilation for that matter – can cause the air to become very dry and increase the water demand of the plants.

Non-electric thermo-expansion devices

There are a few different designs of this device on the market, but all work on the same principle. A special petroleum compound, sealed inside a cylinder, expands and contracts with temperature change, just like the mercury in a thermometer; and this movement, by means of a system of levers and a piston, operates the ventilator. The mechanism can be adjusted to open a vent at any desired temperature, and it is sometimes possible to work both a side and a top ventilator together. Normally one device per ventilator is necessary. Where there are many vents this can therefore prove expensive. Nevertheless, this device has now been in use for many years and has proved reliable and trouble free.

Electric fan ventilation

Fan ventilation is very efficient and ensures a rapid air change in the greenhouse. The fan is best set at one or both ends of the greenhouse in the side high up in the gable. Special greenhouse fans are obtainable. They blow air out of the greenhouse and are fitted with louvres so that wind cannot blow back in when the fan is not running. The arrangement is similar to that used for ventilating in most other domestic buildings or factories. Even so, the louvres are best fastened down during the winter when such automatic ventilation is rarely needed in the greenhouse.

Greenhouse fans are available according to the air change required and the size of the greenhouse. If given the greenhouse dimensions, the makers will advise which of their models should be bought. Control is by thermostat, and this must be the type that switches off when the temperature rises. Some thermostats can be used for heating or ventilation and have terminals for both, but most employed for heating do not have this facility. It is usually best to obtain a thermostat designed to go with the fan. Again, look for reasonable accuracy, but since fans use little electricity there is no need for too great a precision.

AUTOMATIC PEST CONTROL

This is a matter that could lead to problems and that no one is happy about. Much depends on the development of pesticides that can be guaranteed harmless to man and animals but effective over long periods in the control of pests. Unfortunately, many pests develop an immunity to some pesticides unless the dose is high enough for an initial complete kill. Automatic pest control seems to rely on the vaporization of pesticides and it is doubtful whether a concentration certain to kill completely can always be relied on. It would seem that repellent action might be a better property to look for. Some people do not like the idea of the greenhouse atmosphere constantly containing concentrations of chemicals that might be inhaled. Automatic pest control is therefore a matter of personal choice, and one that should be taken up only after careful consideration of the literature issued by the manufacturers of such products and equipment.

AUTOMATIC SHADING

The photo-electric cell can easily be used to control an electric motor operating greenhouse blinds. The equipment, although extremely efficient, is expensive to install and has to be custom made. There are firms which will undertake this, given the greenhouse dimensions.

Greenhouse Gardening

Recently a combination of glass and plastic sheet has been introduced. Sandwiched between the glass and the plastic is a special chemical material that becomes opalescent on exposure to sunlight, and clears again when the intense light ceases. This is still somewhat experimental and at present very expensive.

Experiments have been made using water (alone or with special chemicals added) to absorb heat radiation when pumped as a film over the greenhouse roof; the pump operates by photo-electric or temperature control. This has proved effective, but there are a number of technical difficulties which at present make it of doubtful practicability for the home greenhouse.

6 General Greenhouse Routine

STOCKING THE GREENHOUSE AND DISPLAYING PLANTS

A new greenhouse may look bare at first, but it can soon be filled with colour, beauty and interest. It is wise not to be too impatient, though. Best results are obtained when you start from seedlings or young plants. Large, mature plants that have spent most of their life elsewhere may not take kindly to a sudden change of environment.

A quick way to produce an exciting, colourful display is to sow suitable greenhouse and garden annuals from late winter to early spring (see page 105). Many sowings can be made in autumn, too, for flowering the following spring (see Chapter 8).

Autumn is a good time to procure young plants from nurseries to flower from the following spring to summer. A few examples are auricula, calceolaria, cineraria, cyclamen, fuchsia, impatiens, kalanchoe, primula, schizanthus, streptocarpus and trachelium.

Nurseries and flower shops specializing in house plants are good sources of greenhouse foliage plants and many flowering plants of a sub-tropical nature. Most house plants will in fact grow much better under glass and reveal their true magnificence. Again, small specimens are the best investment.

For specialist plants like chrysanthemums, orchids and carnations it is vital to patronize those firms with a reputation for high quality (see Appendix).

A greenhouse used as a show-place or conservatory will only have a professional look if there are some climbers and plants in hanging containers. Care should also be taken in displaying the plants artistically (see Fig. 8): put taller plants at the back of the staging, and try to get some whose bloom or foliage will tumble

71

over the edge. Climbers can be trained up plastic netting, available from most garden shops; the white kind is best.

When climbers or other plants are trained against the rear wall of a lean-to, the wall should first be rendered and whitened with a waterproof emulsion, to maintain hygienic conditions and eliminate hiding places for pests.

You can give plants extra height by standing them on inverted

8   How to Display Plants
A: on staging with tall plants at rear and short or trailers at front. B: on shelving (trailers). C and D: in front of staging (stand short plants on inverted pots). E: shade lovers under staging. F: hanging pots. G: hanging baskets. H: climbers trained on horizontal wires. I: plants in beds of peat with their pots plunged for natural effect.

flower pots, and tiered staging can be added to the existing arrangements. Pots can often be hidden or disguised with pieces of cork or stone, or sphagnum moss, to create a natural effect, and plants grown from floor level can have their pots plunged in a sunken peat trough (see also page 48). Raised troughs or beds, like pots, can have their sides concealed.

Some plants look attractive displayed on pieces of tree trunk covered with sphagnum moss: for example, small ferns, many bromeliads (page 206) and orchids. The tree trunk should be chosen for attractive branching. It should be cleaned and free from pests and the moss wired on with inconspicuous florists' wire. The plants are then wired on in the same way, their roots surrounded with moss and peat. They must be watered with a spray, and fed with a complete soluble fertilizer such as Phostrogen or Hindglade.

The bulbs provide a wealth of quick colour. As well as the spring flowering kinds, well known outdoors, there are many exotic greenhouse types flowering in summer and autumn (see Chapter 9).

Greenhouses used for utilitarian purposes only are best kept free from all extraneous materials and run on strictly scientific lines. There will then be far less bother from pests and diseases, and fewer cultural problems.

Managing the general-purpose greenhouse

Too many home greenhouses are expected to cope with a vast range of different plants and their growing requirements. A certain amount of restraint must be exercised when building up a plant collection. Plants needing extreme conditions that cannot be provided should be avoided, or disappointment is inevitable (see also Chapter 2, page 18).

Care over positioning plants in the greenhouse can fulfil some of their simplest requirements (see Fig. 8). Shade lovers can go under the staging, or a part of the greenhouse can be shaded for them with a product like Coolglass, easily removable at any time. Tall plants can be grown from floor level, and an area left free of staging for them. You can provide extra humidity by standing the pots on a moist base – a common requirement in summer – or a drier atmosphere by siting plants near the ventilators. Temporary compartments for humidity or even temperature can be improvised with the aid of polythene sheeting.

Overcrowding must be avoided at all costs; this can often be dramatically reduced by using frames as adjuncts (see page 55).

Greenhouse gardeners are urged to be adventurous. Do not be tempted to grow the same things every year to the exclusion of everything else. Even in the case of specialist plants new cultivars appear frequently, and each year brings a wealth of seed novelties. Familiarize yourself with the catalogues of gardening firms and explore all the treasures they have to offer.

CLEANLINESS IN THE GREENHOUSE

If anything could be said to be the essence of successful greenhouse work, it is cleanliness. This is normally ensured by neat, tidy and meticulous working. Anyone who follows these principles cannot go wrong.

Day-to-day checks to ensure that everything is clean and tidy are not too much trouble, and should any pest or disease appear it can be effectively and easily dealt with. When routine care is not given, a chaotic state will eventually have to be faced, and a whole greenhouse full of plants may be ruined. Sickly plants should be removed from the greenhouse, and all dead or decaying plant matter promptly disposed of. Always take a routine look under the foliage of plants where pests first congregate and diseases first appear.

Do not upset compost on the floor or staging and leave it there. Always wash used pots and seed trays, and do not use the greenhouse to store junk and garden implements – these may harbour pests.

If possible, it is wise to give the greenhouse a yearly clean and sterilization, but this cannot be done properly with the plants inside (see page 88). The glass should always be kept as clean as possible (see page 32). Both the inside and outside should receive regular attention, particularly in autumn. For the control of algae and slime, see page 83.

WATERING

Outdoor garden plants are frequently underwatered; merely sprinkling them with a hose or watering-can is a waste of time. With pot plants the reverse is the case, and many people keep them perpetually waterlogged. Most horticulturists agree that more pot plants are killed by overwatering than by any other cultural fault, especially among beginners. Pot plants, unless of the aquatic type, should never stand in water for any length of time – the aim should always be to keep a moist compost. The word 'moist' is important: it must be distinguished from 'dry' and 'waterlogged'.

The water uptake of plants depends on their nature, size and stage of development, and on environmental factors, like humidity, temperature and light. A plant cannot be given fixed doses at specific times. Too often one hears someone say, 'I have given my plant a pint of water each morning, but it doesn't seem to grow well.' Try to understand your plants. Those coming from dry countries are designed by nature to economize with water and to need little. Small plants that are not vigorously growing, and naturally slow growers, also require less. Dormant plants, especially in winter, may not want water at all, whereas large plants, perhaps bearing flowers and fruit (like tomatoes), may demand considerable quantities during summer. On bright, warm days photosynthesis is rapid and plants are able to grow quickly. Then water is in great demand and can be put to good use. When water is unwanted and unused it can cause root rot and interfere with root function by excluding air from the soil or compost. The absence of air also encourages harmful bacteria. Bulbs, fleshy roots and similar storage organs are all prone to rot if they are kept too wet at the wrong time.

The symptoms of root failure brought about by overwatering are leaf yellowing, slow growth, eventual foliage drop and bud or flower drop and wilting. The compost may appear muddy and sticky, and it may have an unpleasant smell. Unfortunately when this happens the plant is often beyond saving. Sometimes the compost can be washed away, all the sick parts removed, and the remains of the root repotted in well-drained, sweet compost, in the hope that new roots will form.

Anything which upsets the function of plant roots will cause wilting. If the compost is nicely moist there is no need to apply more water. Check that the wilting is not caused by high temperature or bright sunlight. If it is, give attention to shading, but do not apply water unless necessary. Spring pot plants, like cinerarias and calceolarias, are very prone to wilt, perhaps because they cannot stand the extra light and warmth at that time of year. Shading is the answer, and just enough water to keep the compost moist.

For assessing the water requirement some simple tricks have been used for very many years. It was at one time common to make a little hammer by fixing a cotton reel on a stick. This was used to tap pots – a high sound indicates dryness, a bass sound indicates that there is plenty of water in the compost. This works well with clay pots but not so well with plastic. You can also lift the pot and see how heavy it is. A moist compost will be very much heavier than a dry one. I prefer to insert a finger into the compost when in doubt, but you can be scientific and use a moisture meter (see page 54).

It is better to water well when you do apply water, but never let it stream from the drainage holes; this will carry away much of the soluble nutrient, such as nitrates and soluble potassium salts (see page 80). For this reason plants should not be watered by immersion in buckets of water as so often recommended – and this includes seed trays and boxes.

Nowadays many potting and seed composts are based entirely on peat, and these can be very difficult to wet once they have become really dry. Peat composts must therefore always be kept moist. Fortunately, because of the fibrous texture of peat and the air it admits, the high water content it holds is well oxygenated and root rot is less likely to occur.

Clean water must always be used. It is pointless to employ sterilized composts which encourage excellent growth (see page 90) if filthy water, perhaps containing animal manure is lavished on your plants. Roof rainwater must not be used (see page 50). Some plants, known as calcifuge – the lime haters – have to be watered with soft water. For these use clean rainwater, which can be collected in clean containers put out just after rain has commenced. It should then be stored in clean closed containers. If much soft water is required, special horticultural water softeners are obtainable – the domestic type may not be suitable. Water can also be partially softened by boiling. But many plants, including orchids, can be watered safely with quite hard water; less damage is likely than if dirty soft water is used. Most woodland plants, such as primulas, azaleas, and many ferns and orchids, prefer water not containing lime.

The temperature of the water given to plants is not so important as people once thought; it does not need to be the same temperature as the greenhouse. On the other hand, some common sense must be used; do not spray icy water over plants growing in sub-tropical conditions.

The watering-can is probably still the most popular method of application. A can with a long narrow spout will make reaching between pots and access to the rear of the staging easier. It is also possible to buy watering lances with a finger-operated valve, which you attach to a greenhouse tap with a length of hose. Many small pots hold water longer if they are plunged in a seed tray containing moist peat or other water-retaining material. The various automatic watering methods described in Chapter 5 should be seriously considered.

HUMIDITY

The term 'humidity' refers to the amount of water vapour in the air. It is often of vital importance to the well-being of plants. When the air is dry water is lost from the surface of plant foliage more quickly than when the air is moist. This loss is called transpiration. As water is 'breathed out', more is taken up by the roots, and this water, which brings with it soluble plant food from the soil or compost, is used for the intricate chemical processes that take place in plant growth. Curiously enough, the business of transpiration has been found to be very wasteful of water. If the humidity is kept high, transpiration is reduced, and hence the water requirement is diminished. Also, many pot plants seem to prefer a moist atmosphere and soon show signs of sickness when the air is dry. This applies to the many flowers and foliage plants that come from countries or areas where it is moist and humid.

Obviously not all greenhouse plants are of this type; most succulents and cacti, for example, prefer the air to be on the dry side. Humidity may also have to be adjusted according to the time of year or the stage of the plants' development. In winter it is generally best to keep the air fairly dry. This lowers the chance of trouble from fungoid diseases and various rots that can affect plants that are scarcely growing or resting dormant.

Humidity is increased by the process of damping down, which merely means splashing plenty of water about the greenhouse and soaking the floor and staging. In summer, plants can often be sprayed overhead with water to wet the foliage. Many choice greenhouse plants need this treatment. However, be careful about wetting blooms, which can sometimes be damaged by browning or rotting if they remain wet for long. This has to be borne in mind when positioning automatic mist damping apparatus (see page 68), or any overhead irrigation.

When water evaporates it absorbs heat. Damping down will therefore result in a cooling effect. The principle is that of the old-fashioned milk or butter coolers. Evaporation is speeded up by increasing ventilation. Staging and the effect of greenhouse design on humidity has already been described (Chapter 2). In winter, staging or floors should generally be allowed to dry out so as not to raise humidity.

TEMPERATURE, VENTILATION AND SHADING

Every attempt must be made to keep the temperature between the limits recommended for particular plants. Extremes for short periods will rarely do much harm, depending upon the type of plant. We still know relatively little about what extremes plants will endure. Some plants classed as warm house subjects at one time, such as strelitzia, will in fact give splendid flowers if kept in a frost-free greenhouse over winter. Other sub-tropical plants can often be acclimatized to quite low temperatures if the conditions are changed gradually. It is, of course, easier to maintain temperatures when there is some form of thermostatic heating. If the weather is severe or there are fuel troubles and shortages, outside blinds can be lowered at night – during darkness only – to help retain warmth and exclude frost; alternatively, sacking or similar textile material can be thrown over the greenhouse roof.

Damping down, as mentioned earlier, is one way of influencing temperature. Another is ventilation which can be used to adjust temperature to some extent in summer. Many home greenhouses have poor ventilation. Perhaps not enough people realize that air contains carbon dioxide, which is vital to all plants' growth and may be considered as a food in the same way as fertilizers absorbed by the roots. The carbon dioxide is used by the plant to form cellulose, sugars and starches, from which its tissues are composed. It is for this reason that carbon dioxide enrichment of the atmosphere has been used to improve growth.

Good ventilation also discourages many fungoid diseases, such as the ubiquitous grey mould, *Botrytis cinerea* (page 84). In winter, always give plenty of ventilation whenever the conditions outside permit. (See also page 45.)

Very few greenhouses can be left unshaded in summer. Even with vents fully open and plenty of damping down the temperature is still likely to shoot up if no protection from the sun is

9   *Shading Brush*
A paint brush fastened to a long stick for applying shading paints to the greenhouse roof. Electrostatic types (Coolglass) can be wiped off with a dry brush (see page 52).

given. The great majority of greenhouse pot plants can be ruined by excessive summer temperatures. Moreover, many come from a naturally shady habitat and even bright sunlight may upset them. Foliage plants are especially prone to turn yellow or to lose their variegation. Often you can shade the glass for the whole of the summer months; the product Coolglass is especially recommended. It can be applied with a brush or sponge tied to a stout cane or pole (see Fig. 9). The white light passed by Coolglass also shows up the colours of flowers and foliage to good effect; this is particularly desirable for begonias, fuchsias and similar show blooms. Special attention must be given to shading in the early spring, and sometimes in late winter. Plants that have been growing in poor light during winter may react to a sudden improvement in weather and sunlight by wilting badly. A low concentration of Coolglass should be applied to the glass until the plants get used to the brighter conditions and the higher temperatures. However, do not allow spring temperatures to rise too high, or the flowering life of plants will be shortened.

In some cases it may be necessary to shade the sides as well as the roof. An east to west house usually needs fairly heavy shade on the south side only.

FEEDING GREENHOUSE PLANTS

(This is covered in greater detail in Chapter 7.) Nowadays animal manures are rarely used; since modern potting and seed composts are being scientifically prepared to provide all the plant's needs for some time. When feeding does become necessary, properly balanced fertilizers should be used. These contain the right ratios of nitrogen, potassium and phosphorus, often with other essential elements added, particularly magnesium.

Liquid fertilizers are recommended. Plants can only take up solutions and any solid material has first to be dissolved by the moisture in the soil or compost. However, much depends on what you want the fertilizer to do. Liquid feeds are usually fast acting; they should be applied properly diluted and frequently, not concentrated at rare intervals. Solid feeds for pot plants are usually compounded to act over a long period, but there is less control over the release of the elements or the concentration reaching the plant's roots.

Modern, scientifically formulated fertilizers can be used as soluble feeds by dissolving them in water, as foliar feeds by spraying them onto the foliage or as fertilizers by adding them in the dry state to potting mixtures (see page 95); and they can be used again in solution, to grow plants in water without soil or compost – called hydroponics (see page 95). This is because they contain other essential elements such as magnesium, iron and manganese, as well as the main nitrogen, potassium and phosphorus requirements.

Plants must never be overfed, or fed when they are in poor health resulting from other incorrect culture. Overfeeding will result in symptoms similar to those for overwatering (page 75). Plants can be safely fed when they are making active growth, not when they are dormant. Whether a plant is fast or slow growing must also be taken into account.

For some plants, special feed formulations have been developed. Examples are tomatoes, chrysanthemums, carnations and others mentioned in subsequent pages of this book. These recommendations should be followed for the best results.

Animal manures are not recommended. They are variable, unreliable, unhygienic, and often a source of serious pests and disease. Certain sterile fertilizers made from natural manures are however permissible. The hit or miss application of 'straight' fertilizers, such as ammonium or potassium nitrate, ammonium sulphate or superphosphate, is only recommended in isolated cases.

A unique combined foliar feed and growth stimulant is the new product Fillip, which incorporates vitamins, trace elements and other compounds that improve growth. In trials it has greatly increased the vigour of plants, and better and larger flowers and vegetables have resulted. Flower and leaf colour are also intensified and improved. The product is specially useful for routine application to pricked-out seedlings since it encourages speedy and healthy rooting. Some plants react to Fillip in a most dramatic way and their growth is very quickly stimulated (see Ficus, page 184). Fillip also improves the size and quality of root crops.

Top dressing

This is an old term still useful today. It means the addition of a balanced fertilizer or some fresh compost containing adequate fertilizer to a plant that has been in the same pot for a year or more. Top dressing is usually done in early spring or just before the plant is expected to begin growing again. Sometimes the surface compost can be removed entirely and replaced with fresh, but top dressing is usually done with plants that dislike having their roots disturbed. It can also be done with some long-term bulbs.

STOPPING, TRAINING AND SUPPORTING PLANTS

Stopping means pinching out or cutting off the growing tip of a plant or plant shoot. It induces more shoots to form from the stem or stems below and hence encourages bushy growth. This may be necessary to produce more flowers or a neat habit. Full details are given where appropriate.

Some plants lend themselves to training. There is a variety of methods including stopping, pruning, tying shoots to suitable supports, and disbudding to produce fewer large blooms (see page 209). Some plants can be trained to form standards. The procedure outlined under Fuchsia (page 166) is generally applicable. Other plants that can be grown as standards include pelargoniums, heliotropium and marguerite.

Pruning is necessary to give plants a particular shape, to keep them neat, to remove dead or diseased shoots or stems, to reduce the space taken up by plants dormant over winter and to keep their size in check, and for special purposes – to induce fruiting or flowering, for example. Recommendations are given where necessary; but if in doubt about when to prune flowering shrubs, do it after flowering.

Supports will be needed for plants from time to time. Twiggy sticks can be used for low, bushy subjects, thin split canes for taller plants and bamboo canes for larger specimens. Various proprietary ties are available, but garden string, cotton and so forth is useful. Always aim at neatness.

COMMON PESTS AND DISEASES

Pests and diseases are easier to control in the greenhouse than outside – provided action is taken in the early stages. If the advice on general cleanliness and greenhouse routine given in this chapter is followed, and sterilized composts are used, there should be few problems. Even so there are some pests and diseases likely to make an appearance even in the best run greenhouses. Special problems (see Index) are described under individual plants.

Algae and slime

These are microscopic plants that can be described as greenhouse 'pests' and, because they are such a nuisance, they are included in this section. They appear anywhere where there is light and moisture coating floors, walls, glass, pots and – what is worse – the surface of compost in seed germination containers and pots, with a green-to-brownish film or slime. They not only make the greenhouse look unsightly and ill-kept: they can interfere with seed germination by impeding air and water entry to the seed compost, and they upset the functioning of automatic watering systems.

A recent product, Algofen, has been cleared for use on food crops by the Ministry of Agriculture, and this is a great help in keeping the greenhouse free of algae and slime. It can be sprayed over any surfaces – including the surface of compost in seed trays and pots. It is best used as a routine measure – before algae has gained a hold. It is also useful for routine applications to the surface of seed compost, both before germination and after pricking out. It is invaluable for treating capillary matting, and was first introduced for this purpose. For capillary sand benches the product Panasand is useful; mix it with the sand before spreading it over the bench.

Aphids

This term includes many species known by common names such as greenfly, plant lice and blackfly. In the heated greenhouse these can breed the year round.

The shelves in garden shops are full of preparations for the control of these pests. I prefer the systemic type, usually based on 'Rogor'. Systemic insecticides are absorbed by the tissues of the plant so that the sap becomes poisonous to sap-sucking insects. Special recommendations may be given on the labels of systemics for the treatment of edible plants, and these must be followed. Malathion insecticides give good aphid control, and so does liquid derris, which is relatively safe.

Botrytis (*grey mould*)

This is caused by the fungus *Botrytis cinerea*. It is very common and can ruin an entire greenhouse of plants. Many ornamentals, such as pelargoniums, are prone to it, and so also are crops like lettuce and tomatoes.

The mould can live on dead plant material and from there spread to living tissues. It is best known as a grey-to-brownish furry mould that releases a cloud of dust-like spores into the air when it is disturbed. These spores are ever-present in the air and their growth depends on the right greenhouse conditions. Damaged plants are especially susceptible to attack. The mould is encouraged by poor ventilation combined with excessive humidity and low temperatures, and it is consequently very likely to appear in winter. Fan-heated houses rarely have trouble from this fungus.

Strict cleanliness is essential and all affected material must be removed from the greenhouse as well as any decaying plant debris. Attacked plants must have the affected parts cleanly cut out. Control is now relatively easy. The product Benlate, containing Benomyl, which has a systemic action, is effective and safe. Routine fumigation can also be given with TCNB smokes (tetra-chloronitrobenzene, or Tecnazine).

Damping-off

This is caused by several fungi that attack the base of seedlings, making them topple over. It can be very serious but its prevention is now a routine matter, requiring sterilized composts and preventive fungicides. The subject is dealt with under composts (page 90) and the care of seedlings (page 111).

Earwigs (*Forficula auricularia*)

The common earwig can be the originator of much 'mystery' damage. It is not generally known that this insect can fly and that it does its mischief at night. Cracks and crevices where it can hide during the day, and from which it flies to the plants at night, must be sought out. It frequently damages flowers by eating the petals, leaving them ragged and holed. Many beautiful blooms such as chrysanthemums may be ruined overnight and seedlings eaten away.

For protecting blooms BHC dusts are effective. Ant bait and killers also destroy the pest and can be put in likely hiding places.

Red spider (*Tetranychus telarius*)

Unfortunately red spider can be seen with the naked eye only when the infestation has become very serious. It then appears as a mass of fine, sticky webbing teeming with minute mites, only visible because of their vast numbers. Any foliage that seems yellow and mottled, and has a tendency to fall, should be carefully examined underneath for mites. A small hand lens will make them more easily visible and may also reveal the very tiny, round, whitish eggs. A dry, warm atmosphere encourages red spider, and infestation is less likely when there is good humidity.

Azobenzene fumigation is an old but still effective form of control, though it may damage some greenhouse plants. Liquid extract of derris can also be used as a spray. Derris dusts are not effective in this case.

Sciarid fly maggots

These tiny worm-like maggots with black heads are the larvae of several species of the fly. The flies themselves are also very tiny and delicate; you may not notice them except in large numbers, or when they fly around when plants are disturbed. The maggots are often found in peat composts and in over-moist conditions. They eat plant roots causing poor growth and eventual yellowing or wilting of the foliage.

An attempt should be made to lower the moisture content of the compost when possible; for initial control you should water them with a malathion insecticide. Most general-purpose greenhouse sprays or aerosols will kill the flies.

Slugs, snails and woodlice

These common garden pests will be a nuisance in the greenhouse if rubbish is left about for them to hide in and decaying vegetation is not cleared. Modern slug and snail baits are extremely effective; woodlice, sometimes incorrectly thought not to cause damage, can be controlled with most dusts containing BHC, for example Topguard Dust.

Thrips (*Heliothrips haemorrhoidalis*)

The thrips is yet another minute pest difficult to see with the naked eye. It makes white patches appear on the foliage, usually surrounded by tiny black specks. If some white paper is placed below attacked foliage, and the plant shaken, the thrips become dislodged and can be seen wriggling on the white surface.

Most pesticides containing the systemics give effective control, and so do derris extract sprays and malathion sprays or aerosols.

White fly

Although very small, white fly is easily recognized as a triangular-shaped winged insect about 1/25th of an inch long and whitish in colour. The larvae suck plant sap in the same way as aphids and cause foliage to become yellow and sickly. They often secrete a sticky substance, upon which a black fungus grows, making plants very unsightly.

In the past this pest was difficult to eradicate completely. Malathion aerosols were probably the most effective, if used repeatedly; liquid derris also gave some control and derris dust acted as a deterrent. Fortunately a new product called Sprayday has recently been introduced. It contains a new insecticide, Resmethrin, which as well as killing a wide range of common pests is particularly effective for white fly control. It also kills ants, which are sometimes a nuisance in the greenhouse, entering pots and disturbing roots. It can be used on the cucumber family without damage.

Application of pesticides and avoiding plant damage

New pesticides are being introduced and recommendations altered and changed all the time. It is unlikely, however, that a universal pesticide will ever be introduced owing to the varied nature of pests and plants. Inevitably, therefore, some pesticides are suitable only for certain plants; it is essential always to read the maker's label very carefully. Plants likely to be damaged by a particular pesticide will be listed on the packaging, and should be removed from the greenhouse or protected with polythene sheeting. Fortunately there are now so many pesticides that it is usually possible to find one that is safe for any particular type of plant. When in doubt the maker should be consulted. Most leading pesticide firms have a technical information department.

Pesticidal dusts are the least effective, but they may have to be used on blooms or where other methods of application will cause damage. 'Puffer packs' are available for most dusts, but there are also special bellows.

Sprays are best applied with a sprayer that delivers a fine mist. Always see that the undersides of the leaves get good coverage. A sprayer with a nozzle that will reach between plants and can be manoeuvred is a great advantage. There are many designs and sizes on the market.

Fumigation is the most efficient way of dealing with pests, but it is often impossible to treat plants selectively. Fumigants are now obtainable in aerosol packs. Pyrotechnic fumigants, which are lit like fireworks, are also common. Fumigating lamps, in which pesticides are vaporized, are rarely used nowadays, but the principle is employed in automatic methods (see page 69).

To assess the dose of a fumigant you must know the cubic capacity of the greenhouse: the dosage is always given in terms of so much per 1,000 cubic feet or similar. To get an approximate idea of the cubic capacity of a greenhouse multiply the length by the breadth by the average height. The average height is the distance from the floor to the mid-point between the ridge and the eaves.

Obviously the greenhouse should be as airtight as possible for fumigation. Wet sacking can be used to block cracks. The roots of the plants should be moist, but the foliage dry. The ideal temperature is usually about 65°F (18°C), but this is not essential, and perhaps not possible in winter. Do not fumigate when there is bright sunshine, when the temperature is excessively high or when the plants are under strain. To do so can cause severe damage and blackening of foliage. Sometimes manufacturers recommend picking blooms or removing flowering plants from the greenhouse; flowers can sometimes be bleached by fumigants. The best time to fumigate is in the evening; leave the greenhouse closed overnight and ventilate well the next morning. Full instructions for the best use and application of fumigants are given on the makers' labels or in leaflets supplied.

Sterilizing greenhouses

Greenhouses left derelict for many years, or greenhouses that have been neglected or become pest- and disease-ridden, are often best cleared and sterilized and a fresh start made. This is often done after, say, tomato and chrysanthemum culture or at a time when the greenhouse can remain empty for a few weeks. It is not possible to properly sterilize a greenhouse containing plants, since all plants are killed by any really effective sterilizing agent.

A simple way to sterilize is to burn sulphur, which produces sulphur dioxide gas – pungent and *poisonous*. About one pound should be burnt per 1,000 cubic feet. Flowers of sulphur can be used (obtainable from chemists) with a few wood shavings to aid ignition. Sulphur dioxide may damage instruments like thermometers with metal scales and automation instruments. These should be removed beforehand.

The structure and ground can be sterilized with formalin, which is sold for horticultural use by garden shops. It should be diluted to give a 2 per cent solution according to label instructions. This solution can be used for washing down the greenhouse interior and for watering into the ground. If the ground soil of the greenhouse is used for growing, it can give some measure of temporary sterilization. The solution can also be used for sterilizing pots, boxes and other containers and tools used in greenhouse work.

It is absolutely vital that all fumes of the formalin (containing formaldehyde gas) have disappeared before the greenhouse is used again. This may take from four to six weeks if the ground soil has been treated.

The pesticide safety code

Do not use pesticides unless you know exactly what you are doing, and have reference to the maker's instructions or other responsible information. Pesticides must not be inhaled or allowed to come into contact with the skin and must be kept out of reach of children. They should be properly labelled and any unlabelled containers with doubtful contents discarded. Pesticides must not be poured into water courses or ponds and the like.

A booklet called *Chemicals for the Gardener*, published by the Ministry of Agriculture, is available from any good bookseller at a very modest price. This will keep you up to date with approved pesticides. Those approved by the Ministry of Agriculture are most strongly recommended. These pesticides have a large 'A' topped with a crown clearly marked on their labels, with the words 'Agricultural Chemicals Approval Scheme' below.

DURING THE GARDENER'S ABSENCE

When you have to leave the greenhouse for long periods, it is nearly always best to get a friend or a professional gardener to come in and keep an eye on things from time to time. Any special instructions should be written down and left with the helper. Failing this, and for shorter periods, the greenhouse is best shaded in the summer, preferably with Coolglass. Some ventilation should be left, but not too much or the atmosphere will dry out. Give the greenhouse a thorough soaking and damping down before you leave, in order to keep up humidity as long as possible. If there is a solid floor, trays or bowls of water scattered around will help to keep the atmosphere moist. Obviously one or more of the automatic aids described in Chapter 5 is the real answer to problems caused by absence.

If possible, cut or remove all flowers before you leave, so that they do not mature and rot during your absence, and give a routine treatment with a systemic pesticide if conditions and plants permit. Often, plants can be kept in excellent condition for long periods if covered with polythene bags.

7   Composts, Pots and Potting

Much of the success and popularity of the greenhouse in recent years is probably due to the development of modern seed and potting composts. These replace the old hit-or-miss mixtures of messy manures and variable ingredients that at one time made the growing of pot plants almost a mystic practice.

In case some beginners are not clear about the meaning of the word 'compost', I must point out that it has nothing to do with *garden* compost made by rotting down vegetable matter. In greenhouse gardening potting and seed composts are specially formulated mixtures that have benefited from much scientific development and study. With their proper use failure can be almost completely ruled out, and even the most inexperienced gardener should be able to grow superb plants. Seed germination is excellent, and damping-off (see page 111) very rare.

JOHN INNES AND UNIVERSITY OF CALIFORNIA COMPOSTS

The growing of pot plants was revolutionized by the introduction of the John Innes seed and potting composts, developed after much research and experiment by W. J. C. Lawrence and J. Newell of the John Innes Horticultural Institute. Their book on the subject, *Seed and Potting Composts* (George Allen and Unwin), should be read for full details.

The John Innes composts showed that composts could be standardized to a considerable extent to suit a very wide range of plants. This means that a few composts can replace the very many different kinds at one time employed and that results are more reliable. The John Innes composts also showed that trouble from pests, diseases and weed seeds can be eliminated entirely by partial sterilization, which allows beneficial soil organisms to survive but kills those that are harmful. Further, they showed that the ideal balance of fertilizers will maintain excellent healthy growth for a long period.

To make the John Innes compost properly some care is needed. Also, in recent years, it has sometimes been difficult to obtain loam suitable for the formulae. For this reason various loamless composts have been introduced. Some are based on peat entirely and others on peat and grit. There are many ready-made composts of this type on sale in the shops, and most can be relied upon to give satisfactory results. However, I still personally prefer the original John Innes, especially for plants that I intend to keep in pots for long periods. The peat and peat/grit composts are better for short-term work, for example annual pot plants and bedding plants (see Chapter 15). The John Innes composts can be bought ready-made too, but it is important to buy from a well-known reliable source since the compost *must* be properly prepared according to the proper formula; there is some very poor material about in apparently reputable bags.

Composts based entirely on peat have the disadvantage of being lightweight, so that pot plants more easily become top-heavy. Also the peat is difficult to wet once it has been allowed to dry. Peat compost must always be stored slightly moist and never permitted to dry out completely. To overcome the difficulty of water uptake, some modern proprietary peat composts have a wetting agent added. Remember that the food content in peat composts has a limited life – you will need to start feeding after six to eight weeks, and feed regularly thereafter.

Peat/grit composts are better, in my opinion, and a good one has been devised by the University of California. This in its seed and potting form, and the John Innes formulae, are given here:

John Innes seed compost
(used for seed germination, page 107)

Parts by volume	Per bushel	Per cubic yard
2 loam (sterilized)		
1 peat		
1 coarse sand		
Calcium superphosphate	1½ ounces	2 pounds
Chalk	¾ ounce	1 pound

John Innes potting compost

Parts by volume	Per bushel	Per cubic yard
7 loam (sterilized)		
3 peat		
2 coarse sand		
John Innes base	¼ pound	5 pounds
Chalk	¾ ounce	1 pound

John Innes base fertilizer

Parts by weight

2 hoof and horn ⅛th inch grist, 13 per cent nitrogen
2 calcium superphosphate, 18 per cent phosphoric acid
1 potassium sulphate, 48 per cent potash

These specifications must be complied with. The base fertilizer is available ready-made, also a Chempak equivalent substituting Nitroform for the hoof-horn. (Nitroform is a modern synthetic long-acting nitrogen fertilizer of reliable composition.)

The John Innes potting compost above is the No. 1. By doubling the amounts of fertilizer and chalk the No. 2 is obtained, which is the most generally useful. Three times the quantity of fertilizer and chalk will give No. 3, and so on. This is to allow for the different possible requirements of plants. Slow-growing plants will be happy with No. 1, whereas fast and vigorous growers should have No. 3. Recommendations are given on the pages which refer to culture.

The University of California composts

The basic composition is an equal mixture by volume of peat and washed sand or grit.

University of California seed compost

Add to each bushel:

Ammonium sulphate	½ ounce
Calcium superphosphate	1 ounce
Potassium sulphate	¾ ounce
Ground chalk (or limestone)	4 ounces

University of California potting compost

Add to each bushel:

Ammonium nitrate	3 ounces
Potassium sulphate	1 ounce
Hoof and horn	3 ounces
Magnesium limestone	2 ounces
Ground chalk (or limestone)	4 ounces
Calcium superphosphate	2 ounces

(For suppliers of horticultural chemicals, see Appendix).

With the University of California potting compost, feeding has to begin rather sooner than with the John Innes. However, the peat and peat/grit composts have the considerable advantage that no sterilization is necessary. Peat and coarse sand and grit, provided they have been properly stored, are relatively free from pests, diseases or weed seeds. Sand is also easily sterilized if necessary by heating.

Making your own John Innes composts

It is not difficult to make your own John Innes composts using the formulae given. For some purposes you can substitute ordinary good garden soil for the loam. The soil should be sterilized as described on page 96. In certain cases it may be possible to use a good garden soil without sterilizing, but this is *not* generally recommended. However, a John Innes compost made up from unsterilized loam or compost will still probably give better results than any other hit-or-miss mixture if the soil used is fertile and clean.

For most home gardeners it is convenient to make up a bucketful of compost at a time, and in any case it is better not to keep the made-up compost too long. For a large bucketful add the following amounts of fertilizer and chalk:

Seed compost

Calcium superphosphate	$\frac{1}{3}$ ounce
Chalk	$\frac{1}{5}$ ounce

Potting compost No. 1

John Innes base	1 ounce
Chalk	$\frac{1}{5}$ ounce

(omit for calcifuge plants) (see page 95)

93

Weighing can be done on a small 'diabetic' balance obtainable from chemists. For the loam, peat and sand you can make a measure with the capacity of 26¾ fluid ounces (1/48th bushel) by simply cutting a plastic bottle. Use a household measure to run the required amount of water into the bottle, mark off the level, and then cut round with scissors. This measure can be filled twice with

10   *Portable Potting Bench*
A three-sided tray of wood or sheet aluminium is useful for mixing composts and potting and can be placed on staging when needed.

sterilized loam, once with peat and once with sand, for the seed compost. Fill seven times with loam, three times with peat and twice with sand for the potting compost. You will find that, in the case of the potting compost, this will fill a large bucket. Usually less seed compost is required.

Make sure the peat used is damp. Black, poor quality decomposing peat must not be used. Mix the fertilizers and chalk with the *dry* sand, and sprinkle this on the mixed peat and loam spread out over the potting bench (see Fig. 10). Then mix everything together thoroughly. Use the compost slightly moist, and store in polythene bags or in closed containers.

Making your own University of California compost and loamless types

The University of California composts are, similarly, easy to prepare. The proportions in the formulae given can be scaled down according to personal requirements. Bushel measures can be constructed as follows:

1 bushel = a box 15 × 15 × 10 inches
$\frac{1}{2}$ bushel = a box $10\frac{3}{4}$ × $10\frac{3}{4}$ × $9\frac{1}{2}$ inches
$\frac{1}{4}$ bushel = a box $8\frac{1}{2}$ × $8\frac{1}{2}$ × $7\frac{3}{4}$ inches

Ready-mixed packs of fertilizer chemicals (such as Chempaks) can be bought for mixing with your own peat or peat/grit. This will save weighing out and having to order several separate chemicals. Certain complete fertilizers containing the necessary trace elements can also be used for loamless composts. For example, Phostrogen can be used to make up a peat/grit compost. The basic mix the makers recommend is three parts by volume of moist peat and one part of sharp sand or grit. To every 5-inch pot of this you should add one level teaspoonful of Phostrogen and one level teaspoonful of ground chalk. The chalk should be omitted for calcifuge plants (see below). For subsequent feeding of plants grown in this compost the same fertilizer should be used, dissolved in water according to the manufacturer's recommendations. Phostrogen can also be used for hydroponics – the growing of plants in solutions of chemicals with no soil at all; an instruction leaflet can be obtained from suppliers (see page 240). A useful book giving full information on hydroponics is *Beginner's Guide to Hydroponics* by James Sholto Douglas (Pelham Books).

COMPOSTS FOR SPECIAL PURPOSES

Although the composts described so far can be used for a vast range of plants, there are – as one might expect – some exceptions. These are mostly dealt with under the entries relating to individual plants in Chapters 8–13. The most common 'special case' is that of calcifuge plants – plants that object to lime and that grow mostly from acid soils, leafmould soils and woodland areas. In such cases the composts already mentioned can be used, provided that chalk is omitted from the formula; there are also special lime-free potting composts on the market. Some mains tap waters contain excessive amounts of lime (hard water) and should this be the case plants potted in a lime-free compost must be watered with *clean* rainwater or specially softened water (see page 76); otherwise lime will soon build up in the compost and raise the alkalinity (pH). The ideal pH (a measure of acidity and alkalinity) for a normal potting compost is pH 6·4–6·5, which is very slightly acid. (pH 7·0 is neutral.) The acid potting composts can go considerably below this figure, but less than pH 5·5 is not recommended for the acid-loving plants most frequently cultivated. For a few renowned acid lovers, such as ericas, a special John Innes acid compost is worth making.

John Innes acid compost

2 parts loam, 1 part peat, 1 part sharp sand, all by volume. To each bushel add $1\frac{1}{2}$ ounces calcium superphosphate and $\frac{3}{4}$ ounce flowers of sulphur.

For plants that prefer very dry conditions, like cacti and many succulents, extra washed grit can be added to any of the normal potting composts. For plants of a semi-aquatic nature a good proportion of crushed charcoal will help prevent souring. Lilies and ferns may enjoy leafmould additions, but this should be sterilized. Generally, it is unnecessary and undesirable to add materials to the standard composts unless there is a very good reason or special recommendation.

STERILIZING SOIL, LOAM AND OTHER COMPOST INGREDIENTS

The loam used for John Innes composts should be prepared by the method described in *Seed and Potting Composts* (see page 90). Sometimes suitable loam can be purchased from garden sundriesmen, or failing this a good garden soil can be used – but in all cases it must be *sterilized* if it is to be used for a true John Innes compost.

The sterilization is actually *partial* sterilization. It is designed to destroy pests, diseases and weed seeds, but not beneficial soil organisms and bacteria which make nutrients in the soil available to plants. Although chemicals can be used, steam treatment is undoubtedly preferable.

Small steam sterilizers can be bought from horticultural sundriesmen at prices that will soon save the cost in compost. The sterilizer is merely a water container in which the water can be boiled by flame heat or by an electric kettle element. The soil or loam is placed in a box with a perforated bottom that fits over the water reservoir, and steam is allowed to pass through.

The loam or soil must be *dry* to begin with. The water should be boiled until a thermometer near the top of the soil reads about 180°F (82°C) and this temperature should be maintained for about ten minutes. It should not be allowed to rise above 200°F (93°C). Ideally, this temperature should be reached within a period of about forty minutes.

Afterwards the loam should be tipped out onto a clean surface and allowed to cool. It can then be used to make up compost immediately, but the compost is best kept for a few days before use.

For small quantities a domestic saucepan can be used. The John Innes Institute suggest boiling half an inch of water in the saucepan and adding dry sifted soil nearly to the brim, and then simmering for fifteen minutes.

Peat does not need sterilizing. Leafmould, if used for special composts, can be sterilized by pouring boiling water over it. Leafmould often contains innumerable weed seeds.

Fertilizers for the standard composts

For feeding plants in the John Innes composts a special liquid feed has been devised:

John Innes liquid feed

Parts by weight

15	ammonium sulphate
2¾	potassium nitrate
2¼	mono ammonium phosphate

Rate of application ½–1 ounce of the mixed powdered crystals per gallon of soft water

The ready-made mixture can be obtained from garden shops or sundriesmen. If it is dissolved in hard water it should be used immediately or some of the phosphate may become insoluble.

The other composts can be used in conjunction with most proprietary pot plant feeds of the liquid or soluble type, such as

Phostrogen. However, the composts contain enough fertilizer to get the plants to a fairly advanced stage. When to begin feeding depends on the nature and vigour of the plant, but a good time is just before flower stems or flower buds are expected.

Some liquid feeds can be applied direct to the foliage provided the maker's recommendations are followed. The plants will absorb them through the leaves and respond quickly. Some feeds including the John Innes liquid feed, may scorch the foliage and should *not* be applied in this way (see also page 80).

For plants grown in John Innes composts the John Innes base fertilizer can be used as a top dressing if required. About one teaspoonful to each 5-inch pot, with a little more or less depending on pot size, is the amount to use.

POTTING, POTTING ON AND REPOTTING

In most greenhouses these operations are carried out at intervals the year round. Clearly, it is of the utmost importance to do them properly. If you learn this from the start it will become automatic, and you will soon get to know your plants' pot requirements.

Choosing pots

Most people now use plastic pots, which are easy to clean and relatively unbreakable. Clay pots seem to be slowly disappearing, which is a pity; a few are useful for plants that need plunging, because clay is porous and lets moisture through. Clay pots should be thoroughly soaked before use. They can be cleaned by soaking overnight and then scrubbing.

Because they are non-porous, plastic pots have the advantage of needing less water. If you have always used clay pots and change to plastic, be careful not to overwater. The growth and development of plants in clay pots and those in plastic pots seems to differ little.

It is wise to stock a selection of various sizes of pots. Pot size is now measured by the diameter at the top. The most useful sizes for general work are $2\frac{1}{2}$-inch, $3\frac{1}{2}$-inch and 5-inch. A few very small $1\frac{3}{4}$-inch pots may sometimes be useful, as well as a few 10-inch pots. There are also what are known as 'half pots' which have the same top diameter as ordinary pots, but only half the depth. This makes them useful for low growing subjects and plants that are naturally shallow rooted. Sometimes half pots are called alpine pots, because alpines and rock plants are usually grown in them. All flowerpots should be well supplied with drainage holes. (See also page 100.)

For plants to be subsequently bedded out or transferred to permanent large pots, various temporary pots of polythene or waterproofed card can be used. There are also composition pots, which are planted with the plant, and rot down afterwards to produce humus for the roots. Unless conditions are kept nicely moist, these composition pots may not always rot as they should and will then restrict the roots.

Never use flowerpots which are larger than necessary. Plants that remain small in excessively large pots look ridiculous. Moreover the excess compost may lose its nutrients with continued watering before the plants' roots can penetrate into it. Sometimes slight under-potting encourages plants to flower.

Hanging pots and baskets

Many plants can be beautifully displayed in hanging containers, and trailing plants may be suited only to them. Pots can be hung by attaching wires. Clay pots can be treated as shown in Fig. 11. Plastic pots can be easily drilled around the edges and wires put through the holes. Baskets are frequently used, and there are now types with a saucer-shaped bottom that holds water for a short time, making watering easier and preventing mess from drips. Ordinary wire baskets have to be lined with moss before you fill them with compost. They tend to dry out quickly and consequently to demand more watering attention. It can be an advantage to place a few pieces of polythene sheet over the moss lining, leaving a few slits for drainage, before filling with compost. This reduces water loss, but the moss tends to go brown quickly. Remember, though, that many vigorous trailers will in any case soon obscure the hanging container from sight.

Take care that hanging containers can be safely supported by the roof. They may be very heavy when watered.

Large hanging containers can be filled with peat and three

11   *Hanging a Clay Pot with Wires*

or four pots of trailing plants plunged in this; they can then be easily placed. This is a particularly suitable method for plants with a short decorative life.

Potting (*see* Fig. 12)

Clay pots must be used soaked, but not wet with free water, or compost may stick, making repotting troublesome. All pots must be scrupulously clean.

Unless pots are to be stood on a capillary sand bench (see page 63), they may need to be crocked. This old term means placing a few pieces of broken pot over the drainage holes, preventing compost falling through and permitting free flow of any excess water. For plants needing specially efficient drainage a few pebbles can be put over the crocks so that there is no risk of the compost causing clogging. Actually the aim should be never to apply so much water that it streams from the drainage holes (see page 76).

Pots with only one drainage hole, like most of the older clays, should always be crocked when necessary. Some of the newer flowerpots made from plastic and other materials have several drainage holes and slightly raised rims at their base to allow free escape of any excess water. These can usually be left uncrocked.

For pots to go on a capillary sand bench it is helpful to place a tuft of peat in the drainage hole or holes. Some gardeners use glass wool. This will admit water by a 'wick' action, but prevent compost soiling the sand of the bench.

There is no need to use broken clay pot for crocking, of course. Plastic or clean, suitably shaped, stones can be substituted. There are also perforated zinc discs and circular plastic or wire mesh available, but sometimes the perforation or mesh is too fine for good drainage and pebbles still have to be put over the top to avoid clogging.

With fast-growing plants that are soon to be repotted, crocking is usually unnecessary (see also Chapter 15, page 228). Several designs of self-watering pot, which hold a reserve of water for

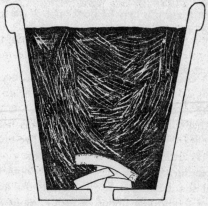

12   *Correctly Filled Flowerpot*
Note that a space is left at the top for applying water. Drainage hole(s) must be crocked or otherwise treated to allow free drainage.

semi-automatic watering, are on the market. These are fine for the isolated specimen plant or small group, but far too expensive for general use.

For potting, a compost must always be moist – not wet. It should have sufficient moisture to enable it to be 'poured' from a scoop or trowel, but not to make it stick to the hands or surfaces. For greenhouse work never pot plants too deeply. The point where roots and stem meet should generally be at surface level. There are a few exceptions, such as the stem rooting lilies discussed later in the book. Many plants and storage organs, bulbs, etc., that would require a fair depth outdoors can be potted with their tops well exposed when they have the protection of glass. This gives plenty of pot depth for their roots to penetrate (see also Chapter 9).

The standardized composts should never be excessively firmed down; you only need to tap the pot gently on the bench as you pour in the compost. With the all-peat composts, firm gently again after filling the pot. Too much compression will impede the entry of water and air.

A pot should never be filled to rim level. Leave a space between the compost surface and the rim to allow for watering, and also to help you judge how much water has been applied. After potting it is usually necessary to water carefully. If there has been much root disturbance it may be better not to water immediately, since damaged roots can rot in wet conditions.

Potting on

This means moving a plant on from a smaller to a larger pot (see Fig. 13). For best results plants should be grown in pots just big enough for them. When the roots fill their pots, they are moved on to another slightly larger pot. This means fairly frequent potting on, but it is good greenhouse culture. The practice ensures that a plant has fresh, fertile compost with the right fertilizer balance available during every stage of its development, and you will be amazed at the excellence of the plants that result. Generally the new pot should give about an inch extra of compost around the root ball.

To pot on, first remove the plant from its pot as described below. Place sufficient compost in the new pot to ensure that when the root ball is rested on it the plant is brought into the new position required – do not forget to remove any crocks, which should be gently disentangled from the roots if necessary. Then run in more fresh compost round the sides. If this compost is moist – not wet – it should run freely from a scoop. A tap of the pot on the bench will usually be sufficient to settle it down, but some of the peat composts may require gentle pushing down with the fingers. Very fibrous compost may need pushing down around the sides and between roots with a short stick known as a potting stick. This may be necessary with orchids and when dealing with plant roots between which it is difficult to get compost. Remember that modern potting composts rarely, if ever, need ramming down firmly.

In many books and articles you will see the instruction 'pot on as required', which means when the plant has filled its pot with roots. This can usually be checked by gently tapping the plant out of its pot in the following manner. After first watering to ensure that the compost is moist, cover the pot top with the hand, allowing the plant stem to pass between the fingers, and invert it; then

 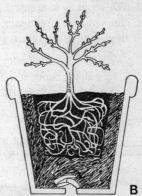

13 *The Principle of Potting on*
A: plant to be potted on. B: the same plant with root ball intact shifted to larger pot.

tap the rim of the pot either on the bench edge or gently with a *small* hammer, and the root ball should slide out cleanly.

The need for potting on does vary, and the knowledge of what to repot and when will come with experience. Recommendations are of course given in this book. Generally plants raised from seed will need frequent potting on. For example, a seedling may begin in a 2½-inch pot (or sometimes in a seed tray; see page 110), and require potting on through about two pot sizes to finish in, say, an 8-inch pot for flowering. Mature plants can be potted on in certain cases, but generally the aim should be to repot rather than pot on. Otherwise it would obviously be impossible to accommodate many plants in the greenhouse. Often you can avoid repotting or potting on mature plants by top dressing (see page 81).

Many annual plants, and a fair number of decorative perennial pot plants flower better if their roots are restricted. Presumably this has something to do with survival, the restriction hastening flowering and the production of seed for propagation. Attention is drawn to this where appropriate later in the book. Suggestions for pot sizes are also given.

Repotting

To repot is to transfer a plant to another pot of the *same* size, at the same time removing as much of the old compost as possible and replacing it with fresh (see Fig. 14). Many dormant perennials can

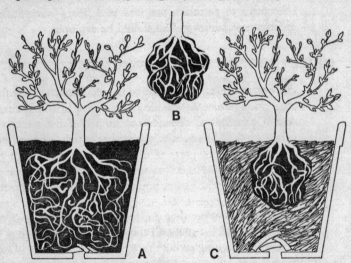

14　*The Principle of Repotting*
A: plant to be repotted. B:1 plant removed from pot and root ball and root reduced in size. C: the plant repotted into same size pot with fresh compost.

be repotted just before they start growing again; in such cases there is little risk of upsetting the plants, but again it is impossible to generalize. Recommendations on the best time for repotting and on which plants to repot are given in this book when necessary.

8 Growing Plants from Seed

Growing from seed is one of the most exciting ways to acquire plants and it is also the cheapest. Nowadays there is an excellent supply of rare seed as well as many delightful novelties which are the result of plant breeders' expertise. It is essential for the reader to consult the catalogues of the firms listed in the Appendix. These will be sent free on request and are always well illustrated. Do not be content to patronize just one seed firm – various firms have different specialities and all should be explored.

GERMINATION REQUIREMENTS

For best results the seed must be bought from a reliable firm. Even then, with rare seeds you may often have to take a chance. Successful germination depends on the age of the seed, how it has been stored, and its condition when harvested. Seeds collected from distant or difficult parts of the world may not always give good germination and sometimes they may not germinate at all. Conversely, the seed of most popular plants, such as those used for bedding and greenhouse display, generally gives germination approaching 100 per cent. Such seed is usually specially produced by the seed firms and tested by them before it is sold.

Always keep a look out for F_1 hybrids. These are obtained by special crossing of selected parent plants and the resulting plants are always much more vigorous. Also of note is tetraploid seed, produced by a special chemical treatment. Tetraploids have much larger flowers and usually greater vigour too.

To germinate properly a seed must have a suitable temperature, moisture and air or oxygen.

The required temperature ranges from about 45°F (7°C) for the more hardy plants, such as garden plants and annuals for bedding, to about 80°F (27°C) for sub-tropical and tropical greenhouse plants. For most of the seed germination in the average green-house you will find about 60 to 65°F (16 to 18°C) adequate.

If the temperature is too low, seed will take a long time to germinate, fail completely or rot. At excessively high temperatures seed can be killed or may germinate too quickly and produce long, spindly, weak seedlings that often prove useless. Follow the germination temperatures suggested in this book.

Air, or the oxygen it contains, is essential to germinating the seed; it is necessary for the chemical processes that take place inside it. Waterlogging after sowing, or sowing too deeply, will suffocate the seed.

Obviously water is necessary too, but it should be present as *moisture*. During germination seed must not be allowed to dry out – another common cause of failure.

SEED SOWING TECHNIQUE

Sow seed as soon as possible after you have received it. Do not store packets in damp places like the greenhouse, or where they may be exposed to extremes of temperature. Specially sealed packeted seed with controlled humidity is now available, introduced by Sutton's, the well-known seed firm.

To aid germination some large seeds can have a tiny part of the outer skin or covering peeled away with a razor blade or very sharp knife. This helps moisture and air to penetrate. Soaking in water overnight may also help to get moisture into some large seeds with woody coverings, but you should never soak them for too long.

For easier handling, some very small seeds can now be obtained in a pelleted form. The seeds are coated with an inert mineral material, like Bentonite, a type of clay, to increase their size considerably. Sometimes a fungicide is included in the coating. Pelleted seed is usually about the size of a small bead and is easy to pick up. It can be sown individually and spaced well in containers, so pricking out (see page 109) may not be necessary. The coating, being designed to give protection but allow moisture and air to penetrate, generally aids good germination.

For seeds that take a long time to germinate, it is sometimes wise to use a seed dressing. This is a fungicidal powder, a little of which can be put in the seed packet and shaken up with the seeds. The coating will protect the seeds from various rots caused by fungi, which may contaminate the seed compost after sowing; even a clean, sterilized seed compost is liable to contamination from the air and surroundings after a time.

Seed must always be sown in a disease- and pest-free compost. For most seeds a special seed compost is preferable and details will be found on page 90. However, some large seeds, which have a considerable supply of plant foods already supplied by nature, can be sown direct in potting compost.

Most small seeds are usually sown in compost in small seed trays or pans. Plastic trays measuring about $8\frac{1}{2}$ inches by 6 inches and about 2 inches deep are freely available and are a convenient size, fitting most of the small propagators sold in the shops. For large sowings the standard seed tray, measuring about $8\frac{1}{2}$ inches by 14 inches and about 2 inches deep, can be used. These seed trays are supplied with drainage holes distributed over the bottom, which is ridged to allow free escape of excess water.

For the majority of seeds 1 to $1\frac{1}{2}$ inches depth of compost is sufficient, depending on the size of the seed. For fine seed you should put a layer of seed compost in first and then a thin covering of seed compost pressed through a sieve of about 10 mesh. The compost should be firmed down very gently – not compressed – and given a level surface. For levelling and firming, you can make a simple tool by bending a piece of metal sheet into an 'L' shape; one side of the 'L' is used as the handle.

The compost must be moist – not wet – before sowing. The seed should be sown thinly so that the tiny seedlings are not overcrowded when they appear. You don't have to sow all the seed in a packet at once. If there is plenty it is a good idea to save some in case the first attempt should fail. In some cases, especially with annuals, it is also wise to 'stagger' sowings so that you have several batches of plants at different stages of maturity; you will then have plants in flower over a much longer period.

To help distribution, very fine seed can be mixed with a little clean silver sand. Large seeds can be set over the compost surface with the fingers or with a pair of finely tipped tweezers; leave about $\frac{1}{2}$ to 1 inch between each seed, depending on the seed size.

Most average seeds can be sown by tapping the seed out of the packet with the forefingers, moving the packet over and just above the compost surface as you do so.

After sowing, the seed should be just covered with some more fine compost – except for very fine seed, which should be left uncovered. A thick covering is rarely necessary and it could be harmful – use a layer of compost roughly the same diameter as the seed. Thus a seed measuring about $\frac{1}{8}$-inch across would have that depth of compost over it. Some seeds germinate better if exposed to light and should not be covered.

TABLE ONE

Seeds needing exposure to light for germination

(These should not be covered with compost)

Anthurium species	Iris species
Bellis perennis	Lettuce
Bromeliads	*Lobelia cardinalis*
Cacti and succulents	Mimulus species
Calceolarias	Nicotiana
Crossandra species	Petunias
Ficus species	Philodendron species
Gesneriaceae (many species)	Primula species
Gloxinias	Saintpaulias
Gramineae (grasses)	Streptocarpus

Once you have sown the seed the next step is to see that there is adequate moisture in the compost. It is usually necessary to apply more, and this is best done with a sprayer giving out a fine mist of water. Do not water seed trays by immersion. The excess of water running away will take valuable soluble fertilizers with it.

To retain the moisture in the seed compost a sheet of glass should next be placed over the seed tray. Before doing this I prefer to cover it first with a sheet of clean white paper; in this way condensation that collects on the glass does not fall onto the seed and soak the surface compost. Another advantage of the paper is that it lets some light through, which may be an advantage for some seeds (see table), but not enough to accelerate the growth of slime or algae.

This can be important in the case of seeds that take a long time to germinate, since such growth can interfere with germination. Instead of using sheets of glass, you could slide the seed trays into polythene bags, or merely cover with a suitable transparent plastic.

To discourage the formation of slime and algae, you could try the product Algofen (see page 239). This is still very new, however, and may possibly damage some tender or fine seeds. So far trials

15 *Preparing a Pan for Seed Germination*
A: seed compost. B: thin white paper. C: sheet of glass.

have been very promising, but the range of seeds and seedlings is so great that there is still much experimentation to be done (see page 83).

SEED GERMINATION, PRICKING OUT AND AFTER-CARE

Most greenhouse plants grown from seed require some form of propagator to supply the necessary warmth for germination. Most bedding plants sown early for summer display in the garden will also need artificial warmth. Home-made propagators have been described (page 57), but any garden centre or shop will usually stock a number of proprietary designs to suit a wide range of requirements. Get the best that you can afford. Thermostatic control to give a range of temperatures and a high maximum temperature are two important features to look for. Some greenhouse plant seeds may require about 80°F (27°C) for initial germination, although afterwards it is often possible to reduce the temperature gradually until the plants are happy in much cooler conditions.

After placing the seed trays in the propagator at the recommended temperature, see each day that the compost is still moist and whether germination has started. If you use the same propagator for several batches of different seed, see that all have the same temperature requirement. As soon as germination begins the paper covering should be immediately removed. Sometimes germination is erratic, but do not wait for all or most of the seeds to germinate before removing any covering and giving them light. However, very tiny seedlings can be left with the glass cover over to help retain moisture. If the propagator is equipped with a cover, the glass or plastic seed tray covering may usually be removed completely, but the propagator cover should be left in position until germination is complete. After germination light is essential or the seedlings will become drawn, spindly and pale in colour. All the same, good light does not mean direct powerful sunlight.

The best results are obtained when the seedlings are pricked out as soon as they are large enough to handle. The term 'pricking out' means removing the seedlings to more permanent quarters, such as small pots for growing on and potting on, as described on page 102, or to large seed trays in the case of bedding plants (see page 228). For slow-growing greenhouse and pot plants it is also often convenient to prick out into large seed trays rather than into small pots. This makes watering easier, and the young plants can be moved out of the seed trays and into pots when large enough.

To handle very small seedlings during the pricking out process I prefer to use a pair of long, finely tipped tweezers, which can be obtained from most chemists' shops. Some people use a thin piece of flat wood or plastic with a 'V' cut at one end to insert into the compost and lift the seedling out. After removal the seedling should be lowered into a small depression made in the compost of the new seed tray or pot and *gently* firmed in position by re-positioning compost around it. Be very careful not to damage roots, especially when a seedling has a long tap root. The sooner pricking out is done, the less likely it is that severe damage will be caused. The seedlings will then grow away much more quickly.

In some cases, when seed is plentiful and inexpensive, or when the seedlings are too numerous and too small to make pricking out very practical, the seedlings can be thinned out by removing and discarding the surplus. However, with most greenhouse seeds this is wasteful.

Some large seeds can be sown directly into small pots if preferred. I will suggest where appropriate how many should be sown, and the best pot size to use.

When modern composts are used the once dreaded damping-off of seedlings is not common. However, the spores of the various fungi that cause the toppling over of newly pricked-out seedlings are probably present in the air. It is wise therefore as a matter of routine to water-in all pricked-out seedlings with Cheshunt compound. This copper fungicide can be bought from garden shops and should be applied according to label instructions. It is best applied with a fine spray, as suggested for watering seed trays, and this operation can replace the normal watering-in of the pricked out seedlings that is necessary to settle the compost around the roots.

After pricking out, the seedlings can generally be transferred to the greenhouse staging or to shelves. Be careful not to expose them to strong sunlight at first and to check that adequate moisture is present each day. However, good light is essential, as I have already pointed out. It is often a good idea to return the seedlings of plants preferring higher temperatures to a propagator until they are well rooted and established.

FAVOURITE GREENHOUSE PLANTS SEED FROM

Abutilon hybrids (flowering maple)

These are easily grown perennials flowering the first year. If the plants are stopped by pinching out the growing tip when a few inches high, they will branch to form a bushy pot plant. If left they may grow tall but flower sooner. Old plants may become scruffy and lose lower foliage. The leaves are maple-like and the flowers pendent on short stalks and about 2 inches in diameter. Colours are shades of pink, crimson, orange and yellow, and the petals are often attractively veined. A large cluster of yellow stamens enhances their beauty. Germination is easy at about 60/65°F (16/18°C), one plant per pot. Pot on to final 5-inch for first year flowering. Best in cool greenhouse, but will survive in frost-free. With March sowings, flowers can be had from summer to winter.

Acacia (mimosa)

The most popular acacia is *Acacia dealbata*, the mimosa of the florist. It is an easily grown pot plant, usually grown only for its graceful foliage, since the flowers only appear after some years, when the plant is well established in a small tub and takes up considerable room. The yellow fluffy balls of flower are well known, and in a large, frost-free greenhouse with good light they will be borne freely in spring. For foliage, first-year plants can have a 5-inch pot. Germinate at about 65°F (18°C). Plants that have become inconveniently large can sometimes be planted outside in the milder sheltered parts of the country. Other species of acacia are listed in the seed catalogues and some of these make more compact pot plants, but few flower quickly. Sow any time from spring to summer.

Annuals (hardy garden types)

Choice varieties of many garden annuals make excellent pot plants. By taking extra care and protecting the potting compost with glass, you can produce the most spectacular results. A cool airy greenhouse is essential so that the plants can be raised under almost hardy conditions. Best results are obtained by sowing in autumn and growing on over winter. Very early flowers can be had. Generally it is convenient to prick out the seedlings, several to a 5-inch pot. Recommended for growing in this way are *Phlox drummondii* (most varieties), *Clarkia elegans* ('Salmon Bouquet'), calendula ('Golden Gem'), nemesia ('Unwin's Hybrids' and 'Funfair'), nicotiana ('Idol' – this is compact and remains open all day) and larkspur ('Dwarf Hyacinth Flowered'). The several F_1 hybrid types of antirrhinum make fine pot plants. The large flowered forms can have all side shoots removed to produce single enormous specimen spikes. For this, put one plant to each 5-inch pot. 'Double Column' stocks, which produce a single spike, can be grown similarly. 'Beauty of Nice' stocks are useful for winter flowering. For stocks get the Hansen's type. The seedlings have light and dark green leaf colouring to indicate which will be double flowered; keep only the light green seedlings. Best germination temperature is about 50°F (10°C), which gives the most noticeable colour contrast in the seedlings. Some of the taller annuals will need thin canes for support as they grow, but here I have suggested the more compact and dwarf forms, which should always be selected for pot work.

Asparagus (so-called 'asparagus ferns')

These are not ferns (see page 121). Most commonly seen are *Asparagus sprengeri*, which has pendent fine needle foliage and goes well with flowers in hanging baskets, and *A. plumosus*, which has even finer foliage but stands erect. The foliage of the latter is often used with buttonhole flowers like carnations. However, more recently a delightful species, *A. meyersii*, has become available. This has foliage similar to *A. sprengeri* but it is very neatly erect and much more compact. Give it a 3½-inch pot the first year and a 5-inch the second. It is much slower growing than *A. sprengeri*. All these species are suitable for a frost-free greenhouse. Germinate the seed in early spring at about 60°F (16°C).

Begonias (see also pages 142, 160, 180)

All begonias are best sown as early as possible, for early flowering and a long period of bloom. The fibrous-rooted kinds popular for bedding make excellent pot plants. The large flowering forms of these, such as 'Muse Rose', are especially suitable. 'Colour Queen', a variety with green and cream variegated foliage, is also interesting. There are many F_1 hybrids giving a wide range of flower and foliage colour.

Exhibition double begonias can be grown only from tubers of named varieties (see page 142). However, quite decorative tuberous sorts can be had from good strains of seed. The multi-flora doubles, such as 'Double Fiesta', are particularly recommended. These will flower – prolifically – from summer to autumn if sown early; the flowers are about 3 inches in diameter. It is also possible to grow from seed several types of pendulous begonias for hanging baskets; these, too, flower the same year from early sowings. An excellent species, simple to grow from seed, is *Begonia bertinii*. Again, this is quick flowering, although tuberous. The flowers are brilliant scarlet and very striking indeed although single. A compact form and a strain of seed giving white, yellow and orange colours as well as red shades is also available.

B. rex is a handsome foliage plant with large heart-shaped foliage, variously coloured and marked, but it does best in a warm, shady and humid greenhouse.

Begonia seed is very fine and can be mixed with some dry silver sand to assist even sowing. Do not cover with compost. Germinate at about 65°F (18°C). Keep the seed trays in a warm propagator until the seedlings are large enough to handle, after which the fibrous sorts can be transferred to large seed trays until ready for potting.

Browallia

Browallia speciosa is a free-flowering perennial which gives a splendid show of winter bloom in the warm greenhouse. In the cool greenhouse you should allow the plants to remain dormant over winter by keeping them only slightly moist and they will flower from spring to autumn. The blue flowers are small but plentiful. Sow in early summer, when no extra warmth will be necessary for germination. In the cool greenhouse keep the plants in small pots over winter. Do not worry if they deteriorate slightly. In spring new growth will begin, and it is then advisable to nip out any remains of the previous year's growth to within about 4 inches from the base, otherwise straggly plants will result. In a warm greenhouse growth will continue over winter and the plants should be potted on as required. Generally a 5-inch pot is suitable for flowering plants. The seedlings are best stopped several times to encourage branching growth and to prevent them from becoming tall and straggly.

B. viscosa is a pretty annual with blue, white-centred flowers in great profusion. Sown in spring, flowering will occur in autumn. Put several seedlings to each 5-inch pot and stop them when they are a few inches tall to induce bushy growth.

Calceolaria

With herbaceous calceolarias it is easy to produce a dazzling display from seed. There are a number of varieties from dainty neat plants

114

with masses of small flowers to huge specimens with clusters of enormous pouchlike flowers. The varieties can be chosen to suit your greenhouse size, but for the best effect display some of each together. In spite of their exotic appearance – the inflated flowers are often speckled or spotted with contrasting colours – calceolarias can be grown in merely frost-free conditions. However, you must keep the frost away or the plants will be blackened and ruined. For earlier bloom a cool greenhouse may be necessary. The time of flowering also depends on variety and time of sowing. It is possible to have flowering plants from November to late spring.

Generally seed should be sown from May to June. Compact and small flowered multiflora varieties usually flower sooner than the huge exhibition types. The F_1 hybrid, 'Glorious Formula', is especially early. No extra warmth is needed for germination. Prick out the seedlings into large seed trays, spacing them well. Put the trays in a cool, shady place over the summer months, such as a north-facing cold frame. Keep them watered and watch for aphids (page 83), to which these plants are especially prone. When the plants are large enough for potting, transfer to $3\frac{1}{2}$- or 5-inch pots, depending on size. Take care not to damage the brittle foliage. The F_1 hybrids can be flowered in $3\frac{1}{2}$-inch pots. Large varieties can be potted on as required to 5- to 7-inch pots. As the plants gain height provide a cane. Feed with a liquid feed at the first sign of buds. During winter watch for botrytis attack (page 84). From late winter onwards you may need to apply Coolglass shading to the glass at times; the plants are likely to wilt with an increase in the sun's intensity. Cool, shady conditions with good ventilation are essential. Do not use pesticidal smokes on these plants, and avoid spraying the flowers. After flowering the plants should be discarded.

Calceolaria rugosa 'Sunshine' is a new F_1 hybrid shrubby type. Before it was introduced shrubby calceolarias could only be satisfactorily raised from cuttings. The F_1 seed yields splendid sturdy plants for summer bedding from February sowing, but the plants are also excellent for pots. In 5-inch pots in the frost-free greenhouse they will form large specimens, evergreen in winter and flowering from early the following year.

Campanula (see also page 163).

The most popular greenhouse campanula is *Campanula isophylla* (page 163). This cannot be grown from seed. However, a very similar species, *C. fragilis*, is easily grown from a spring sowing, and generally no extra warmth is required. It has large, pale blue flowers and can be used for the same purposes as *C. isophylla*.

Very spectacular when well grown is *C. pyramidalis*, the chimney bellflower. This can be sown in May with no extra warmth. Prick out the seedlings first into seed trays, and then into 5-inch pots. Keep them in a shady cold frame until autumn. Then transfer them, singly, to 8-inch pots or, in threes, to 10- to 12-inch pots and keep them in a frost-free greenhouse over winter. From spring on the plants will quickly increase in height; by summer tall spikes of flowers will be produced, making an impressive sight. Both blue and white forms are available, and they grow to between four and five feet.

Capsicums and solanums

Although two very distinct species of the same family, the culture of these can be described together. Capsicums usually have green to red elongated or slightly elongated fruits; solanums, better known as winter cherries, have spherical berries of a similar colour. Solanum berries can be poisonous, however, and children should be warned not to eat them.

For a good crop of berries it is important to sow early. Late February to early March is best. Germinate at about 60/65°F (16/18°C) and prick out into small pots in the cool greenhouse. Some varieties may need stopping when they are a few inches high to promote bushy growth. Pot on as required to final 3½-inch pots. During summer keep the temperature down to the minimum. When the plants flower stand them outside or plunge the pots in a tray of moist peat outside. Solanums especially need good pollination or the berries will not form. Outside, insects will do this, but it also helps to spray the open flowers with a fine mist of water to distribute pollen. If this fails to produce berries, try using a tomato set (see page 194). Capsicums usually set much more easily than solanums.

Solanums are prone to magnesium deficiency. For this reason

it is wise to add Epsom salt (magnesium sulphate) to the potting compost, about ½ ounce per bushel. Magnesium deficiency will result in leaf yellowing and fall.

In October return the plants to the greenhouse. Solanum berries are usually beginning to turn red at this time. Capsicums may develop much earlier, depending on the variety, and some may be ready for decoration by late summer. Good varieties of capsicum, sometimes incorrectly listed in catalogues as 'peppers', include 'Red Fangs', 'Fips', and the multi-coloured 'Chameleon'. A notable large-berried solanum is 'Red Giant', which has bright orange fruits.

Chrysanthemum (see also pages 210 and 230)

The greenhouse chrysanthemums usually grown from seed are the 'Charm' and 'Cascade' types. The former is easy, the latter needs care and training. Both have masses of small starry flowers in a variety of beautiful colours, and both can be started from seed sown in February with a germination temperature of about 60°F (16°C). Transfer seedlings first to large seed trays, then to small pots and pot on as required. The seedlings should be stopped by removing the growing tip, when about three leaves have been formed, to promote bushiness. During summer the plants can be accommodated in cold frames and some time during summer they will need a final potting into 8- to 10-inch pots, depending on their development. They flower from late summer to autumn. The Charms form large cushions of bloom up to about 2½ feet in diameter on plants about 1½ to 2 feet high. The Cascades are taller, and those plants with flowers poor in colour or form should be discarded. Keep the best ones for cuttings and subsequent training into the cascade form.

During late autumn basal shoots will form on the Cascade plants you have saved. These should be taken as cuttings (see page 219) about 3 inches long, and rooted as described in Chapter 14. When rooted, pot into 3½-inch pots and grow on over winter in the cool greenhouse. By spring the plants will need 5-inch pots of John Innes No. 3 compost. When the plants are about a foot tall they should be hardened off and moved outside the greenhouse. When about 1½ feet tall pot on to 12-inch pots, insert a stout cane

117

in the ground at an angle of about 45°, and tie the plant to the cane at a height of about 6 inches from the plant's base. In the lower leaf axils side shoots will form as the plant develops. These should have the tips removed when about three leaves have formed, thus encouraging more shoots to form on the new side shoots; these are again stopped, as already described. The process should be repeated until about late September. As a result of the stopping the plant should be bushy at the base and tapering at the top, and the leading shoot will have been tied to the cane as it developed. The final stopping should be arranged so that the lower parts of the plants are pinched out during about mid September, the middle parts at the end of this month, and the upper parts about a week later. This is to ensure that the flowers are evenly distributed over the whole plant, appearing simultaneously at the top and the base.

In October you should move the plants to a frost-free greenhouse – an operation needing great care to avoid damage. The plants should be from about 3 to 5 feet long and covered with buds. The cane must be carefully removed and the plants lowered gently so as not to snap the stem. At this stage it is useful to have a helper. With your assistant supporting the plant take the pot into the greenhouse and place it on a shelf or on the staging where the hanging plant will be able to cascade. To prevent breakage of the stem it is best to bend a piece of very stiff wire into a 'U' shape and insert one end of this into the compost at the pot's side. The base of the plant can then be tied to this. In some cases it may also be necessary to slope a cane from the staging or shelf to the floor to support the plant.

It has only been possible to give a rough outline of the training procedure here. Success comes with practice and your technique may have to be altered to suit your particular growing conditions. The plants should be fed as described on page 212.

Cineraria

This is another pot plant with outstanding colour. It can be easily grown along the lines suggested for calceolaria on page 114 – the two are often grown together. The same germination temperature and pot sizes apply. Cinerarias bear masses of daisy-like flowers in many colours and sometimes the petals are banded in white.

Colours can be rich and vivid, or pastel and delicate. There are many varieties, embracing multi-flora types with lots of small flowers, intermediate kinds and huge exhibition forms. There are also Stellata types that have masses of small, starry flowers. An important new variety is 'Spring Glory'; this has large flowers but the plants are compact. It has an exceptionally long flowering period – up to ten weeks – and can be sown in June for Christmas flowering or later for spring use. 'Gubler's Double' is a double-flowered variety, but is somewhat clumsy-looking and limited in colour.

Cinerarias are even more prone to flagging than calceolarias. In late winter the sun may be intense enough to cause considerable wilting of the foliage. Should this happen, apply Coolglass to the glass and wipe off during dull weather. Do not give the plants more water if the compost is already moist; in shadier and cooler conditions they will quickly recover.

Cinerarias are also liable to serious aphid infestation and it is wise to apply a systemic insecticide as a routine precaution. Generally the plants do not need canes for support unless they are being transported. Discard after flowering.

Coleus (flame nettle)

This popular foliage plant, with its gloriously coloured leaves, is simple to raise from seed sown from any time up to early summer. However, fully grown plants need warmth over winter, or the foliage will fall. For this reason it is best to sow early and discard the plants at the end of the year. Germinate at about 60/65°F (16/18°C) and prick out into seed trays. Allow the plants to develop sufficiently to show their true colours – the tiny seedlings may not look very exciting. The best colours can then be potted and the others discarded. Pot on as required and remove flower spikes as they form. The flowers are not particularly decorative and may even give an untidy appearance. Many beautiful varieties are now available, including fancy kinds with frilled or laced foliage. Of special note is the new F_1 hybrid 'Carefree'. This seed gives an outstanding range of rich, contrasting colours, many unusual to the normal coleus strains. The plants are compact and vigorous.

Cuphea ignea (*Mexican cigar plant*)

This is a neat pot plant with numerous small, elongated, scarlet flowers with black and white tips. It is very quick flowering and even as a seedling is impatient to bloom. Sow in early spring at 60/65°F (16/18°C) and prick out the seedlings into 3½-inch pots in which they will flower. This species is good for a bright greenhouse or sun room, but is also tolerant of shade. You can keep the plants over winter if you wish, but they are so easy to raise from seed it is hardly worth while.

Cyclamen (see also page 144)

From a September-to-November sowing, good flowering specimens of cyclamen can be grown in about fourteen months. There are a number of varieties in the seed catalogues, ranging from miniatures to large flowered sorts. Some strains are noted for scent, but not all cyclamen have this desirable quality. Some varieties are also of special interest for their attractive foliage.

Place the seed on the compost surface and cover with about ½ inch of fine moist peat. Germinate at about 65°F (18°C) and keep this temperature steady. Germination may be erratic, but when the seedlings have formed two leaves prick out into 2½-inch pots. Keep the temperature at about 65°F until the seedlings are well rooted and then lower to about 60°F. During April pot on to 5-inch pots. For summer transfer the plants to a shady cold frame. When potting cyclamen at any stage see that about one-third of the corm protrudes above the compost surface, since this lessens the chance of rotting. In September take the plants back into the greenhouse and treat them as described (page 144). Remove any premature flower buds to conserve the plants' resources for the main display from December to spring.

Recently, varieties with frilled petals have been introduced, and some of them are very attractive. Very new is the F_1 hybrid double, but this lacks the charm and grace of the single cyclamen flower. A dainty new miniature which I recommend is 'Puck': it is very free flowering, has a good colour range and pleasingly marked foliage, and grows to only about 8 inches tall.

Exacum affine

This has small but plentiful lavender-blue flowers with orange-yellow anthers. In the cool greenhouse it can be sown in spring for autumn flowering; in the warm greenhouse it will flower in winter. It is of special interest for its delightful fragrance, but unfortunately I have found that some new, so-called improved varieties, developed for compact habit, have lost their scent. Sow from February onwards, germinating at about 65°F (18°C). Prick out several seedlings to each 3½-inch pot and grow on in warmth for early results. Transfer to the greenhouse staging in spring when the temperature is rising generally. Exacum like shade, warmth and humidity.

Ferns (see also page 183)

Ferns are grown from spores which are botanically quite different from seed. Most seed catalogues offer spores of mixed ferns suitable for cool or warm greenhouses. The spores are very fine indeed and

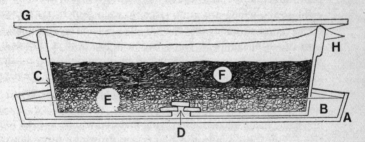

16 *Arrangement for Germinating Fern Spores*
A: shallow pan. B: water kept topped up. C: half pot. D: drainage hole covered with crocks. E: coarse washed grit or crushed pumice stone. F: seed compost. G. sheet of glass. H: thin white paper.

can be mixed with a little silver sand for sowing to get better distribution. Sow in spring on a lime-free compost; preferably peat or grit. Place the compost in a well-drained half pot (page 98), and stand this in a shallow dish or tray of water so that the compost is kept really moist. After sowing cover the half pot with a sheet of glass and place in a shady part of the greenhouse. Germination may take some time and the tray of water must be kept topped up during this period. (Two months is not unusual.) After this time the compost surface may appear to become covered with a greenish lichen-like growth. This is the first stage in fern growth, the pro-thallus stage.

Close inspection will reveal that each prothallus consists of a tiny heart-shaped filmy growth. It is at this stage that fertilization takes place and for this to happen a film of water on the prothalli is essential. Leave the glass cover in place on top of the half pot to keep in moisture. After fertilization the tiny first fern frond will begin to rise from the prothallus. The sporeling can then be pricked out in the usual manner into small pots and potted on as required. For composts and general culture, see page 183.

Freesia (see also page 145)

From a January sowing freesias can be expected to flower from summer to autumn. They do not make tidy pot plants, but the blooms are useful for cutting and you can save the corms from any plants notable for size, colour or fragrance. Sow about seven to eight seeds, which are quite large, to each 5-inch pot and give a temperature of about 60/65°F (16/18°C). Cover with about their own depth of compost. Germination is hastened if the seeds are soaked overnight in tepid water before sowing. After germination leave the pots in the propagator for a week or so. Then move to the staging of a cool greenhouse where the temperature preferably does not fall below about 50°F (10°C) for long periods. A few thin canes and some inconspicuous thin tying material will be needed to keep the foliage neat while the plants are growing. After flowering, continue to water and feed from time to time until the foliage begins to die. Then allow the pots to dry and separate the corms from the compost. Spread out the corms in the sun for a few days to dry and 'ripen' – a treatment which improves flowering. The corms can then be stored in a dry, frost-free place and potted as described on page 145.

Gerbera jamesonii (*Transvaal daisy*) (also see page 168)

An early spring sowing will often give plants flowering from autumn into winter. It is essential for seed to be reasonably fresh. It should be sown on end (it is elongated in shape) or at any rate only covered very slightly with compost. Germinate at about 70°F (21°C), prick out into small pots and pot on as required. Generally, 5-inch pots are suitable for flowering specimens in autumn. Although the *jamesonii* hybrids are interesting to grow – you can get some good colours and save the finest plants – there are two other important new introductions. The first is the 'Ramona' strain, which has very broad petals and strong stems for cutting. The second is 'Thurman's Double'. This has a wide colour range, and the flowers are often surrounded with a ring of thin petals greatly increasing in number towards the centres. Since 'Thurman's Double' is specially produced for the seed trade by hand pollination and prompt harvesting, the seed is extremely fresh and germination is usually 100 per cent. This is just as well because the seed is expensive.

Gloxinia (also see page 147)

At one time beginners often had difficulty in growing these magnificent plants from seed. However, the introduction of F_1 hybrids with their increased vigour has now made the job quite easy. Sow in January. Do not cover the seeds with compost since germination is better if some light reaches them. Germinate at about 70°F (21°C) and keep the seed trays in the propagator until the seedlings are large enough to handle. Germination is usually very good, so sow thinly. The seedlings can be pricked out into large seed trays or into small pots if preferred. The young plants are best kept in the warmth and humidity of a propagator until the general rise in greenhouse temperature allows their transfer to the staging. Gloxinias like warmth, shade and humidity. Pot on as required, taking care to leave the tops of the small corms just above the compost surface. A final 5-inch pot is suitable for flowering, which should occur from late summer to early autumn. After flowering dry off the corms as described on page 147, and thereafter treat as for growing from corms. You will have the finest flower display the second year.

Grevillea robusta (Australian silky oak)

Although this ultimately grows to a considerable size, it is a decorative foliage plant when it is young. It can also be kept more compact by stopping when it is beginning to reach an inconvenient height. Sow from early spring to summer, germinating at about 70°F (21°C) and transferring the seedlings to 3½-inch pots. A lime-free potting compost must be used for best results. Pot on as required. In winter the plants may deteriorate unless you can maintain cool-house conditions, but plants that lose their foliage due to chill may grow again with the return of warmer conditions in spring.

Heliotropium peruvianum (cherry pie)

Often used for summer bedding, the new varieties of this sweetly scented plant are excellent for pots. The best is 'Marine', which is compact and has deep-blue flowers. Sow from January to spring, germinating at about 60°F (16°C) and pricking out into 3½-inch pots. Pot on as required to 5-inch pots. Generally no stopping is required for this variety. Flowering is from late spring to autumn, depending on the time of sowing. The plants can be saved over winter in the cool greenhouse, and they should be cut back. They will begin to grow again in spring, but nowadays it is probably best to raise new plants from seed each year.

Hibiscus

There are numerous beautiful hibiscus for the greenhouse, but the one to raise from seed is the F_1 hybrid 'Southern Belle'. This remarkable plant has enormous flowers the size of dinner plates, in beautiful shades of carmine, pink and rose – also pure white with a carmine centre. Sow as early in the year as convenient – preferably January. Germinate at about 65/70°F (18/21°C) and prick out into 3½-inch pots. From then on pot on as required to a final 10-inch pot. Growth is rapid and you should bear in mind that the plants will eventually grow to a height of from 4 to 5 feet and produce their great flowers from summer onwards. The plants can be kept over winter, but to get the best flowers you should raise new plants from seed each year. This is a splendid plant for the cool conservatory, and one that will amaze the grower.

Impatiens (busy lizzie)

This is probably one of the most commonly seen of all pot plants, but often it is either not very well grown or is allowed to become straggly. There are many excellent varieties now available and you get the best results by sowing frequently so that young plants can be used for decoration instead of old ones. The dwarf forms are the most suitable for pots and they are very quick flowering, even very young seedlings bearing bloom. Sow at almost any time of the year if you have a cool or warm greenhouse. Germinate at about 65°F (18°C), pricking out into $3\frac{1}{2}$-inch pots. Plants will flower in this size pot quite well, their neat growth almost hiding the pot from view. Notable new varieties include 'Zig Zag', which has white flowers striped with pink, salmon, scarlet and orange; 'Minette', which is low and spreading; 'Elfin', which is also dwarf and is very brightly coloured; and 'Treasure', which has exceptionally large flowers. All these are F_1 hybrids.

Ipomoea tricolor (morning glory)

This is one of the most beautiful of the easily grown climbers. It is usually listed in catalogues as *Ipomoea rubro-caerulea*, although this name is not correct. The plant is typical of the convolvulus family, but the flowers are often at least 4 inches in diameter. Although several colours ranging from crimson to white striped blue are now available, I still think the original intense blue is the finest. The flowers are seen at their best in the morning – hence the name morning glory. By afternoon they have usually faded, although there will be plenty of buds ready to open the next day. Sow in early spring, germinating at about 65°F (18°C), and prick out the seedlings into $2\frac{1}{2}$-inch pots. Prompt pricking out, before a long tap root is formed, is essential or the seedlings may die or deteriorate. Try to maintain warm conditions for the seedlings in the early stages. Pot on to a 5-inch pot for flowering, and provide a cane for the plant to climb up. Alternatively, put several plants in a 10-inch pot and train them up wires, strings or plastic netting fastened to the wall of a lean-to or the greenhouse side. Morning glory likes a position in good light. If grown in a 5-inch pot, stop the seedling when it is a few inches high to encourage several shoots. This will reduce the ultimate height, which can be as much as 8 feet – absurd for a small pot. In recent years a disease believed to be of the virus type has affected ipomoeas. The seedlings are pale, whitish or white-striped instead of green, and lose vigour. If this happens, a higher temperature sometimes helps to boost the seedlings so that they recover. Try buying your seed somewhere else. The variety 'Heavenly Blue' is an old favourite. 'Early Call' is a new rose-pink form, 'Flying Saucers' is white with blue stripes. To hasten germination, soak seed in water overnight.

Jacaranda mimosaefolia

Like grevillea this makes a handsome foliage plant. Although less frequently seen it is probably more decorative. It can be raised from seed in exactly the same way, but does not need a lime-free compost. The foliage is delicate and ferny in appearance, and a large, well-grown specimen is very beautiful.

Kalanchoe blossfeldiana

In recent years this has become a popular house plant. It is easy to grow and even suffers some neglect without apparent ill-effect. Being a succulent, it does not mind if you occasionally forget to water it. Numerous varieties are available, with scarlet, orange, magenta and yellow flowers borne in large panicles. The foliage is dark green, thick and succulent. Sow in spring, germinating at about 65°F (18°C). Prick out into $2\frac{1}{2}$-inch pots and pot on as required. The plants will flower in winter in the cool greenhouse or indoors, but you will get the finest results the following year. You cannot always predict when they will flower; they are affected by the day length and the amount of light they receive. After flowering the plants are best cut back to some extent, otherwise straggly specimens will result.

A trick to get early flowering is as follows: sow in January and grow on the seedlings until June at 45/50°F (7/10°C). Transfer to a cold frame that is blacked-out. Remove the black-out so as to regulate the daylight to only nine hours per day. Continue until flower buds form – usually after about ten weeks. Since old plants can become woody and straggly, it is wise to propagate from small cuttings or raise new plants from seed frequently.

Lobelia tenuior

This species is a tender but very glamorous form of the well-known garden lobelia and has very large showy flowers of a beautiful blue colour. It is useful for hanging baskets or for trailing from shelves or from the staging edge. Sow as early in the year as possible, germinating at about 65°F (18°C). Prick out into large seed trays and return to the propagator until well established. To encourage bushy growth, stop the seedlings when they are about 3 inches high. Transfer the little plants to 7-inch half pots or other containers, setting about four or five plants to each 7-inch pot. If you do not want them to trail, use a few twiggy sticks to keep the plants upright. Flowering begins in summer and continues until autumn. This species enjoys warmth, and may fail if sown too early under cool conditions. If no suitable propagator is available leave sowing until later; flowering will then of course also be later. During summer, shade the greenhouse where this lobelia is placed and keep up the humidity. Discard the plants after flowering.

Mimosa pudica (sensitive plant)

This is an exciting curiosity that everyone should grow at some time or other. Children find it especially interesting. The attractive foliage is made up of numerous leaflets. These fold up dramatically on being touched, and a more vigorous disturbance causes the whole plant to collapse. The plant recovers after half an hour or so and is then ready for a repeat performance. Sow in spring, germinating at about 65°F (18°C), and prick out into 3½-inch pots, in which they can remain for the year and produce their small, solitary, pale purple to pinkish mimosa-like flowers – by no means showy. A height of about 9 to 12 inches is usually reached by autumn. The plants can be kept and grown on over winter in a warm greenhouse. However, young plants are more sensitive and it is better to raise new plants each year from seed. The seed is fairly large and can be soaked overnight to improve the speed of germination.

Nierembergia caerulea

This is almost hardy, and useful for the frost-free greenhouse. It grows to a height of about 9 inches and bears masses of blue

127

campanula-like flowers, about $\frac{1}{2}$ inch in diameter, with yellow centres. Sow in spring, germinating at about 60°F (16°C). Prick out the seedlings into 7-inch half pots, setting about four or five to each pot. The plants will flower during summer; but if they are saved over winter, after being cut back to within about 2 inches of the compost surface, and given just enough water to keep the compost moist, they will grow again the following year and flower much more profusely. The variety 'Purple Robe' should be obtained if possible.

Palms (see also page 186)

A number of palms are easy to grow from seed. One of the easiest is the magnificent *Phoenix canariensis*, which is hardy in the Isles of Scilly. Two hardy palms are *Trachycarpus fortunei* and *Chamaerops humilis*. Useful for the small greenhouse is *Phoenix roebelinii*, the dwarf date palm. *Butia capitata*, a near relative of the coconut, *Howea belmoreana*, the curly palm, and *Howea forsteriana*, the flat palm, are others worth growing. The seed is very large and is best germinated by immersion in moist peat at a temperature of about 80°F (27°C). When the seed shows signs of germination by sprouting or cracking, plant in 5-inch pots. For general culture, see page 186. For ease and tolerance of cold conditions I recommend *Phoenix canariensis*, although this will eventually become too large for the greenhouse. You can then try it outside in mild, sheltered places.

Pelargoniums ('geraniums') (see also page 171)

It is usually best to buy regal pelargonium s as named varieties and until recently this was also true of zonals ('geraniums'). However, the recent introduction of F_1 hybrid seed has altered the situation. Very fine plants can now be simply raised from seed to flower in one year. The Carefree hybrids give a range of beautiful colours including white, pink and scarlet; the flowers are handsome and the plants strong and vigorous. Separate colours are also now obtainable. I recommend two F_1 hybrid dwarf forms: 'Dwarf Carefree', which has a variety of colours, and 'Sprinter', which has well-formed flower-heads. Both are very early. From January sowings plants can be ready for summer flowering. Sow in a temperature of about 65°F (18°C). Transfer to 3½-inch pots and then pot on to 5-inch pots. For general culture, see page 171.

Petunia

There is little point in growing the ordinary multiflora bedding petunias in pots under glass, but the grandiflora types and the doubles, often spoilt by weather outdoors, will flourish in the greenhouse. The doubles have a delightful clove-like fragrance, similar to that of carnations. The double 'Giant Victorians', an F_1 hybrid, makes a magnificent pot plant. Sow as early in the year as possible at about 60/65°F (16/18°C). Do not cover the seed with compost since light aids germination. Prick out into large seed trays and transfer the seedlings to 3½-inch pots when large enough. For flowering, a final 5-inch pot is adequate. For best results, petunias like plenty of light and an airy greenhouse. The doubles will, however, tolerate some shade.

Pharbitis, see Ipomoea

Polyanthus

The polyanthus, one of the primula family, is well-known for its brilliant outdoor colour in spring. It also makes a splendid pot plant for the greenhouse and is especially useful where there is little or no artificial warmth. Under glass the pleasing fragrance of the polyanthus will also be better appreciated. There are many exquisite forms available, and again the F_1 hybrid seed is recommended. The recently introduced F_1 'Regal Supreme' is particularly fine; it has larger and better flowers than the more popular 'Pacific Giants', as well as a wonderful scent. Of the separate colours the blue strains are perhaps the most beautiful, especially the ones with the central yellow eye. Other fancy types can be had too, including 'laced' forms whose petal edges are delicately bordered with a contrasting colour.

Sow during February to March, germinating at about 55/60°F (13/16°C). A higher temperature than this is undesirable. Prick out into large seed trays, allowing plenty of space around each seedling. The trays can be kept in a shady cold frame until they are ready to transfer to 5-inch pots – probably from late summer to autumn. In autumn take the potted plants into the frost-free or cool greenhouse where the temperatures should not rise higher than 45/50°F (7/10°C). Over winter slow growth will continue and you should give sufficient water for this without waterlogging the compost. In early spring, when you first detect the flower buds, begin feeding with a liquid feed. After growing the plants as pot specimens you can transfer them to the garden where they will usually multiply. However, for the finest pot plants it is better to grow freshly from seed than to divide up existing outdoor plants.

Primula

From a very large number of primulas, three are most commonly grown in the greenhouse: *Primula malacoides*, *P. obconica*, and *P. sinensis*. If sown in May these flower from early winter (starting with *P. sinensis*, the Chinese primula) to late spring. *P. obconica* often continues to flower for many months, becoming a perennial. *P. kewensis* is worth growing because it is the only one that contains yellow.

Beginners' attempts to grow primulas from seed often result in failure, but if you follow these instructions disappointment should be avoided. Make sure that your seed is from a reputable firm and reasonably fresh. Do not cover the seed with compost since light is necessary for the best germination. Germinate at about 60/65°F (16/18°C) and promptly prick out into large seed trays. Keep moist and well shaded during the summer, and keep the temperature down. In autumn pot into $3\frac{1}{2}$-inch pots. *P. malacoides* can be left in this size for flowering, but the other two will need potting on to 5-inch pots. When potting do not plant too deeply. Press the compost down firmly round the roots, or rotting may set in at the base. Do not use hard water for watering. It is best to use *clean* rainwater – not collected from roofs or stored in dirty butts (see page 76) – if the mains water is hard or limey. The compost should also be checked for alkalinity. A pH of about 6·5 is ideal, but in some cases an acid compost (see page 96) may give better growth. In alkaline compost, containing too much chalk or lime, growth will be very slow and weak and the foliage will turn yellow and sickly.

The minimum temperature for these primulas should not fall below 45°F (7°C).

Numerous varieties of these primulas are described in the seed catalogues. Both *P. obconica* and *P. sinensis* can cause an unpleasant skin rash in people allergic to them; if you notice any redness or irritation of the skin when handling them, it is best to have nothing more to do with these two species. *P. malacoides* and *P. kewensis* appear to be harmless.

Saintpaulia (African violet) (see also page 174)

This is another plant that the introduction of F_1 hybrids has made worth growing from seed. Mixed colours are available in the F_1 form – giving blue, pink and white, as in the variety 'Fairy Tale', and there is 'Blue Fairy Tale' or 'Pink Fairy Tale'. Sow as early as possible to yield plants flowering the same year. Germinate at about 65/70°F (18/21°C), but sow thinly because germination is usually very good. Do not cover the very fine seed with compost. Prick out the seedlings when large enough to 2½-inch pots and return them to the propagator until established. In the cool greenhouse it is wise to leave the seedlings in the propagator until warmer weather arrives. Pot on as required, but take care not to snap off the brittle foliage. It is usually best to pot on just before the leaves protrude over the pot rim. Young plants will flower well in 3½-inch pots, but they can be potted on to 5-inch. Since the plants are not deep rooted they often look better in half pots. For general culture see page 174.

Salpiglossis

This extremely colourful annual, which bears a multitude of richly hued trumpet flowers often exotically veined with golden yellow, is very easy to grow. If you sow in autumn you will get very early flowers on large plants the following spring. If you sow early in the year, flowers will bloom from summer onwards. There are a number of fine varieties listed in the catalogues, but the one to produce a fantastic display is the F_1 hybrid 'Splash'. This is compact, early and vigorous. Germinate at about 60°F (16°C) and prick out into 3½-inch pots. When the seedlings are about 2 to 3 inches high stop them to encourage branching growth. If you sow

131

in autumn, the shoots that grow after the first stopping should again be stopped; early spring-sown plants may not need a second stopping. Pot on spring-sown plants to 5-inch pots for flowering. Autumn-sown plants may need a slightly larger pot since they make larger plants. The height is from about 1½ to 2½ feet and a cane is usually needed for support. Good light and airy conditions are important. A frost-free greenhouse will give excellent results.

Schizanthus (*butterfly flower, poor man's orchid*)

This easily grown annual is outstanding for free flowering and colour over a very long period. You can sow in autumn for spring flowering and early in the year for early summer to late autumn bloom. The flowers, although small, are extremely pretty and come in many colours; they are beautifully marked and veined, and so numerous that they almost obscure the foliage. The foliage itself is highly decorative, being ferny and delicate. Germinate at about 60°F (16°C). For autumn sowing the large flowered varieties are recommended. 'Pansy-Flowered' and Sutton's giant hybrids, which used to be called 'Cattleya Orchid', will give exhibition results. For sowing early in the year select these and several dwarf varieties. 'Hit Parade', which grows to a height of about one foot, is remarkably easy to grow. It needs no stopping and flowers with amazing speed; stagger the sowings so that you can see it flower over many months. Prick out autumn-sown seedlings into large seed trays and, when they are big enough, transfer them to 5-inch pots: three seedlings a pot, or one to a pot if you are prepared to carry out more stopping. Stopping the seedlings is important to get as much branching growth as possible. Stop them when they are about 2 inches tall; stop all side shoots at a similar length. Further stopping can be carried out: it depends on the vigour of the plants and on how soon you want them to flower. Pot on if necessary to 7-inch pots. A cane will be needed for support since autumn-sown plants can reach a height of 3 feet. The plants from January to spring sowings can usually be put three to each 5-inch pot. One stopping may be sufficient for the taller varieties; the dwarf types can be left alone. Over winter schizanthus are susceptible to botrytis (see page 84) and they are also sensitive to paraffin fumes. Give good ventilation, and shade in spring. Ideal for the cool house.

Streptocarpus (*Cape primrose*) (see also page 177)

Raising this from seed is sometimes difficult for beginners, but the following method should reduce failure. Sow as early in the year as possible at about 65°F (18°C). Use sifted John Innes No. 2 compost and do not cover the seed. The seedlings grow very slowly at first and should be left in the seed trays in the propagator until they are large enough to handle and well rooted. Sow thinly so that there is plenty of compost around each seedling; this can be removed with the seedlings when they are transferred to 2½-inch pots. Do not plant the seedlings in the pots too deeply or they may rot at the base. Keep them in a propagator after potting, maintaining about 65°F (18°C) until they are well rooted and growing healthily. Often the seedlings may appear slightly distorted and one leaf may grow more than others. This is not unusual, and need cause no alarm. Once established the plants usually grow quickly and can be potted on and transferred to the staging. If you sow in January, you can have flowers by autumn. 'Triumph' hybrids are recommended. These have an excellent colour range and the flowers stand well above the foliage on strong stems. Pelleted seed is now available. For general culture, see page 177.

Thunbergia alata (*black-eyed Susan*)

This is another very easily grown quick-flowering annual that will charm everyone with its orange to cream flowers with contrasting matt black centres. It can be used in hanging baskets although by nature it is a climber. It is by no means rampant and can be trained up a fan of canes set in a 5-inch pot. Sow from about February onwards at about 60/65°F (16/18°C) and prick out directly into 5-inch pots, one to three plants to a pot; alternatively, you can set them around the edge of a hanging basket. A good strain of seed should give a high percentage of flowers with black eyes, but sometimes this desirable feature is missing. This species will do well in bright conditions or in shade. However, in a dry atmosphere it is prone to red spider attack (see page 85). It can be expected to reach an ultimate height of about 3 to 4 feet.

Torenia fournieri (wishbone flower)

The flowers of this species are of unusual shape, and their deep blue colour contrasts with a golden yellow throat. They are small but numerous and the plant is neat and compact. Sow in spring at about 65°F (18°C) and prick out the seedlings into 2½-inch pots, or if preferred into large seed trays for the early stage of growth. Subsequently put about three to four seedlings to each 5-inch pot. The plants can be grown upright, with a few twiggy sticks for support, but they also make a neat trailer for hanging baskets. In the warm greenhouse you can have flowers almost the year round by staggering sowings. Since you need a congenial temperature for the best growth, do not sow in the cool or frost-free greenhouse too early unless you can keep the seedlings in a roomy propagator. They grow to about one foot.

TABLE TWO

More interesting plants to grow from seed
(recommended)

Sow during spring. Germinate at about 65°F (18°C) unless otherwise stated. Pot sizes are for flowering-size plants.

Ardisia crenulata   Shrubby plant with bright red berries.
7-inch pot.
Asclepias curassavica   Attractive heads of orange flowers.
5-inch pot.
Asclepias physocarpa   Spiky inflated seed pods second year.
7-inch pot.
Boronia megastigma   Scented purple-yellow flowers second year.
7-inch pot.
Brunfelsia calycina   Scented lilac flowers. Evergreen. Sow 70°F.
Caesalpinia gilliesii   Small shrub. Showy scarlet stamens. 10-inch
pot.
Caesalpinia pulcherrima   Shrub. Showy orange-yellow flowers.
10-inch pot.
Cardiospermum halicacabum   Inflated pods. Trail or climb.
Foliage.

Clivia miniata (see page 165)   3–4 years to flower from seed. Sow 75°F.

Coffea arabica   Shiny foliage. White flowers in warmth. Sow 75°F. 5-inch pot.

Cordyline terminalis tricolor   Foliage tinted red or rose. Sow 75°F. 5-inch pot.

Crossandra undulifolia   Pink flowers over long period. Evergreen. 5-inch pot.

Cyperus alternifolius   Foliage like umbrella spines. Aquatic. 5-inch pot.

Datura suaveolens   Short tree. Scented white trumpets third year. Warm. 10-inch pot.

Desmodium gyrans (*telegraph plant*)   Terminal leaflets move. Very curious. 5-inch pot.

Dracaena indivisa   Palm-like foliage. Sub-tropical bedding plant. 5-inch pot.

Eccremocarpus scaber   Easy climber. Showy orange/scarlet flowers. 10-inch pot.

Eucalyptus citriodora   Lemon-scented foliage. Minimum winter temperature 50°F. 7-inch pot.

Eucalyptus globulus   Glossy eucalyptus-scented foliage. Almost hardy. 7-inch pot.

Gossypium herbaceum   (*Cotton*)   Short-lived yellow flowers followed by fluffy cotton balls. 5-inch pot.

Heliconia hybrids   Handsome foliage. Small flowers like strelitzia. 8-inch pot.

Hippeastrum (hybrids and species)   Handsome flowers; see page 148.

Hypoestes sanguinolenta   Foliage spotted red. Very pretty. 5-inch pot.

Luffa cylindrica   Elongated gourds – bathroom loofah. Curious. 10-inch pot.

Musa coccinea   Handsome foliage like banana. Sow 80°F. 10-inch pot.

Nertera granadensis   Cushions of bead-like orange berries. 5-inch pot.

Passiflora caerulea (*Passion flower*)   Vigorous climber. Hardy. 10-inch pot.

Passiflora quadrangularis   Exotic version of above. Warm only. 10-inch pot.

Petrea volubilis   Climber. Long racemes, blue flowers. Sow 75°F. 10-inch pot.

Philodendron bipinnatifidum   Glossy foliage plant. Sow 70°F. 5-inch pot.

Rechsteineria leucotricha   Tuberous. Silver-grey leaves, salmon flowers.

Rehmannia angulata   Bright-red flowers over long period. 5-inch pot.

Rosa, miniature   Easy from seed, flowering first year. 5-inch pot.

Schefflera digitata   Large shiny pale-green foliage. 5-inch pot.

Sesbania punicea   Racemes of salmon pea-like flowers. 7-inch pot.

Sparmannia africana   White flowers in winter. Minimum temperature 45°F. 7-inch pot.

Limonium (*statice*) *suworowii*   Long pink tail-like flowers. Everlasting. 5-inch pot.

Vinca rosea   Glossy foliage, pink or white flowers. 5-inch pot. (Also known as *Catharanthus roseus.*)

All these plants are normally easy and give quick results from seed except where stated. However, those taking several years to flower are so beautiful they are worth waiting for.

9 Growing Plants from Storage Organs

HOW TO BUY

It is not possible to enter here into the botanical explanation of the differences between bulbs, corms, tubers, rhizomes, tubercules, pseudobulbs and so forth. However, a common factor is that they store plant food in the form of chemicals such as starches, sugars and the like. They are therefore collectively known as 'storage organs'.

Because of this, you will appreciate that when you buy a bulb, or storage organ of some kind, its quality will depend on how it has been grown. It is vital to buy from reputable firms or nurserymen. Never buy storage organs that are soft or spongy, show signs of rot, have holes, or are covered with 'corky' tissue as is possible in the cases of cyclamen and gloxinia. Bulbs that may be covered with loose scale, such as narcissus or tulip, and bulbs like lilies composed of segments, should be closely examined for signs of mould or mildew. Fairly large bulbs are more likely to be of flowering size, but some corms and tubers can deteriorate with age and their size may not be significant (see under individual species headings).

The time of year of planting is often important. A good nurseryman will not dispatch material until the proper time. You should then plant as soon as possible.

GENERAL CULTURAL HINTS

Bulbs or other storage organs should not be grown in 'bulb' fibre which contains no nutrient – use the potting composts described in Chapter 7. The storage organs grown in the greenhouse fall into two classes – spring-flowering 'bulbs' (not all are true bulbs), grown in pots and often forced, and half hardy or tender types. The culture of these is different and is described here separately.

Spring-flowering 'bulbs'

Nearly all the spring-flowering bulbs commonly seen outdoors can be grown in pots in the greenhouse. Grown in this way their beauty can be better appreciated and their fragrance is more noticeable. They can also be made to flower earlier. Some, called 'prepared' bulbs, are given special treatment by the growers so that they flower considerably earlier, generally at Christmas or soon after. To get earlier flowers some ordinary bulbs can be 'forced'. This means giving a slightly higher temperature for a time. However, not all bulbs can be forced, and some so treated may go 'blind' – produce no flowers at all. Varieties that can be forced are always marked in the catalogues of the bulb suppliers.

Ornamental pots and bowls are often used for potting bulbs. Care must be taken with undrained containers to see that they do not become waterlogged. A few pieces of lump charcoal at the bottom may help aeration and keep the compost from 'souring'. For the greenhouse, clay bowls or half pots are usually best.

The number of bulbs to plant per pot or bowl varies with type and personal preference. The larger bulbs like hyacinths can be individually planted if desired. When planting more than one, try to select bulbs all near enough the same size and quality – otherwise they may flower at different times. Any loose debris adhering to the bulbs should be removed before potting and any dead roots trimmed off. Pot so that the tops of the bulbs are just level with or slightly above the compost surface (see Fig. 17). Large bulbs like hyacinths and narcissi can have at least half showing above the compost. This is to give a good depth for the roots to penetrate. You should remember that since the bulbs will be grown under frost-free conditions there is no need for deep planting.

After potting, the containers must be put in the cool and in darkness. They should be immersed in the 'plunge' described on page 56. See that the compost is kept moist, but on no account allow waterlogging. Plunging is essential to stop top growth being formed before an adequate root system has developed.

If it is not convenient to plunge the containers, heap as much moist peat as you can on top of them and cover with a polythene bag or piece of polythene held in place with an elastic band. Stand the covered pots outdoors in a sheltered place, free from frost.

Whilst frost and freezing must be avoided, high temperatures at this stage are harmful. Inspect the containers from time to time to see that they are moist. It usually takes from six to eight weeks for shoots to appear. If the bulbs appear to be rising out of the containers it is probably because the containers are too small, the bulbs have been planted too deeply, or the compost has been firmly pressed around them. If this happens, repot the bulbs now

17 *Positioning Greenhouse Bulbs*
Most greenhouse bulbs should be potted with at least half above compost surface to give maximum depth of compost for roots.

in larger containers. Attempts to push them down will damage the roots.

When shoots have appeared, remove all covering and stand the containers in a shady, cool place. After about a week they can be gradually introduced to full light and then given as much light as possible to prevent pale, drawn foliage. For flowering from early spring onwards, most spring-flowering bulbs should be potted from September to November. In spring every attempt must be made to keep temperatures in the greenhouse down, and slight shading with Coolglass may be required.

Forcing spring-flowering bulbs

Forcing does not mean subjecting bulbs to hot, humid conditions as so many beginners seem to think. If this is done most bulbs will fail. At first the potting and plunging procedure already outlined must be carried out so as to get a good root system. When there are signs of top growth and there are plenty of roots, transfer the containers to a greenhouse where the temperature does not exceed about 60/65°F (16/18°C). Gradually build up to this temperature over a week or so, and at the same time introduce to full light. To see whether there is adequate root growth, the bulbs can be tapped out of their pots. If the compost is moist it should come away cleanly without disturbing any roots that have formed. Unless there are adequate roots it is unwise to begin forcing. When flowering occurs the temperature can be considerably lowered to extend the life of the blooms. Bulbs to be forced should be planted from August to September.

Prepared bulbs

Full instructions and the best temperatures are usually provided by the suppliers of the bulbs. Sometimes plunging is necessary for a time, and sometimes it is not. Since preparation of bulbs for early flowering needs care and experience, they are necessarily more expensive. If saved after flowering they can be potted the following year or transferred to the open garden. However, they may fail to flower until they have settled down to a normal sequence of growth again.

Greenhouse and summer-flowering storage organs

These are potted as already described. They are left in the greenhouse and not plunged. Specific cultural notes are given later in this chapter.

Often these bulbs, corms, tubers, rhizomes and so on have to be 'started' into growth. This is usually done by immersing them in moist peat in a warm propagator. As soon as the shoots or roots appear, you should pot them in potting compost. In some cases starting in this manner ensures that they are planted the right way up, for it is often difficult to locate the tops of, for example, gloxinia corms.

After-flowering care of storage organs

After flowering, the foliage of bulbs, corms and the like should be looked after. Then is the time to water and feed well, for it is usually then that food for future growth and flowering will be stored in the organ and development there will take place. With true bulbs the flowers will usually be formed inside in the 'embryo' state. As the foliage deteriorates, you should water less and less, and finally allow the pots to go dry. There are exceptions (see below) for which it is necessary to give just a little water when the organs are dormant. However, in general the organs can be stored dry during dormancy or over winter, and suggestions for storage are given under the individual species headings.

TABLE THREE

Spring-flowering bulbs, etc., for pots

Many of the following have small storage organs and should be planted 5 to 7 per 5-inch pot or *pro rata* according to size. They are generally best grown in half pots, except for the larger bulbs like hyacinths, narcissi and tulips.

Allium (1 to 3 per 5-inch pot)	Hyacinth
Anemone	Leucocoryne
Babiana	Leucojum
Bulbocodium	Muscari
Chionodoxa	Narcissus (includes daffodil)
Crocus	Puschkinia
Eranthis	Scilla
Erythronium	Tecophilea
Fritillaria	Tulip (there are many species)
Galanthus	Urginea
Hermodactylus	

BULBS AND OTHER STORAGE ORGANS FOR GREENHOUSE DECORATION

Achimenes

There are numerous species and varieties of these charming flowers, in many colours. Some grow upright and others are trailers, ideal for hanging baskets; some can be grown either way and if wanted upright can be given a few twiggy sticks for support. They are grown from tubercules, which are small catkin-like storage organs. These can be started into growth from late January to April by immersion in moist peat in a propagator at 60/65°F (16/18°C). As soon as they sprout, set about three to five plants to a 5-inch pot, just covering with compost. If you wish, you can use half pots for the upright types. If you use baskets, you will need ten to fifteen to a basket of average size. After planting, the temperature should be allowed to fall as little as possible. In the cool greenhouse, planting is best left until March or April. When growth is under way, water generously and in summer see that humidity is kept up. Slight shading from direct sunlight will be required. Flowering usually begins in June and may continue until late autumn. When the foliage begins to die down water less and gradually allow the pots to become dry. The tubercules can be stored, with the dry pots on their sides, in a frost-free place over winter. The following January, separate the compost from the tubercules, which should have increased in number considerably, and start again as already described.

Most catalogues list the Michelssen hybrids, which have large flowers in bright colours and a neat habit. A fine variety for hanging containers is 'Cattleya', with blue and white flowers. 'Purple King' is an old favourite of dwarf habit and easy for beginners. Also easy is 'Paul Arnold', violet-purple with strong stems. 'Peach Blossom' has rich pinkish flowers with dark eyes. Very many beautiful forms can be obtained from specialists.

Begonia (see also pages 113, 160 and 180)

Among the tuberous begonias can be found some of the most impressive greenhouse blooms. You should obtain a catalogue from a specialist firm for descriptions of the numerous named varieties; new varieties are introduced frequently. These choice varieties have enormous blooms in wonderful colours but are necessarily expensive. The beginner would do well to start with some of the cheaper, but quite good, varieties offered in the catalogues of seed firms. They are usually listed at the end among miscellaneous bulbs, tubers, etc., and include pendulous and multiflora sorts.

Start the tubers by immersing them in moist peat at a temperature of about 65°F (18°C). This should be done as early as possible for summer to autumn flowering the same year. If possible maintain a temperature of about 55°F (13°C) after transferring the tubers to 5-inch pots when they show signs of growth. The top, which is usually the concave or flat side, should be level with the compost surface. If you want large exhibition blooms, allow only one shoot per tuber to develop; others can be used as cuttings and should be carefully broken off where they meet the tuber. As the plants grow the stems will be very brittle and a cane should be given for support. Start feeding when the buds begin to form. The male flowers are the showy ones and, to encourage the resources of the plant to be directed towards them, the female buds should be removed. The females usually form each side and can be easily identified by their winged seed pods. Summer shading is important, especially when the plants are in bloom. Coolglass is ideal for begonias since, as well as giving excellent light for growth without the risk of scorching, it brings out the colours of the blooms.

After flowering, water less and less until the pots go dry, but, while the foliage is still in good condition, do not be in too much of a hurry. When the pots are dry at the end of the year the tubers can be removed, freed from adhering compost and top growth, and stored in a frost-free place in a box of clean, dry sand over winter.

Canna (see also page 232)

The best canna for pots in the greenhouse is the low growing *Canna* 'Lucifer'. This variety is very neat and sturdy, reaching a height of only 1½ to 2 feet. The huge gladiolus-like flowers are brilliant vermilion and orange. This variety and other taller named varieties, some of which have beautiful bronzy-coloured foliage (see also page 232), can be started from fleshy rhizomes, again immersed in moist peat early in the year at about 60/65°F (16/18°C). When you see that they are growing, transfer the rhizomes to the smallest pot that will take them comfortably and keep them as near 60°F as possible. *Canna* 'Lucifer' will flower well in 7-inch pots, but the larger varieties will need 10-inch pots. The earlier the rhizomes are started the longer the plants will be decorative – from summer to late autumn. Water and feed well during summer and gradually reduce watering in autumn. Cut off the faded top growth and store the pots in the greenhouse under frost-free conditions. Do not allow the pots to go 'dust dry' in winter; if the rhizomes dry out completely they sometimes die or do not start well again. The following year the rhizomes can be removed from the pots and started again. It may be possible to separate them into several segments to increase the number of plants. In general, cannas like plenty of warmth, light and feeding, but they are easy summer greenhouse plants.

Cyclamen (from seed, see page 120)

Beginners find it easy to grow cyclamen from the corms of young plants offered by specialist nurserymen. Old 'corky' corms may flower badly or not at all, although there have been exceptions, with plants continuing to flower for many years. Start the corms from July to August, planting them in 5-inch pots of potting compost. The convex side of the corm should be put downwards in this case and about a third of the corm allowed to show above the surface of the compost. No extra warmth is necessary at this time of year and the pots can be placed in well-shaded frames. Water cautiously at first and more generously as the plants make active growth. Bring the pots into the greenhouse in September and try to keep a minimum temperature of about 50°F (10°C). Remove any premature flower buds if you want the main display during winter and early spring. The corms can be kept for further flowering for one more year if desired. To do this, continue watering and feeding for a time after the plants have flowered. Then gradually water less until the pots are moist enough only to keep the foliage in good condition. Rest the plants in a shady cold frame, standing the pots on a layer of shingle to keep out worms, and return to the greenhouse in September, treating them as before. Some people recommend drying off the corms completely after flowering, but I have had better results by cultivating the plants as described here. The corms usually offered are choice greenhouse varieties, mostly with large flowers. However, some of the hardy cyclamen species are worth growing in the cold greenhouse (see page 16), and also in an alpine house (see page 205).

Eucharis

The species usually grown is *Eucharis grandiflora*. It is a very large, long-necked bulb that should be potted like hippeastrum (page 148). This bulb dislikes chilly conditions and will grow better in a warm greenhouse. The large, powerfully fragrant flowers are white and reminiscent of those of the daffodil in shape. In warm conditions they are produced several times a year, including winter, in a warm greenhouse. Minimum temperature should be about 60°F (16°C). The bulb likes a fibrous compost, and if the John Innes is used some extra peat can be mixed in. In summer give plenty of water and feed when the plant is actively growing; in winter water enough to keep the foliage in good condition. This bulb must never be allowed to become completely dry. A certain amount of potting on can be done, but at a later stage it is better to apply top dressing than to disturb the bulb.

Eucomis (*pineapple flower*)

The species we grow is *Eucomis bicolor*. Its common name is derived from the strange pineapple-like cap of foliage at the top of the flower spike. The bulbs are easy to grow in the cool greenhouse. Pot direct into 5-inch pots early in the year, leaving the nose exposed. Water cautiously until growth is seen. In the cool house no extra warmth is necessary, since the bulbs are almost hardy. The flower spikes, which appear in July or August, are borne hyacinth fashion on one-foot stems, and are greenish with lilac edges. Although the flower is attractive, it can sometimes give off a very offensive carrion-like odour, and is then best put outside. This fact rarely seems to be brought to the growers' attention.

Freesia (from seed, see page 122)

Corms planted during summer, about six to a 5-inch pot, should flower during winter. The large flowered hybrids, which are not hardy, should be obtained. No extra warmth is needed in summer, but a winter temperature of about 55°F (13°C) is desirable. After flowering treat as though you were growing from seed (see page 122). Freesias like plenty of light or the foliage will become pale and inconveniently long. Very choice named varieties are available as corms, and some like 'Blue Banner' and 'Souvenir' are specially noted for fragrance. 'White Swan' is an excellent cut flower, and 'Pink Giant' is exceptional for free flowering. Not all are scented.

If you wish, you can plant again in late September for winter to spring bloom. In this case the pots should be plunged as for spring-flowering bulbs (see page 138).

Gladiolus

The ordinary garden gladioli are not very successful in small pots and there is little point in growing them in this way. An exception is 'Nymph', a variety of the dwarf species *Gladiolus nanus*. Other named varieties of this species can, however, be tried. Plant about three to each 5-inch pot in late autumn, just covering with compost. Keep in a frost-free house or frame until March, when they can be put on the staging and gradually given extra warmth. Water freely only when they are growing healthily. *G. colvillii* 'The Bride' can be grown similarly and is early flowering. Both these varieties are white, but 'Nymph' has bright carmine streaks.

Gloriosa *(gloriosa lily)*

The most readily available and most common is *Gloriosa rothschildiana*, a delightful species that can be easily grown from large elongated tubers. It is by nature a trailing plant and can look effective in hanging containers provided that there is enough height to the greenhouse – the plant may hang down 5 feet or more. Generally, it is more convenient to grow it as a climber. The leaves have tendrils at the ends to give support, but it usually needs a cane and tying. The flowers are like those of reflexed lilies – brilliantly coloured crimson and yellow, freely borne, and very attractive indeed.

The tubers are often very long. Start them growing by immersing them in moist peat at about 60/65°F. If you have a warm greenhouse do this as early in the year as possible for early flowering. If the house is cool, leave it until later. April to May starting will result in flowers from late summer to autumn. Check the tubers each day and at the first sign of rooting transfer to 7-inch pots. Set the tuber so that the rooting end is centrally placed. Keep warm and water well as soon as top growth becomes vigorous. Just before flowering start feeding and continue until the end of the year. When the foliage begins to deteriorate – this may not be until early winter – let the pots go dry and remove the remains of the top growth. The following year the pots should be carefully tipped out – the tubers are brittle and easily damaged – and you will usually find that at least one extra tuber has been formed. Shade the greenhouse slightly in summer and maintain a good humidity. A similar species sometimes grown is *G. superba*.

Gloxinia (see also page 123)

These wonderfully exotic and showy flowers with pleasing velvety foliage are easily grown from tubers started in early spring, or earlier if there is general greenhouse warmth. It is often difficult to distinguish the 'top' and 'bottom' of the tubers, but if you start by plunging them in moist peat at about 60°F (16°C) it soon becomes apparent where roots and where shoots form. Pot them in 5-inch pots, and leave them there to flower. If you do this early in the year, leave the pots in a warm propagator. The plants like warm, humid and shady conditions. Water well when growth is rapid; it is best to keep water off the foliage, though a fine mist that does not collect on the foliage in droplets will improve the humidity. After flowering, which is usually from late summer to autumn, gradually reduce watering and allow the pots to dry out. Then tip out the tubers, free from compost and remains of top growth, and store in a dry, frost-free place until starting time the following year. Two-year-old tubers usually give the best results. After this they may become 'corky' and should be discarded. You can propagate the plants you wish to keep from leaf cuttings (see page 221). Catalogues list a number of named varieties.

Haemanthus

The species generally grown is *Haemanthus multiflorus*. This has an extraordinary flower like an enormous crimson dandelion clock, and bright green foliage often coming after the flower. Pot the bulbs in spring as for hippeastrum. Give little water until the bulb starts to shoot. Once this occurs, growth is usually remarkably rapid. It usually flowers in late summer and afterwards sprouts its luxuriant foliage. This is the time to feed and water well, gradually reducing the amounts as the foliage deteriorates. During winter keep the bulbs almost dry or they may rot, and at a temperature of not less than 40/45°F (7/10°C). If potted in spring, no extra warmth is usually needed to get the bulbs growing. If you have a temperature of not less than 50/55°F you may be able to keep the bulb going all winter – if so water freely.

Hedychium (gingers)

Several species can be grown from rhizomes. The most commonly seen are *Hedychium coccineum* with scarlet flowers, *H. coronarium*, which is white and scented, and *H. gardnerianum*, which is powerfully fragrant, has red and yellow flowers, and is probably the best. Height is from about 3 to 4 feet and the flowers are borne in spikes during late summer to autumn. Pot the rhizomes in March, choosing pots large enough to take them comfortably. Pot on as required. Ultimately you will need very large pots or small tubs. You will obtain the best results by letting the plants become established in these and leaving them undisturbed. Water well in summer, sparingly in winter. The plants may take a few years before they flower freely, but the foliage is attractive and tropical looking. Although they are called 'gingers' and belong to the ginger family, these species are not the source of commercial ginger.

Hippeastrum (so-called amaryllis)

This is an important and impressive indoor bulb that has now become extremely popular. It can be had in the 'prepared' form for Christmas and early flowering, and is available in a number of named hybrids with enormous trumpet flowers in beautiful colours. Bulbs for normal flowering should be potted in early spring. The very large bulbs should be given a 7-inch pot and potted so that about two-thirds protrude above the compost surface. The flower bud may soon appear and grow rapidly. During this time you should water cautiously since it is not until the foliage begins to appear that there is substantial root growth. For this reason you must take great care, when the great flowers are formed at the top of the stem, to see that the whole plant does not topple out of its pot – there may be no roots for anchorage. When the foliage forms, you can water generously. If potted in spring, the natural greenhouse warmth may be adequate for growth. Earlier in the year you will need more warmth, and often an indoor window-sill can be used to grow excel-

148

lent plants. A first-quality bulb may produce two flower stems, each bearing four flowers. Sometimes it will flower later, in autumn.

Hippeastrums, like many other members of the Amaryllidaceae, prefer to remain undisturbed for as long as possible. For this reason repotting should be delayed for at least three years, if possible, and top dressing carried out. Although some people dry off the bulbs over winter, you can get much better results by giving them just enough water to keep the foliage in good condition. However, this can be done only in a greenhouse with a temperature minimum of 40/45°F (7/10°C). Prepared hippeastrums are potted from October onwards, usually for Christmas flowering. Full instructions are supplied with the bulbs. Hippeastrums can be grown from seed, although flowering may take from three to five years. They can also be propagated from offsets, the small bulbs that often form around the side of the large parent. These bulbs can be separated when repotting (see page 223).

Hymenocallis (Ismene) (Peruvian daffodil)

The species usually grown is *Hymenocallis calathina* and the variety available is called 'Advance'. This can be treated exactly like hippeastrum, to whose family it belongs. The flowers are like daffodils in structure and have a delightful fragrance. Sometimes you can get *H. festalis*; the variety 'Zwaneburg' is particularly fine. The flowers of these species are white, but a very pale yellow form is sometimes seen. Hymenocallis is frequently listed in catalogues as 'Ismene'. Pot up early in the year and maintain a temperature of about 55/60°F (13/16°C). The temperature requirement is somewhat higher than for hippeastrum, so it is less suitable for the cool greenhouse. Flowering occurs from March to April. A good-sized bulb will flower year after year, but small bulbs will have to be grown on before they flower satisfactorily. Keep almost dry in winter and leave undisturbed for as long as possible.

Ixia (corn lily), Tritonia (blazing star), Sparaxis

Since the culture of these is similar, they are described together here. They are grown from small corms and have dainty, many-coloured flowers borne several to a spike on stringy, wiry stems. They make good early cut flowers, but also look attractive in pots;

they are rather like freesias, and can be planted in the same way, preferably in October. After this they should be treated like spring flowering bulbs and plunged. During January the pots can be transferred to the cool greenhouse and very gently forced if desired. Culture is similar to freesia (see page 145), and flowering can be expected in spring. There are many named varieties of ixia and the nurserymen's catalogues should be consulted for details. The tritonias usually grown in the greenhouse are *Tritonia crocata* varieties: 'Orange Delight' is recommended. *Sparaxis tricolor* and *S. grandiflora* are mostly grown in the greenhouse and the variety 'Fire King' is an old favourite. These corms are not expensive, and after flowering it is a good idea to plant them out in the garden, where they should be well covered with soil in a warm, sunny site.

Lachenalia (*Cape cowslip*)

Several species are grown from small bulbs. These look particularly attractive in baskets and their flowers are long lasting. The best for baskets is *Lachenalia bulbifera*, usually listed as *L. pendula*, whose flowers are coloured in a combination of yellow, red and purple. Either plant the bulbs through the sides of wire baskets, with 2 to 3 inches between each bulb, or place them on the moss lining, with their tops pointing downward, before you add the compost. Put a few more bulbs at the top and around the edge. Such a hanging container will become a globe of colour when the plants flower from December onwards. Other species can be given bowls or pots with about five or six bulbs to each 5-inch container or *pro rata*. Just cover with compost. Potting is best done from August to September. Put the containers in a cold frame or cold greenhouse and transfer them to the cool greenhouse where the temperature does not fall to below 40°F (7°C). Temperatures in excess of about 55°F (13°C) must however be strictly avoided or the plants may not flower. After potting see that the compost is moist but do not be too free with water until the foliage is well on its way. Best for pot culture is 'Nelsonii', a variety of *L. aloides*.

After flowering put the containers in full sunlight and when the foliage dies down allow them to go dry. They may be left dry until the next potting time, when any offsets can be separated for propagation.

Lilium

Most lilies are excellent for pots. In recent years some wonderful hybrids have been introduced, some of which are expensive and may not survive outside in the garden. Success is usually assured under glass provided simple cultural care is taken. The majority of lilies grow well in the potting composts recommended in Chapter 7 (page 90). However, they do not like richly manured or fertilized soils or composts. A simple, special one which is easy to make consists of 4 parts fibrous loam, $3\frac{1}{2}$ parts sterilized leafmould, 2 parts grit, and $\frac{1}{2}$ part of crushed charcoal ($\frac{1}{4}$-inch lumps). Some lilies form roots at the base of the stem. To provide compost for

18   *Lily Collar*
Stem roots of lilies can be given more compost by adding a collar of bent zinc, aluminium or plastic.

these as they develop it is possible to increase the depth of the pot by adding a collar of metal sheet or plastic, or by cutting a plastic pot to suitable shape (see Fig. 18). When potting lilies, leave the 'nose' of the bulbs protruding slightly in order to give maximum useful depth for the basal roots; if any stem roots appear you can give them compost immediately, tipping it into the extra space provided by the collar. Autumn to spring is the best time for planting. After potting, the bulbs must be kept cool by plunging, as described for spring-flowering bulbs (see page 138). Take

151

care that there is not too much moisture or rotting may occur. When growth begins bring the pots into the cool greenhouse, but avoid high temperatures. Usually, the best pot size is from 6 to 8 inches, depending on the size of the bulb. The larger lilies need a pot to themselves, but some of the smaller types can be planted in threes. For descriptions of the enormous range of lilies available, consult the catalogue of a specialist firm (see Appendix). Specially recommended are Mid-Century hybrids, oriental hybrids and Fiesta hybrids. The following species and their varieties are also excellent.

Lilium auratum

Very exotic and powerfully scented. Stem rooting. Has some fine named varieties with rich colouring.

L. brownii

White trumpet-flowered with outside shaded chocolate-brown. Stem rooting.

L. formosanum pricei

This trumpet-flowered lily is remarkable for its ability to flower the first year from seed. It is best to acquire your stock this way, because the bulbs that form the first year can be saved for even better bloom production the following year. The first year, plant about five seedlings to a 10-inch pot, and in subsequent years, about three bulbs to the same-sized pot. Other lilies normally take some years to reach flowering size. Sow L. formosanum as early in the year as possible. Germinate at about 55°F (13°C), prick out into small pots and pot on. You will be delighted with this lily that is so easy, free flowering and fragrant.

L. iaponicum

Trumpet-flowered, white-tinted pink, fragrant, about 2–3 feet high. Plant three or four to each 8-inch pot.

L. longiflorum

The Easter lily forced by professional growers for Easter. Stem rooting. A good variety is 'Holland's Glory'.

L. regale

Very well known in gardens, but also good in pots. Stem rooting to some extent.

L. speciosum

Reflexing petals, fragrant and often flushed pink or crimson. Flowers in autumn when many others have finished. Most are stem rooting.

L. tigrinum

The tiger lily, an old favourite. 'Splendens' is good for pots, and there is also a double form.

L. umbellatum

A low-growing lily for limited space. Erect, colourful flowers, often very exotic. There are many named varieties.

Nerine

For the greenhouse the exquisite named varieties of nerine should be obtained, not garden forms. Beginners often fail through incorrect culture of these bulbs. They should be potted as soon as they are received in August, one bulb to a 5-inch pot. Pot as for hippeastrum, leaving the top of the bulb above the compost surface. Place the pots outdoors in a sunny frame and give no water until flower spikes or foliage start to grow. At this stage water generously, ensuring that the compost is thoroughly moistened. I suggest the John Innes No. 2, or a peat/grit compost. The all-peat type are difficult to wet once they have dried out. Bring the pots into the cool greenhouse for flowering from autumn to December. The flowers are borne as umbels of six to ten, on stems about one foot high, and have graceful, slender petals. The colours are glorious shades of rose, pink and salmon, often with a glistening metallic lustre.

After flowering cut off the dead umbels and continue watering until the foliage yellows. Then reduce watering, allowing the pot to go dry, and store dry in a frost-proof but sunny place until next starting time. Do not repot for several years – the bulbs prefer to remain undisturbed. Top dress before starting into growth; and if repotting is necessary, do it in August.

A number of beautiful species and other forms of nerine are worth growing under glass. Their culture may differ slightly from the popular named varieties and depends on the time of rainfall in their natural habitat. For descriptions and full details of individual culture consult a specialist nursery catalogue (see Appendix).

Polianthes tuberosa (tuberose)

This is noted for its sweet scent, and it also makes a fine cut flower but it tends to be an untidy pot plant. The variety 'The Pearl', which is double flowered, is usually grown. The species itself is single and quite pretty. Both are white with the flowers borne as spikes. As soon as you get them, pot the bulbs with the tips just protruding from the compost, one to a 5-inch pot or three to a 7-inch pot. Water cautiously at first and try to maintain a temperature of about 55/60°F (13/16°C); this will not be difficult in the cool greenhouse in spring. However, the tuberose can be forced at almost any time of the year if this temperature is attainable. The bulbs often fail to flower if saved for another year, possibly because most are imported from Mexico and it is difficult to give the best ripening conditions here. After flowering, try exposing the bulbs to as much sunshine as possible, then store dry over winter in a frost-free place.

Smithiantha (temple bells)

Modern smithiantha named varieties embrace some of the most beautiful combinations of flower and foliage colours, and often give very dramatic effects. The leaves are also a delightful velvety texture. The flowers are borne as spikes and are like foxglove in structure. There is a wide range of colours – shades of salmon, pink, cream, orange, yellow, red and purple, and the foliage is a rich shade of green, olive green, red or purplish, possibly with an iridescent sheen.

Start the rhizomes in late winter at 55°F (13°C) by immersing them in moist peat. When they start to grow, immediately pot one rhizome to a 5-inch pot or three to a 7-inch pot. Cover with a thin layer of compost, and make sure they are placed flat. If the greenhouse is cool, return the pots to the propagator until the plants are well rooted. Then water generously. If the weather is cold it is best not to start until March. Feed well when the flower spikes begin to form. Flowering will be from late summer to autumn. After flowering gradually allow the pots to go dry, and then store them on their sides in a frost-free greenhouse over winter. The next year, tip out the pots and separate the rhizomes, which should have increased in number. Pot and start again as already described. During summer try to maintain a moist atmosphere, and shade the greenhouse well. Plants started early can be stopped to produce bushy plants, but this delays flowering for a couple of months. The many named varieties are described in the specialist growers' catalogues.

Sparaxis, see *Ixia*

Sprekelia formosissima (*Jacobean lily or Aztec lily*)

This bulb has quaint, thin-petalled flowers, a colourful rich crimson, on stems about one foot tall. Pot with neck protruding, as for hippeastrum, in February. A 5-inch pot is adequate. Try to maintain about 45/50°F (7/10°C) and water cautiously at first. The flower will usually appear before the foliage in June. When the foliage is growing well, water freely and feed. In autumn allow the pots to go dry slowly and store the bulbs in their pots until starting time the following year.

Tritonia, see *Ixia*

Vallota speciosa (*Scarborough lily*)

Buy this species as large, flowering-sized bulbs, and pot them in August, one to a 5- or 6-inch pot, with the tops protruding as for hippeastrum. Water carefully at first, increasing as growth becomes vigorous. In autumn the trumpet-shaped scarlet flowers appear at the top of strong stems; each stem may carry as many as ten buds with about four or five open at the same time. The flowers are large and showy. Treat vallotas like hippeastrum (page 148), and keep them slowly growing in winter in the cool greenhouse. They usually produce offsets, which can be separated during repotting. These may take three to four years to reach flowering size.

155

Veltheimia capensis

This species has an attractive rosette of foliage from the centre of which rises a flower like a small red-hot poker. It is a very easy bulb and looks interesting, but the flower colour is a rather drab shade of pink. Pot in autumn in 5-inch pots, leaving about half the bulb above the compost surface. The pots can be put directly on the staging of a cool greenhouse and kept just moist. Flowering is sometimes erratic and may occur from winter to early spring. Continue watering and feeding until summer and then rest the bulbs by keeping them almost dry until autumn.

Zantedeschia aethiopica (arum or calla lily)

This is the well-known arum 'lily' of the florist – although it is not a lily. The rhizomes should be potted from September to October, one to each 6-inch pot or about three to a 10-inch pot. Mix some crushed charcoal with the potting compost, as you will have to keep it very moist. Just cover the rhizomes and keep the pots in a cool greenhouse, making sure the compost is kept nicely moist. Flowering is from March to June, but depends on the greenhouse temperature. If you force the plants a little, they can flower considerably earlier. After flowering and during summer, stand the pots outside, gradually reducing the amount of water and allowing the pots to go dry in autumn. Until this time, however, always water very generously indeed, and feed the plants well when they are growing vigorously. The dry pots can be turned out in September and the rhizomes, which should have multiplied, repotted as already described. There are several other ways that this plant can be grown, but this is the easiest.

TABLE FOUR

More summer to autumn flowering bulbs for pots

	Plant	Flowering time
Acidanthera	May	July
Brodiaea	Autumn	June
Calochortus	Spring	Summer
Camassia	Autumn	July
Chlidanthus	Spring	July
Crinum	Spring	July/September (1 per 10-inch pot)
Crocosmia	Spring	July/August
Galtonia	Spring	July/August (3 per 8-inch pot)
Habranthus	March/April	June/July
Iris	September/October	May/June (Dutch, English, Spanish)
Ixiolirion	September/October	May/June
Lapeyrousia	Spring	Summer
Lycoris	Spring	August
Ornithogalum	September/November	Summer (Chincherinchee)
Oxalis	September/October	May/July
Ranunculus	Early spring	June/August
Sternbergia	September/November	September/October
Zephyranthes	February/March	September

Pot five to seven to each 5-inch pot or *pro rata* according to bulb size unless otherwise stated.

10 Favourite Greenhouse Plants for Flowers

The following plants are generally best obtained as small specimens from nurseries or as rooted cuttings. Some are sold as 'house plants' and they will grow to their full glory in the greenhouse. Remember that it is better to buy small plants than large, mature ones; it is not only cheaper, but also gives the plants a chance to get used to the conditions of your greenhouse. Buy the more tender plants during the warmer months of the year. Beware of buying plants that have been standing outside flower shops during chilly weather. Reputable nurseries send out plants at the right time of year. The plants are carefully packed and may be in pots or wrapped in moist paper. Pot up immediately you get them, but be careful not to over-water at first; damaged roots may rot if waterlogged. There is a vast range of greenhouse plants and it is only possible to make a selection here. I have therefore concentrated on subjects that should be freely available; too often plants that are almost unobtainable are recommended. See Appendix for suppliers.

Acalypha hispida (red-hot cat tails)

This is sometimes sold as a house plant, for which it is hardly suited. Its attractive feature is the long, catkin-like, pendent, crimson flowers. Unfortunately, without warmth and a very high humidity it rarely succeeds. It likes an abundance of moisture during the summer and should be well shaded. Minimum winter temperature: 55°F (13°C). Add some crushed charcoal to the compost. In ideal conditions it will eventually reach a considerable size and it flowers from spring to summer.

Aeschynanthus speciosus (trichosporum)

This is also sold as a house plant and if kept on the dry side will survive a winter minimum of about 45°F (7°C). The species is good for hanging pots or baskets, and is better in the latter because it likes an aerated compost. Add some fibrous peat and moss to a peat/grit potting compost. During summer, spray frequently with water and shade well; it will grow best in warmth and humidity. Groups of bright orange tubular flowers are borne from summer to autumn and at other odd times.

Agapanthus (African lily)

Although there are several agapanthus that can be grown, the Headbourne hybrids, which are practically hardy, make excellent greenhouse plants. They are ideal for the unheated greenhouse where they will flower earlier and remain in good condition longer. Give each plant a 10-inch pot. Water and feed well in summer, but keep on the dry side over winter. They bear large umbels of beautiful blue flowers from July to September, and the plants are noted for their neat compact habit, which makes them ideal for pots. These hybrids are available from any good centre or hardy plant nursery.

Astilbe

The hybrids are fine plants for the unheated greenhouse, but given slight warmth they will produce graceful feathery plumes from April to May (compared with June to July for outdoor plants). Not all astilbes are suited to pot culture. The low-growing types are best, and for forcing the varieties 'Fanal' (red plumes) and 'Deutschland' (white) are especially recommended. Five-inch pots are suitable and it is wise to add crushed charcoal to the potting compost since plenty of water is needed the year round, and they are semi-aquatic. Pot the plants during autumn and keep them in a cold frame until December. From then on the plants can be taken into the greenhouse and forced for early bloom at temperatures from 50 to 60°F (10 to 16°C), allowing the maximum temperature to be reached slowly over a couple of weeks. Cut off faded top growth in autumn and propagate by dividing the roots before re-potting. Roots that freeze during dormancy can be forced earlier.

Azalea

Beginners often confuse the tender and the hardy azaleas grown in pots. Most of the hardy evergreen outdoor dwarf types make excellent plants for the cold or unheated greenhouse where they will bloom earlier. These are available from any good garden centre, and a wide selection of varieties is usually stocked. They are usually container-grown and merely need transferring to proper flowerpots, using a lime-free potting compost. Flowering lasts several weeks during the spring months. Unfortunately the 'Indian azalea', often labelled *Rhododendron indicum*, but really *R. simsii*, that appears in florists' shops around Christmas time, is often also expected to be hardy, whereas it is best suited to the warm greenhouse. Moreover, the plants that come onto the market in flower have been forced commercially by special techniques. Sometimes, owing to chill and sudden temperature changes, bought plants may drop their flowers and foliage. To save these plants, keep them warm, humid and shaded until summer. You can then stand them outdoors in a shady place and keep them well watered. If in autumn the plants are placed in a greenhouse with a temperature of about 55°F (13°C), they may flower again in December. At low temperatures they will flower later. A winter minimum of about 40/45°F (4/7°C) is desirable. Water with clean rainwater and always use lime-free or acid-type potting composts. Repot when necessary in autumn.

Begonia (tuberous, see page 142; from seed, see page 113)

There are numerous species with delightful flowers, often combined with decorative foliage, and many are sold as house plants. *Begonia corallina* is easy and impressive and *B.* × 'Lucerna' is similar. These have heart-shaped olive-green leaves spotted white above and flushed with red below. On established plants the flowers are borne very freely in large clusters, from spring to autumn. They are deep pink and they have conspicuous winged seed-pods attached. Small plants will flower well. After some years in the cool greenhouse they can reach a height of several feet and viewed from below the hanging flowers look most impressive. *B. fuchsioides* is a compact, winter-blooming shrub, with fuchsia-like flowers, as the name implies. *B. coccinea* grows very tall and has flowers similar to *B. corallina* but bright scarlet in colour; it flowers from spring to autumn. Its hybrid, 'President Carnot', has spotted foliage and grows more vigorously but the flowers are paler. *B. haageana* has foliage coloured dark-green on top and red below, and pretty pale pink flowers. *B. boweri* has foliage edged with chocolate-coloured streaks; it is somewhat hairy and has pale pink flowers in spring. *B. manicata* bears delicate panicles of pink flowers in winter; the foliage is also interesting, with tufts of red hairs below, and red borders. All these species are happy in 5- to 8-inch pots and with a winter minimum of about 50°F (10°C). For some the temperature can fall considerably, though they will usually suffer by dropping foliage and taking on a leggy, scruffy appearance. However, they usually recover in spring. Keep well watered and shaded in summer, and keep up the humidity. In winter keep only just moist, depending on the minimum temperature. The lower this is, the less water should be applied. Propagate by taking stem or leaf cuttings, or simply by dividing the roots or rhizomes.

Beloperone guttata (shrimp plant)

This is frequently sold as a house plant. Its common name derives from the strange shrimp-like appearance of the bracts surrounding the insignificant flowers, which flourish from spring until late winter. (The botanical name is now *Drejerea*.) Give the young plants 5-inch pots and remove the first flowers and bracts to encourage general growth. Although you are often recommended to shade in summer, the plants can in fact be put outside in full sunlight – provided watering is not neglected. The sunlight develops a fine rich colouring. Return the plants to the greenhouse in early autumn. A winter minimum of about 45°F (7°C) is advisable to keep the plants in good condition, and watering should then be slight. Overwintered plants that have deteriorated can be cut back in early spring; they will usually grow to large specimens during the summer.

Bougainvillea

Some of the most showy climbers or wall shrubs are found among the species of this genus. Again it is the highly coloured bracts that give the display and the actual flowers are very modest. Although the plants can eventually cover large areas they will in

161

fact make very attractive plants when quite small, even in 5-inch pots. By constant pruning you can keep them as neat shrubs if you have limited space. However, they are at their best when grown against the wall of a lean-to or trained up wires to the greenhouse roof. For this purpose put the plants in large pots or small tubs. When grown against a wall, a trellis or plastic netting should be given for support and the plant's stems tied to this. Water well in summer and keep up humidity by frequent spraying with clean rainwater. In winter keep on the dry side and try to maintain a minimum temperature of about 50°F (10°C). *Bougainvillea glabra* has mauve bracts, and flowers well when very young; so also will *B.* × *buttiana*, of which the finest variety is 'Orange King'.

After the plant has flowered, you can do some pruning, but February is the time for close pruning and the removal of all weak growth.

Callistemon (*bottle brush*)

A number of species can be grown. The one usually recommended is *Callistemon citrinus*, which eventually takes up considerable room. In fact *C. linearis* is much easier and more practical for the greenhouse. It is also hardy in mild areas and is ideal for the unheated greenhouse where its bright red 'bottle brush' flowers will not become bedraggled from rain – a common trouble when grown outdoors. This plant can be kept neat, although the less pruning the better. It can be trained to form a short standard if desired. It flowers in July. It is available from some garden centres in containers and it should be potted in a 10-inch pot. Water well and give maximum light and air. In winter give less water to keep conditions just slightly moist. Do not allow the roots to dry out completely. Ultimate height can be kept to about 4 feet.

Camellia

These well-known evergreen shrubs are splendid for the cool or unheated greenhouse and, contrary to widespread belief, they flower freely as quite small plants, sometimes even in 5-inch pots. There are many named varieties, usually derived from *Camellia japonica*, and a specialist nursery should be consulted before you make your selection. Although most of them are perfectly hardy, under glass they bloom earlier, unblemished by weather, and also last longer. The pot size depends on the size of the plant purchased, but camellias can be grown in pots that seem far too small provided they are fed well. An acid compost is best. In alkaline conditions the foliage may become yellow and growth poor. Never allow the roots to dry out, especially when the buds form. Erratic watering, with extremes of dryness and wetness, is a common cause of bud dropping and leaf fall. Beginners often experience this trouble, which may result from ill-treatment the plants have received months before. Shade them well; like all hardy plants under glass they object to 'oven temperatures', and must be well ventilated. The plants benefit from spraying with clean rainwater in summer, and they should also be watered with this in hard-water districts. Flowering usually takes place from February to May but in the greenhouse can be considerably earlier. You will have to prune the plants eventually to keep them in shape and to control their size; do this after flowering and before the start of active growth. At this time any necessary potting-on can also be done. It is usually advisable to stand camellias out in the garden during summer to give more room in the greenhouse. Choose a shady, sheltered place, stand pots on shingle to keep out worms, and do not forget to water and feed.

Other species are sometimes available. The early flowering *C. sasanqua narumi-gata* is very fragrant. The large white blooms appear from October to November. There are a number of varieties derived from *C. saluenensis* × *C. japonica*, all of which are even less tolerant to lime. The late-flowering *C. reticulata semiplena* has huge salmon-red flowers and *C. taliense* has waxy white flowers.

Campanula (*bellflowers*)

Most greenhouse campanulas can be grown from seed (see page 116). The one most usually purchased as a plant is the very old-fashioned *Campanula isophylla*. This is an outstanding plant for hanging baskets, or for pots at the edge of the staging, where it will form a cascade of bloom from late July to autumn. It is happy in a frost-free greenhouse provided that it is kept on the dry side over winter. The blue form is probably the most attractive, but there is also a white form. Often leaf variegation occurs spontaneously, the foliage becoming edged with cream. If a piece is removed and treated as a cutting a new variegated plant will result, but in my experience such plants are less vigorous and the flowers smaller. You can only propagate *C. isophylla* by taking cuttings or by dividing the roots in spring. It cannot be grown from seed.

Citrus (*orange, lemon, grapefruit, lime, etc.*)

Many people try to grow these from seed and are disappointed with the outcome. Success cannot be guaranteed because in commerce special techniques are used to produce plants suitable for cropping. These do not always come true from seed. Lemon and grapefruit are best to grow from seed; you can rear quite good lemon trees in only a frost-free greenhouse if there is enough space. Sometimes citrus species appear on the market, but they are not common.

By far the best investment is *Citrus mitis*, the dwarf orange, also known as Calomondin orange. You can normally obtain this easily, since it is sold as a 'house plant', and you will get the best results in the cool greenhouse with a winter minimum of about 45°F (7°C). In these conditions the waxy, fragrant white flowers, and little oranges in various stages of ripening, will be on the plant almost the year round. The plants are expensive to buy, but they are well worth the money and will give pleasure for many years. Buy them in early spring. Shade only slightly to protect from intense sunlight, and keep well watered during active growth from spring to summer. Keep only slightly moist in winter. If subjected to sudden changes or allowed to dry out, the foliage may turn yellow or fall. Over-watering will also cause yellow foliage, as will a compost that is not acid enough. Do not pot on too frequently and certainly not until the roots are slightly pot-bound. Use an acid compost. It may be an advantage to water the plant with a solution made by dissolving a pinch of aluminium sulphate (from a chemist's shop) in a pint of water. Use clean rainwater for general watering, and treat with aluminium sulphate only if the leaves turn yellow. Scale insects can be killed by dabbing with methylated spirit. Fortunately the dwarf orange is remarkably resilient, and even if all the branches become bare it will usually spring to life again when treated properly. It can be very vigorously pruned if desired and trained to shape easily. Even if cut back severely it will usually grow new shoots in a short while.

The little oranges, about the size of walnuts, can be preserved in syrup and used in cocktails, and a well-established and well-grown bush will give an excellent crop. There are few seeds, but they will germinate at a temperature of about 65°F (18°C).

Clivia

For some unknown reason clivias are sometimes said to be grown from 'bulbs'. The plants actually have fleshy roots. The species usually grown is *Clivia miniata* (Kafir lily), but this has several varieties. It is an easy but extremly impressive plant, with bold strap-like foliage and enormous umbels of large, erect, trumpet-shaped flowers of showy orange shades, produced in spring. If small plants are purchased they should be given 10-inch pots. Plants can be grown from seed but may take at least three years to flower. Splendid plants can be grown in a cool greenhouse, but over winter they will survive in a frost-free house if kept fairly dry. When in active growth they should be well watered and fed. Once established, they grow vigorously and soon fill their pots with roots and form side growth. When this happens, turn the plants out of their pots, carefully separate the side growth by disentangling the roots, and repot. If there is difficulty it is better to cut through the roots with a *very sharp* knife, or razor-blade – this will not cause bruising of the tissues. After repotting water very cautiously until the plants are growing well.

Daphne

The daphne most suited to the greenhouse is *Daphne odora*, which does well under frost-free conditions and is a neat evergreen. It bears heads of very pale purple flowers from January to April and these have a delightful spicy fragrance. This species is usually obtainable from garden centres, particularly in the south and west, where it is hardy in sheltered places. Once potted in 10-inch pots it needs little attention apart from watering and an occasional feed when it is actively growing.

Drejerea, see Beloperone

Erica (*heather*)

Several greenhouse species come onto the market at around Christmas time. The most common are *Erica gracilis*, which has pink flowers and a white form, and *E. hyemalis*, which has long foliage and pink tubular flowers. These may have been forced for early flowering. The plants should be potted on when necessary in an acid potting compost (see page 96). Stand them outdoors in summer, and water and feed them generously. In September return them to the greenhouse, where a temperature of about 45°F (7°C) is adequate. Water with clean rainwater. (Many nurseries now have named hybrids – the species mentioned here are the parent species.)

Erythrina crista-galli (*coral tree*)

This is a spectacular herbaceous shrub that has recently become more widely available. It should be potted in 10-inch pots in spring. You need a temperature of about 50/55°F (10/13°C) to start it growing; then water more and more generously. From June to July the large, waxy-textured, pea-like flowers are freely borne. They are a glistening red, and very showy and unusual. In summer, keep the house cool, shade slightly, and spray the foliage with water from time to time. During a good summer you can stand the plants outside to give more greenhouse space. In autumn, return the pots to the greenhouse, where the winter minimum should be about 40°F (4°C) and the plants should be kept fairly dry. Remove faded top growth, since new growth is formed each spring.

Fuchsia

This favourite is so well known that no description is necessary. There are many named varieties that can be grown as shrubs or standards, or as hanging basket plants; and there are also types for training against greenhouse walls and some noted for beautiful foliage. Some fuchsias, especially those related to the species *Fuchsia triphylla*, may not always be instantly recognizable as fuchsias – their flowers are long and tubular.

There are numerous firms specializing in fuchsias and you should consult their catalogues when making a selection; there is a fantastic range embracing the varieties of many famous breeders. In recent years the American fuchsias have been given much publicity because of their great size and often double form with marbled colours on the petals. However, our own developments have probably done the fuchsia greater service by preserving the flower's natural grace and beauty. You can buy most varieties cheaply as rooted cuttings in spring; pot them in $3\frac{1}{2}$-inch pots as soon as you receive them.

Fuchsias can be grown in several ways and when ordering some consideration should be given to this. Some varieties are ideal for training as standards, especially those with elongated single blooms, or for hanging baskets. Some are best kept to the bush shape and others can be formed into fancy shapes like pyramids. All good catalogues will help in selection. All fuchsias need a certain amount of training; you may have to start with the newly potted rooted cutting.

To grow a standard the tip of the plant must be retained intact at all costs. The plant must be grown on and potted on with this as the object. Remove all side shoots and provide a cane as support for the stem until the required height is reached. It may be necessary to grow the plant on over winter, and in this case a growing temperature of about 55/60°F (13/16°C) is essential to prevent it from becoming dormant. When the required height is reached nip off the top of the stem. Branching shoots will then form immediately below. Stop these also to encourage further branching, and so on, until a bushy head is developed. At this time, and not before, remove the foliage on the supporting stem.

Hanging baskets of normal size usually require about three plants set around the edge. Once the leading stem is well over the basket side it should be stopped to produce plenty of branching growth.

As ordinary pot plants, fuchsias only need stopping from time to time to encourage bushy growth and a neat sturdy habit. Weak and unwanted growth should be cut out without hesitation. Do not stop for too long, as this may affect flowering; plants are best left to grow unmolested for about eight weeks before the required flowering time. In the case of large plants or standards, you may have to devote a whole year to the process.

Many of the choice greenhouse fuchsias are not hardy, and they may be severely checked or damaged if left outdoors. All those, whether hardy or not, used to decorate patios, terraces and window-boxes, should be put into frost-free conditions for the winter. The plants can be trimmed back to save space and kept only slightly moist in a winter minimum of about 40° (4°C). When the natural temperature begins to rise in spring more water can be given and any repotting or potting on carried out. When new growth is under way, you may have to cut out some of the shoots to improve the shape. These shoots can be used as cuttings for propagation.

Give as much light as possible, while protecting the plants from intense sunlight to get the best flower colour. Slight shading with Coolglass gives excellent growing conditions. Do not neglect feeding or watering. Varieties with ornamental foliage need particularly good light to develop foliage colour. In summer overhead spraying is beneficial. Remove all faded flowers and their seed pods promptly.

Gerbera (from seed, page 122)

When bought as plants, named hybrids should be obtained from specialist growers (see Appendix). They should be potted into $3\frac{1}{2}$- or 5-inch pots, depending on their size, as soon as received. Plant so that the crowns are very slightly above the compost surface, as this lessens the risk of rot. Water thoroughly but only when necessary. In winter little is required – just sufficient to keep the compost slightly moist. The plants also need plenty of light, but protect them from intense sunlight in summer. Do not expect to get masses of flowers the first year. It may take three years before a good crop is obtained, but the blooms are so beautiful that it is well worth waiting. There should be a plentiful supply during the winter months. When removing the flowers, do not cut them. Pull the stems sharply so that they come away from the crowns. If a piece of stem is left it may start a rot, which can spread down to the crown. Gerberas can be easily grown in the cool greenhouse with a winter minimum of about 45°F (7°C).

Hydrangea

Most of the hydrangeas seen in pots are varieties of *Hydrangea macrophylla*. *H. paniculata*, which bears large creamy-white panicles of bloom during late summer and early autumn, is also attractive.

Greenhouse hydrangeas are frequently bought from florists as pot plants intended for home decoration. When flowering is over, dead flowers and any weak stems or growth should be cleanly cut off. The plants should then be stood outdoors in a shady place, with their pots plunged in moist shingle or peat; this should be well over the rim, if the pot is plastic, so that the compost is kept moist. During summer, cut out shoots that have flowered to a point just above the highest of any new side shoots. The best flower heads for the following year will appear on these new shoots. Give liquid feeds from time to time, as the plants grow during summer.

Take the pots into the greenhouse in autumn when the foliage falls and give very little water during winter. Temperatures over about 50°F (10°C) should not be allowed since this may inhibit flowering later. During February, pot on if necessary, and raise the temperature slightly if early flowering is required. At this time more generous watering can begin.

A special technique is used to raise flowering specimens from cuttings. The cuttings should be taken from flowering shoots about 4 inches long, and should be treated in the standard way (see page 219). Roots will quickly form at 65°F (18°C). Pot on to 2½-inch pots of acid or lime-free potting compost. When the plants are well rooted stop them so that only two pairs of leaves remain. After potting on to 5-inch pots a few weeks later, plunge the pots outdoors as already described. In early July stop the plants by reducing all shoots formed after the first stopping to two pairs of leaves. This should result in bushy plants, producing about five heads of flowers in summer, or in spring if the plants are gently forced. To force, maintain a temperature of about 60°F (16°C) from late December.

To obtain plants with one enormous flower head, strike cuttings in early autumn and treat as described, except for stopping so that only one stem develops.

Most hydrangeas become too large for the greenhouse after a time and they can then be transferred to the open garden. *H. paniculata* should be treated differently from *H. macrophylla*. Remove blooms after flowering and do not prune until autumn, when each growth should be cut back to about three buds from the base. Untidy growth, basal suckers, drooping shoots and weak wood must be cut out.

Some varieties of *H. macrophylla* can be 'blued', but do not attempt to blue the varieties that are naturally pink, white or red. Generally, blue varieties tend to turn pink or become of poor faded colour in alkaline soil or compost. This is why acid compost should always be used. You can get good blue colours by mixing aluminium sulphate with the compost or by watering with a solution. Dissolve $\frac{1}{2}$ ounce aluminium sulphate in one gallon of clean rainwater and water the plants with this every two weeks throughout the growing period. Normal watering should also be done with lime-free water.

A number of specifically coloured named varieties are described in nurserymen's catalogues.

Jasminum

The most common greenhouse jasmine is *Jasminum polyanthum*, which has an extremely powerful scent and bears masses of white flowers late in winter. In the cool greenhouse it is evergreen and is rather rampant if unchecked. It can be grown in 10-inch pots and trained up wires or a plastic mesh fastened to a wall. Do not hesitate to stop shoots to get neat growth, otherwise this climber will get quite out of hand. The best minimum temperature is about 40/45°F (4/7°C). Choose a well-lit position, and water well during summer. Be careful not to overfeed or there will be too much foliage and too few flowers.

Lapageria rosea (*Chilean bellflower*)

This is not a common species, but I include it in the hope that some publicity will bring it to the fore. It is an extremely beautiful evergreen climber with large, elongated, waxy, bell-like flowers, usually bright red. There is a white form and recently a pink has been developed. The flowers appear from September to late November, and the plant is quite at home in merely frost-free conditions. It is easily grown in 10-inch pots and it is easy to train, requiring little attention apart from an occasional tie. The plant is stocked by some nurseries and garden centres, particularly in the south and west, where it is hardy in sheltered places.

Nerium oleander (oleander)

This easy evergreen shrub usually begins flowering in early summer and continues until late autumn. It can reach a considerable size in the cool greenhouse, but you can check it by severe pruning if you wish. Normally the plant should be given plenty of water at all times, but in cool or frost-free winter conditions it should be kept on the dry side. Good specimens can be kept in 10-inch pots for many years. If you cut the tops off when they are too high, new basal growth will develop. Proper pruning is important. Shoots that grow from the bases of the flower trusses should be removed as early as possible. After flowering cut back shoots of the previous year's growth to within 3 inches of their base.

There are single- and double-flowered varieties in white and shades of red and pink. Cuttings will grow roots if you simply stand them in a glass of water. Indeed, many plants are acquired from friends in this way. Considering their ease of culture and their showy flowers, produced in large numbers over a long period, oleanders ought to be more popular.

Pelargonium (so called 'geraniums') (see also page 128)

These can be divided for convenience into three groups: zonal pelargoniums (the so-called 'geraniums'), ivy-leaved pelargoniums, and regal or show pelargoniums. The last are ideal for greenhouse decoration. Some of the ivy type look attractive in hanging containers or trailing from shelves or the staging edge.

Zonal pelargoniums

During the summer there is little point in growing these in a greenhouse. Under glass they will flower well in winter – a fact not generally known. Take cuttings early in the year from plants that have been overwintered in the greenhouse. For rooting the cuttings use a propagator at about 60°F (16°C) and follow the general procedure (see page 219). Pot on the rooted cuttings into $2\frac{1}{2}$-inch pots, and later pot on as required. In summer, plunge the pots outdoors in a sunny position, taking care to keep the compost moist. Stop the central stem when about 4 inches high and remove any premature flower buds. In autumn, take the plants into the greenhouse where, with a minimum temperature of about 45°F – though preferably about 50°F most of the time – they should bloom well all winter. Ventilate the greenhouse well whenever outdoor temperatures permit, and keep a watch for *Botrytis cinerea* (grey mould, see page 84). Plenty of winter light is desirable.

Ivy-leaved pelargoniums

Varieties with variegated foliage are particularly attractive – 'L'Elegant', for example. Three or four plants will be needed for each hanging container, depending on its size. The plants need very little attention after planting: simply remove dead flowers and stop occasionally to encourage branching.

Ivy-leaved varieties can be trained up the wall of a lean-to, or up the side of a greenhouse, if some plastic netting is provided. In a 10-inch pot they will grow to a considerable height.

Regal pelargoniums

The very showy and exotic blooms of the regals need greenhouse protection, but after flowering they should be plunged outside like zonals. Cuttings can be taken during July and August, rooted as described and kept over winter in $2\frac{1}{2}$-inch pots at a temperature of about 50°F (10°C). Rapid growth will start in spring; the plants should then be stopped to encourage branching and potted on to 5-inch pots. Old plants from which cuttings have been taken should be drastically pruned back – don't be afraid to do this. Place the cut-back plants in a frame and give frequent overhead sprays of water, rather than applications to the roots. When the new growth appears reduce the root ball and repot, using the same size pot. This process will result in very nice bushy neat plants of show standard.

Pelargoniums of all types are often straggly and untidy because the growers are afraid to cut back and prune severely when necessary.

Plumbago

The favourite is *Plumbago capensis*, which has very beautiful phlox-like masses of bloom from spring to autumn. It is a wall shrub, and is seen at its best when trained against the wall of a lean-to. However, with constant pruning it can make a neat, bushy shrub. In both cases you will eventually need a 10-inch pot. If allowed to grow unchecked it will reach a height of about 12 to 15 feet and look very impressive in flower. It is very easy to grow in the cool greenhouse, where it should be kept just moist in winter and well watered in summer. After flowering, prune by reducing all growth by about two-thirds. In the cool greenhouse this species is evergreen, but if chilled it may lose its foliage in winter. In a warm greenhouse the blue or white flowers often appear over a longer period.

Rosa

Roses grown in pots in the greenhouse can produce flowers in early spring. Procure high quality HT roses in October in the usual way. Clean the roots under running water to remove soil, and pot into a potting compost using 8-inch pots. Trim the roots to fit the pot if necessary and cut away cleanly any that are damaged. After potting, stand the pots in the open garden on a layer of shingle until December. Return the pots to the greenhouse and prune the plants if necessary, with the object of getting several good shoots rather than lots of weaker ones. Drastic pruning will give better results than a hesitant, cautious trim.

Only cool conditions are required: temperatures over about 50°F (10°C) should be avoided. Ventilate whenever possible. In these conditions flowering should commence during April. Some growers prefer to stand out the pots for a year, removing most of the flowers in the early bud stage so that the plants' resources are directed to development. When they are stood out all summer the pots are best plunged (see page 56). Plants so treated can be returned to the greenhouse earlier, in November, and gradually forced in January. Again, 50°F should not be exceeded and the plants should be pruned, but this time much more leniently. Some of the floribunda and polyantha roses make good pot plants. Some climbers can also be used on walls of lean-to houses or conservatories. There are of course innumerable rose varieties, and the catalogues of the specialists, usually beautifully illustrated, should be consulted.

Saintpaulia (*African violet*) (see also page 131)

In recent years African violets have become very popular house plants. With the right conditions – a congenial temperature and moist atmosphere – they will continue to flower almost the year round. Do not try growing them in chilly, draughty or very dry surroundings. Special cases with thermostatic heating and artificial lighting supplied by a fluorescent tube are available to provide just the right growing environment; use these in the home and in cold or cool greenhouses to get the best results. A large enclosed propagator also makes a suitable home for these plants, which are always neat and take up little space (see page 59).

Many fine named varieties can be had from specialist nurseries (see Appendix). You can also grow from leaf cuttings begged from friends (see page 221), or from seed (see page 131). In the latter case colour and form are very limited. The plants will not be dispatched from a nursery until the weather is warm enough for safe delivery. Be careful about buying from florists and garden shops in case the plants have been chilled. Pot size depends on the size of the plants obtained; generally a 3½-inch pot will accommodate a flowering plant for a long time, but a 5-inch may be needed for large specimens. The plants usually look better in half pots when they reach an appreciable size.

Mature plants often produce suckers a short distance from the parent plant. Remove these by tapping the plant out of its pot and cutting away the sucker, leaving some roots attached; then repot both the parent plant and the sucker. Another method of propagation is from 'side crowns', which appear as tiny rosettes of leaves formed between the leaf axils of mature plants. Always remove these side crowns, whether you want them for propagation or not, with a pair of pointed tweezers or vine scissors. This encourages flowering and keeps the plant neat. The side crowns root very easily if just pressed into compost in a propagating case.

All propagation is best done at about 65°F (18°C). In general, African violets like warm, shady conditions and high humidity. They will endure a winter minimum of about 50°F (10°C) if they are very carefully watered, but it is safer to keep choice varieties warmer, in a propagating case if necessary. During active growth, spray them overhead with a fine mist of clean rainwater. Hard tap water will mark the foliage. If plants are exposed to sunlight when the foliage is wet, brown marks may appear.

Schlumbergera (*Christmas cactus*)

Often known by the old genus name *Zygocactus*, several species are grown, including the frequently confused and very similar Easter cactus, *Rhipsalidopsis gaertneri*, once included in the genus *Schlumbergera*. The plants have succulent flattened stems and very showy pagoda-shaped flowers. The Christmas cactus, *S. × buckleyi*, blooms from December to February and is magenta in colour. *S. truncata* (crab cactus) is also winter flowering, but there are several colours, including white and blue shades. All are trailers, useful for hanging containers, though they are often grown to trail over the sides of ordinary pots. Rhipsalidopsis is considerably more erect and the flowers are usually bright red. All these species are sold as house plants. They are easy to grow provided you can maintain a winter minimum of about 50°F (10°C). Do not allow the compost to dry out at any time, but keep only slightly moist during winter. In summer the plants benefit from standing outdoors in a *partially* shaded place. Propagate by breaking off pieces of the succulent stem and inserting in a cutting compost during summer. A case can be used to keep in moisture but no extra heat is required.

Stephanotis floribunda

This is also sold as a 'house' plant, and is often trained around a wire hoop. It is a delightful twiner which, given a free run in the greenhouse, will attract much attention and fill the house with fragrance. The foliage is evergreen and the creamy white flowers tubular, with starry petals at the end. These appear from early summer to autumn. It is usually much more successful in the greenhouse because it likes a very high humidity. It should be sprayed frequently with water during summer and slightly shaded. In winter see that the compost is moist and maintain not less than 50°F (10°C). The plants flower best after two or three years. Give them 8-inch pots and train them up wires into the greenhouse roof, so that the flowers hang down. Prune them, if necessary, in February. Leading shoots can be reduced by about half their length, and lateral shoots reduced to about 3 to 4 inches.

Strelitzia (*bird-of-paradise flower*)

Strelitzia reginae is a greenhouse treasure and perhaps one of the most highly prized plants. Unfortunately, its unique exotic flower and tropical-looking foliage have made many people associate it with high temperatures and difficult culture. This is in fact nonsense: I have grown it as a greenhouse plant in little more than frost-free conditions and as an indoor house plant. Indeed, it is a very accommodating plant, and will even put up with some neglect.

The flowering-sized plants are expensive, but sometimes advanced seedlings come onto the market. It is possible to grow strelitzias from seed easily (germinate at 80°F), but they take at least four years to reach flowering size, depending on overall growing temperature. For flowering, the plants can be slightly pot bound, and you need 12-inch pots, small tubs or some other drained ornamental container. The plants need plenty of water in summer and very little in winter. The lower the winter temperature, the dryer you should keep them. In the cool greenhouse or in the home they flower twice a year, in early summer and from November onwards. Sometimes there may be Christmas flowers.

Leave strelitzias in their flowering-sized pots for as long as possible. Eventually, they become fan-shaped; divide them then, potting each segment of the 'fan' as a new plant. Dividing such a large specimen is a mammoth job, but not too difficult. You may have to break the pot away from the roots if these have penetrated the drainage holes. Use a very sharp knife to cut through the fleshy roots; this does less damage than trying to disentangle them. The best time to divide is just after flowering in early summer.

The plants enjoy slight shade in summer and their foliage, which is large and spade-like, can be sprayed with clean rainwater during warm weather. The flowers are coloured bright orange and rich blue like the plumage of an exotic tropical bird; the shape of the flower also resembles a bird's head. *S. parviflora* is worth growing too. It is generally smaller and thus more suitable where space is limited. A so-called 'dwarf' form of *S. reginae* is now available from seed.

Streptocarpus (Cape primrose – see also page 133)

Beginners may prefer to buy the streptocarpus hybrids as small plants. They are sometimes advertised by nurseries in the gardening press and the best time to buy is in autumn. If these plants are kept in a cool greenhouse over winter, with a minimum temperature of about 45/50°F (7/10°C), they will make rapid growth in spring and should then be transferred to 5-inch pots. In summer, keep the plants well watered and shaded, using an overhead spray with a fine mist of clean rainwater to maintain humidity. Feed when you first detect buds forming. After flowering gradually water less and less and keep only very slightly moist in winter. Plants that have been saved for several years can be propagated by simply dividing the roots in early spring. If the plants are left too long without division they may become so leafy that they cannot produce flowers. You can also propagate from leaf cuttings. A beautiful named variety to look out for is 'Constant Nymph'; its numerous flowers, smaller than those of the hybrids, are lavender with deep purple throats. Beautiful named hybrids in many colours have also been developed by the John Innes Institute. These and other choice forms are available from special nurseries (see Appendix).

Tibouchina semidecandra (T. urvilleana)

This is another superb shrub for the cool greenhouse, with a winter minimum temperature of about 45°F (7°C). The plant actually sold under this name is in fact *Tibouchina urvilleana* but this error seems to have persisted in all catalogues. The true species, *T. semidecandra*, is very rare. Plants are often sold as rooted cuttings. These should be potted on and have their growing tips removed. Stop the laterals that form when they are about 4 inches long. Pot on as required to 7-inch pots. A stout cane will eventually be needed for support. Water well and maintain a humid atmosphere while the plants are actively growing. Keep only just moist in winter. The magnificent violet flowers, like enormous pansies, are borne freely from July to November. The attractive foliage often turns red in autumn. In late February, cut the plants severely. Leading shoots can be reduced by half and laterals to two pairs of leaves. To take cuttings, choose non-flowering lateral shoots, about 4 inches long, from March to April. These will root easily by

177

the usual methods (see page 219) at a temperature of about 65°F (18°C). Seed is also available now.

TABLE FIVE

More recommended flowering plants

Abutilon megapotamicum   Easy climber. Lantern-like red/yellow flowers.

Acacia armata   Mimosa-like flowers. Compact and better pot plant.

Acacia dealbata   Mimosa – only suitable for spacious greenhouse.

Clerodendron thomsoniae   Climber. Red/white flowers. Warm only.

Columnea   Several species for baskets. Red/orange flowers. Warm.

Euphorbia fulgens   Stems of orange/red flowers in profusion.

Euphorbia splendens   Thorny plant. Scarlet flowers.

Gardenia jasminoides   White fragrant flowers, but not easy. Warm.

Globba winitii   Stems of rosy bracts. Long-lasting.

Hibiscus rosa-sinensis   Variously coloured showy flowers.

Hoya carnosa   Climber. Pink flowers. Shiny bronze leaves. Scented.

Hypocyrta glabra   Semi-trailing. Orange/yellow flowers.

Isoloma amabile   Orange-red tubular flowers. Hairy edged foliage.

Ixora   Heads of showy orange to pink flowers. Small shrub. Warm.

Jacobinia carnea   Heads of rose-coloured flowers. Showy. 50/55°F.

Jacobinia pauciflora   Yellow/red flowers, pale green foliage.

Jacobinia suberecta   Orange flowers, grey felted foliage.

Manettia bicolor   Climber with tubular orange flowers.

Medinilla magnifica   Spectacular pink flowers. Warm/humid only.

Pentas   Various hybrids with starry flowers. Pink to white.

Spathiphyllum wallisii   White arum-like flowers. Warm only.

These plants are suitable for a cool greenhouse unless otherwise stated.

11 Beautiful Foliage Plants

Owing to the popularity of house plants we can now buy many delightful foliage subjects that were at one time very difficult to obtain. There are so many that I have concentrated here on some of the most beautiful, mostly with coloured or variegated foliage, and those especially suited to greenhouse culture. In most cases, house plants will grow much better under greenhouse conditions. Some like shady places and can be grown under the staging. All will respond well and give great satisfaction if you follow the general rules on care and feeding outlined in Chapter 6.

Aglaonema

There are a number of attractive species, often sold as house plants. Generally they prefer warm conditions but will survive a winter minimum of about 50°F (10°C). One of the easiest and most vigorous is *Aglaonema robelinii*. This has very large spear-shaped foliage, silvery green with a dark border. In cool conditions in winter aglaonema should be kept almost dry.

Aphelandra (zebra plant)

The most common species is *Aphelandra squarrosa louisae*. This has a very striking foliage – large, dark-green, glossy leaves contrastingly veined with creamy white. When the plant is established and slightly pot bound, it produces curious yellow flowers of angular appearance. Remove these flowers when they turn green; afterwards the many new shoots can be used as cuttings. Although this plant likes warmth and will grow vigorously in such an atmosphere, it can be acclimatized to very low temperatures. In the winter at a minimum temperature of about 40°F (4°C) it may look unhappy, turning its foliage down, but in spring when the temperature rises it will soon recover. In winter give very little water; in summer water generously. Never let the roots dry out completely. It likes a position with good light.

Aralia, see *Dizygotheca*

Begonia

There are innumerable begonias with ornamental foliage, many with delightful flowers too (see page 113). One of the most popular is *Begonia rex* with large, heart-shaped leaves, beautifully marked and coloured. Another favourite is *B. masoniana*, called the Iron Cross begonia because of its characteristic leaf marking. A begonia that could be more extensively grown is *B. cathayana*. The foliage is reminiscent of *B. rex*, but the veins are red and the stems covered with red hairs. In the greenhouse this house plant usually makes a splendid specimen. For the descriptions of the many other foliage begonias, consult the catalogues of the specialist nurseries. Most of the plants prefer some shade and cool greenhouse conditions in winter. They need plenty of water when in active growth, with roots just moist in winter. A humid atmosphere is always beneficial.

Caladium

These magnificent plants are mostly sold as named hybrids. They are grown from tubers started into growth in March in a propagator at 75°F (24°C). Pot then and keep them as warm as possible until there is a good head of growth. They may be kept in the greenhouse or used as house plants during the summer, but they quickly deteriorate in cold conditions. The large, showy leaves are arrow-shaped and strikingly coloured or striped in green, cream or bright red. In autumn the foliage dies down and the pots should then be stored almost dry – but not quite – over winter, at a temperature not lower than 55/60°F (13/16°C). Often you can buy plants already in leaf during summer, and it is then possible to select the finest colours. This is not an easy subject unless you have a warm greenhouse, especially if you intend to grow the same plants year after year.

Calathea

There are a number of species of this genus with the most wonderfully coloured foliage, and leaves beautifully marked with stripes and blotches. *Calathea zebrina* is so named because of its stripes. *C. ornata* has cream veins lined with pink against a dark-green background. *C. bachemiana* has vivid green blotches contrasting with silvery grey-green, and *C. picturata* has bright green bordering with a rich maroon colour below. *C. makoyana* is perhaps the most beautiful of all. Its oval leaves are reddish-purple below with silvery and dark green markings on top. When viewed with the light shining through there is a spectacular colour effect – hence the name peacock plant. This species needs more warmth than most. The culture of this genus is almost identical to that of maranta (page 185). The plants are similarly ideal for the understage area and shady places.

Cissus

The most popular and easy of this genus is *Cissus antarctica* (kangaroo vine). The most beautiful is, however, *C. discolor* which unfortunately is more difficult to grow. It needs a winter minimum of about 55°F (13°C) if it is to remain in good condition and not shed foliage. It is a delightful climber and has bright green foliage marbled with a variety of colours including pink, crimson, purple and white. The undersides of the leaves are a rich crimson. This species makes a splendid plant for a hanging basket. It is a good choice for a small greenhouse run at a higher temperature for a special collection of sub-tropicals, but in a cool greenhouse it will certainly be disappointing.

Codiaeum (*croton*)

The plants sold in florists' shops under the name of 'croton' are usually *Codiaeum variegatum pictum*. It is very variable indeed, but the foliage is nearly always exotically coloured with various combinations of orange, red and pink. Most varieties have long oval leaves rather like *Aucuba japonica*, the well known 'laurel', but there is one with quite different thin foliage. Again, these plants cannot stand temperatures below about 55°F (13°C). Wide temperature fluctuations should also be strictly avoided or the foliage will fall. Those varieties with narrow foliage are generally easier than the others. Unlike the majority of the foliage plants described here, the codiaeums should be given plenty of light, especially when they are growing actively. If, through an accidental drop in temperature, the foliage should fall, cut the plants right

181

back; they will grow again if the temperature is restored. Do not buy these plants during the winter months.

Ctenanthe

For some obscure reason these often appear on the market labelled calathea, which they resemble, although they have a closer, upright habit. They are also similar to maranta (page 185). Of the several species, *Ctenanthe lubbersiana* seems the most common, probably because it is a comparatively easy plant and will survive in a cool greenhouse with care. It has longish stems and foliage mottled with light and dark green and cream. It enjoys quite gloomy conditions and grows well under the staging.

Dieffenbachia picta

There are a number of varieties with handsome, spade-shaped leaves in various shades of green, usually marked or mottled with cream and sometimes veined. All are suited to partial shade rather than full light or the gloom under the staging. They are all rather tender and need a winter minimum of 55°F (13°C). A moist atmosphere is also essential to maintain reasonably fast growth and the production of new foliage, which does not remain in very good condition for long. All parts of the plants are extremely poisonous. Ingestion of the sap is said to inhibit the power of speech for some days, hence the common name – dumb cane.

Dizygotheca elegantissima (spider plant)

Although often listed under the name *Aralia*, this plant has now been consigned to a new genus: *Dizygotheca*. It has very delicate thinly serrated foliage; a well-grown specimen is very beautiful. Unfortunately, as a house plant it commonly drops most of its leaves, and will do the same if subjected to sudden temperature changes. Unless you can provide a congenial warmth fairly constantly, winter minimum about 55/60°F (13/16°C), and maintain a high atmospheric humidity, it is a waste of time trying to grow this species. However, given the right conditions it is no trouble at all and will reach the proportions of a shrub, producing much side growth.

Dracaena

Most dracaena species are happy with a winter minimum of about 50°F (10°C). Most of them have narrow or strap-shaped leaves and may eventually take on a palm-like appearance. *Dracaena parri* is sometimes used outdoors in summer for a sub-tropical bedding effect. The foliage of most species is usually coloured or attractively striped. During summer, encourage them to grow by maintaining warm and humid conditions with good watering and feeding. In winter keep the plants on the dry side. They need a little shade in summer, but generally like bright conditions. Grow them in 5- to 10-inch pots, depending on species and size. Cuttings, which root at 75°F (24°C) in a propagator, can be taken from basal shoots in spring. Note that the first leaves that form on the cuttings are usually plain green, the true colours forming later.

Ferns (see also page 121)

Many ferns can be grown in a cool shady greenhouse – one that is overshadowed by a house, for example, or a lean-to facing north. *Pteris quadriaurita argyraea* is unusual for its silvery variegated fronds. *Nephrolepis exaltata*, the ladder fern, is ideal for hanging baskets, but it is important not to let it dry out in winter when it has lost its fronds. This fern can be easily reproduced from runners, which it forms freely. *Athyrium filix-femina*, the lady fern, is hardy though deciduous. *Dryopteris filix-mas*, the male fern, also makes a beautiful pot plant and is indigenous to this country. *Polypodium vulgare* (adder's fern) is hardy and a fine pot plant too. *Asplenium nidus* (bird's-nest fern) has plain, sword-shaped fronds – unlike one's usual conception of a fern. A tiny graceful species is *Davallia mariesii*, which is also hardy, at least in the south. You can make 'fern balls' by winding this species in moss and fastening the balls with fine wire; they can then be hung from the greenhouse roof. During the summer they must be sprayed with water. In winter the fern is deciduous and the balls can be dried off and stored in a dry place. The various species of adiantum – the maidenhair ferns – are very pretty and popular but unfortunately rather unpredictable and difficult to grow. They need plenty of humidity (though no direct spraying) and a light position.

In a warmer greenhouse the strange stag's horn fern (or elk's horn) *Platycerium bifurcatum* can be entwined in moss, fastened to cork and hung from the wall.

Ferns like a moist but well-drained compost at all times; most need shade and a moist atmosphere. In summer, give an overhead misting with clean rainwater from time to time. Although most ferns will grow well in the potting composts described in Chapter 7 (page 90), they generally prefer acid conditions. Some also benefit from the addition of sterilized leafmould to the compost.

Ficus

The popular rubber plant is *Ficus elastica decora*. The variety 'Doescheri' is beautifully variegated in pale green and cream. It is said to be more difficult, but I have not personally found it so. Both, if ill-treated by erratic watering and wide temperature change, will drop their lower leaves. Although these plants are often grown in very small pots, it is better to match the plant to the pot; this will give more even conditions of moisture at the roots. You will get the best results with a temperature of 55 to 60°F (13 to 16°C). *F. benghalensis*, the Bengal fig, is easy and very resistant to cool conditions, also simple from seed, but not so decorative. *F. diversifolia*, the mistletoe fig, is so named because it bears yellowish berries. A very impressive plant is *F. lyrata*, the fiddle-back, which has large leaves shaped like a violin. All these grow to a considerable size in a warm greenhouse. Should the lower foliage fall, the tops of the plants can be cut off to encourage new growth from the base. If you are reluctant to do this, you could try air layering (see page 224). Sprayed on existing foliage, the bare stem and any subsequent shoots, I have found that the product Fillip greatly encourages the growth of lower shoots and leaves (see page 81): the effect has been quite dramatic. Spray in summer for the best results. Most varieties seem to grow best in partial but not excessive shade (with the exception of *F. pumila*, creeping fig, a small creeper that is almost hardy).

Fittonia

Among the smaller foliage plants *Fittonia argyroneura* is one of the most charming. It has oval-shaped green leaves with an intricate network of creamy white veins, giving a lace-like effect. Unfortunately you must keep this delightful species warm, but since it is small and compact this is easy to do with the aid of a propagating case. It is a good plant for bottle gardens or plant cases, where a moist atmosphere, a winter minimum of about 60°F (16°C) and moderate shade will keep it in good condition.

Maranta (prayer plant)

The marantas, like most other members of the family, are beautiful plants. When growing they all like warmth, humidity and shade. They go well under the staging, and do not grow as tall as the calatheas. They are called 'prayer plant' because at night the leaves fold and become erect, like hands closed in prayer. Several varieties of *Maranta leuconeura* are commonly grown. *M.l. massangeana* has large chocolate-brown spots on the foliage. *M.l. kerchoveana* has a herring-bone marking. Both these are easy and will survive in a cool greenhouse over winter; indeed I have had them in a greenhouse that was only frost-free, and they have both grown again in spring. However, in the cool they will become very tatty and may lose all their foliage. The most beautiful is *M.l. erythrophylla* which has larger foliage flushed with red. This is far less tolerant of cold and needs a winter minimum of about 55°F (13°C). All marantas and the other members of the family should have plenty of moisture and a humid environment when actively growing. Overhead misting with water is beneficial. In winter, water according to prevailing temperature; the cooler it is, the less water you should give and in very cool conditions you should keep the plants almost dry. If the fleshy tuberous roots rot they will not grow again in spring. 3½- to 5-inch pots are usually adequate.

Monstera

Monstera deliciosa and *M. pertusa* are sold as house plants. The latter is often incorrectly given the name of the former, but is easily distinguished by its more compact habit and more rounded foliage. The leaves are large and have perforations or slits. Because of their size, they are best seen in a greenhouse or conservatory. Fortunately, they will survive a winter minimum of about 45/50°F (7/10°C) if kept only slightly moist in winter. They will begin growing vigorously when the temperature reaches about 65°F (18°C), so in the greenhouse they can reach a considerable size. They may, in fact, even flower and fruit. The flower is an arum-like spathe and the fruit like a small elongated pineapple without the crest of foliage. The fruit, which takes at least a year to ripen, is said to be delicious, hence the name *deliciosa*, but I find it unpleasantly fibrous. *M. deliciosa* is a good plant to train up a roof support or a trellis on a lean-to wall. It will produce aerial roots, which should be trained back down to their 12-inch pots or small tubs. Monsteras are quite unsuited to a small greenhouse unless you want to grow nothing else!

Palms (see also page 128)

The palms are among the most graceful and elegant of all foliage plants. Unfortunately, in the relatively small greenhouses of today it is rarely possible to show them to their best advantage. The nomenclature of palms is often confused and species appear on the market with a variety of names, frequently incorrect, and with an assortment of common or fancy names such as 'fan palm', 'Chinese palm' and so on. This makes identification difficult, particularly since many very young palms can look alike. Usually sold as 'Kentia' palms are *Howea belmoreana* (curly palm) and *H. forsteriana* (flat palm). Both are splendid greenhouse or house palms and they will be happy with a winter minimum of about 45°F (7°C). *Phoenix roebelinii* (dwarf date palm) has also come onto the market as a pot plant (see page 128), but the true date palm, *Phoenix dactylifera*, which some people grow from date 'stones', is not recommended. It grows too large and demands too much warmth. *Neanthe bella* is an attractive palm when young, and takes up little room. It is probably the most compact palm for the home greenhouse, and quite easy. (It is also known as *Chamaedorea elegans*, but its proper name is *Collinia elegans*.)

Most palms prefer plenty of light, and they do not mind pots that appear far too small. They like plenty of water, but perfect drainage. The compost should be acid. The John Innes with the chalk omitted, and with a more fibrous peat, has given me good results. It is also a good idea to add some crushed charcoal. During summer a spray with clean rainwater or a wipe with wet cotton wool keeps the fronds in good condition. When repotting choose a pot to give only about one to two inches of extra compost around the root ball. I prefer clay pots which can be plunged in a larger, possibly ornamental, container of moist peat.

Peperomia

There are numerous species giving a remarkably wide range of leaf variation. All are charming and excellent for a small greenhouse. Most, with the exception unfortunately of one of the most delightful, *Peperomia sandersii*, are easy to grow and will thrive in a greenhouse with a winter minimum of 45/50°F (7/10°C). *P. sandersii* has delightful spear-shaped leaves banded with silver and green. It needs careful watering or it may rot, and it prefers a draught-free, moist atmosphere, and a little extra warmth. It is a good bottle garden or case plant. *P. caperata* is a small, bushy plant with tiny corrugated dark-green leaves and catkin-like creamy-white 'flowers'. *P. glabella* is a trailer with smooth oval leaves. The variegated form is the best. *P. scandens* is similar but has larger foliage, which tends to drop when the plant is young, though this is less likely as the plant matures. *P. magnoliaefolia* has large, oval, variegated foliage in green and cream. There are several others that are sufficiently different to be well worth collecting. In general they like shade and careful watering. Water well when necessary, but do not keep the compost too moist. In winter special care is required: in cool conditions give them just enough water to prevent drying out.

Pilea cadierei

P. cadierei (aluminium plant) is one of the most attractive house plants easily grown, and it has become popular. The dainty foliage is prettily marked with glistening silver. In the greenhouse it can be grown to a fair size in a 5-inch pot, but to keep a neat habit you should propagate new plants from time to time. Cuttings root with extreme ease. For best results water and feed well during active growth. It is liable to suffer from magnesium deficiency and an occasional watering with a solution of Epsom salt, about 1 ounce per $\frac{1}{2}$ gallon of water or *pro rata*, will ensure excellent leaf colour and prevent crinkling or distortion. Shade is essential. A minimum winter temperature of about 40/45°F (4/7°C) is desirable.

Another pilea sometimes seen is *Pilea muscosa*, the artillery plant. This looks completely different from *P. cadierei*, having delicate, very 'ferny' foliage and flowers that may not be noticed. When the plant is shaken, these distribute pollen in clouds like smoke – hence the popular name. It needs the same culture as *P. cadierei*. *P. mollis* (*P.* 'Moon Valley'), which has wrinkly leaves with gold on green, is a new and pretty plant.

Rhoeo discolor vittatum

This is an attractive plant with a rosette of strap-shaped leaves, and in the greenhouse it can become fairly tall. The upper side of the leaf is boldly striped with cream and the lower side a deep rose colour. It prefers slight shade and needs careful watering in winter or it may rot at the base. The flowers are hardly showy, but are of interest because they are formed in little cup-shaped structures at the base of the stem. A winter minimum temperature of about 50°F (10°C) is desirable. When well grown the plant will form offshoots around the base that can be separated and used for propagation.

Sansevieria (snake plant)

The most common species is *Sansevieria trifasciata laurentii*. This is often lost through overwatering in winter, when it should be kept almost dry, particularly if the temperature is low. In summer it can be watered freely, but even then should be allowed to go almost dry between waterings. With very careful watering the plant can be grown in a cool greenhouse, but it is really better suited to a winter minimum of not less than 55/60°F (13/16°C). You can propagate easily in summer by cutting a leaf in pieces and inserting each piece in the usual cutting compost, in a propagator covered to retain moisture. Plants grown like this will be unlikely to have the same variegation – to get identical plants you need to separate offshoots from mature plants. Whichever method you use, you must keep the young plants very warm until they are well established. Well grown sansevierias, with their tall spiky leaves bordered in cream, are very attractive.

Setcreasea purpurea

This is one of the easiest to grow of all beautifully coloured foliage plants and can be revived even after months of neglect. Although it will endure merely frost-free conditions and erratic watering, given care it will look decorative the year round. If badly grown it often becomes leggy and untidy. If you keep it as a pot plant you can propagate frequently from cuttings or by root division; in this way the young plants will retain an erect bushy habit for a long time. But the plant also makes a fine trailer for hanging containers if properly fed and watered and stopped from time to time.

The plant has the habit of tradescantia but the leaves are very long and pointed, slightly hairy, and a glorious purple colour; it also produces small magenta flowers. This species prefers slight, not too heavy, shade; in excessive gloom the colour does not develop so well. It has been used for outdoor sub-tropical bedding during the summer months.

Tradescantia (*wandering Jew*)

Various forms of *Tradescantia fluviatilis* are well-known house plants, but they often have poor colour or variegation caused by overwatering and dark conditions. For the greenhouse, the species *T. blossfeldiana* is a better choice and a good hanging basket plant. It is, however, not so tolerant of ill-treatment and it prefers a warm, moist atmosphere, though it survives in a cool greenhouse over winter. The leaves are larger and covered with white hair, dark green above and purple below; the stems are also purple. It prefers slight shade. Well grown plants produce purple to rose pink flowers from spring to summer. A form with cream variegated foliage is sometimes also available. Young plants can make neat pot subjects and they can be grown on for hanging containers.

Zebrina pendula

This is another easy trailer and a popular house plant. In the greenhouse, it is of special value because it will grow under the staging. Unlike the tradescantias, it develops its best colouring in poor light. It is also a marvellous hanging basket plant for a shady greenhouse. Gardeners often overwater to the detriment of the colour. If you want it as an ordinary pot plant you should

189

propagate frequently from the easily rooted cuttings. The young plants usually retain an erect habit for some time. 'Quadricolor' is probably the best known variety. Its leaves are striped with rose-pink, silvery white and varying shades of green above and are purple underneath. This particular variety should be given plenty of light for the best colour contrast to develop.

12 Fruit and Vegetables in the Greenhouse

There are a number of fruits and vegetables which are ideally suited to the greenhouse. However, to grow well they need space and often special environmental conditions; there is often trouble when people try to grow them with a variety of other plants and ornamentals. Bear in mind also that low-growing vegetables, like lettuce and early salad crops, can just as well be accommodated in frames (or cloches in some cases), saving much valuable greenhouse space for crops that need extra height.

Tomatoes

This is undoubtedly the most important of all greenhouse fruits, and extremely popular, so I am giving a little extra detail here. For best results, give the crop a house of its own. A glass-to-ground house is best. There must be good light and ventilation.

Although basically an easy plant to grow, the tomato is subject to all manner of setbacks in the form of pests, diseases and cultural problems. By taking care, and selecting the vigorous modern varieties, you can avoid most of these.

The first thing to remember is *not to grow the plants in the greenhouse ground soil and not to use crude unsterilized animal manures*. The great majority of disasters can be traced to these origins. To overcome soil problems it was customary in the past to sterilize the greenhouse soil each year before planting, or change it for fresh. This was time-consuming and not always satisfactory. Nowadays, the home grower is advised to use special tomato composts, available from most garden shops, or potting composts in 9- to 10-inch pots. In recent trials I have found that the easy-to-make and inexpensive Phostrogen potting compost (page 95) also gives excellent results, provided the subsequent feeding is not neglected, especially in the later stages. Fibre or composition pots are good enough, and all

191

pots should be stood on plastic to isolate them from the greenhouse ground soil and to prevent roots penetrating. Tomato pots that can be thrown away at the end of the season can be obtained from most garden shops. Fibre rings for ring culture (see below) are also available. By discarding pots and composts at the end of the season and taking care over general hygiene, you will prevent the build-up of diseases or pests over the years, and a satisfactory crop can usually be guaranteed. A simple new method is to grow

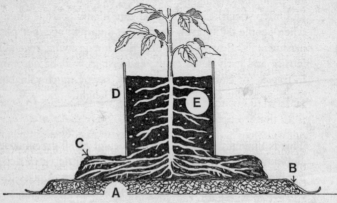

19   *The Principle of Ring Culture*
For large installations spread a layer of gravel (A) on greenhouse floor and cover with sheet polythene (B), holed for drainage at intervals. For small installations the gravel and holes in the polythene can be omitted. C: 4 to 6 inches of peat. D: ring pot. E: tomato compost.

the plants in 'tom bags' – plastic bags of special tomato compost. You lay a bag flat on its side, cut out sections with scissors as marked, and set the tomato plants in the spaces. As the plants grow, a few slits are cut low on the bag's sides for drainage. At the end of the season remove and burn the top growth. The used compost in the bag can be dug into the outdoor garden to provide humus. It should *not* be used again: this should be the rule with all tomato compost of any description.

Ring culture

This system allows for more even watering and there is consequently less trouble with fruit splitting and premature flower and fruit drop (see Fig. 19). The first step is to prepare the 'aggregate', a layer of moisture-retaining material which will supply water to the roots. At one time ballast (from a builder's merchant) was recommended. This is composed of small stones, to support the weight of the rings (see below), and finer particles of grit to convey water to the compost in the rings by capillary action. This can still be used, but again you should sterilize or change each year. Peat will do the job as well, if not better. It is lightweight and easy to use, and it can be dug into the garden at the end of the season. Weathered ashes have been used, but ash often contains harmful chemicals and is of variable composition.

Spread out the aggregate over polythene sheeting or other material to isolate it from the greenhouse floor. A 4- to 6-inch layer is all that is necessary. Keep it thoroughly moist *at all times* – but not waterlogged, as so many people suppose. One of the automatic systems described in Chapter 5 is highly recommended (see pages 63–7). To prevent waterlogging you need a few slits in the polythene sheet, and the ground should be well drained below so that any excess water can run away freely.

Stand the rings on the aggregate and fill them with potting compost. Any proper potting compost will do, but a special tomato compost, or the John Innes No. 3, which in trials has given first-class results, is best. After planting, keep the compost moist until the roots have reached the aggregate (though if the system is working properly sufficient moisture should be taken up by the ring compost automatically). When you see that the ring compost is staying moist, give no more water – only liquid feeds.

General tomato culture

Although you can buy tomato plants, it is a simple matter to grow your own from seed. For suggested varieties see Table 6 (below). Sow and germinate as described in Chapter 7, with a temperature of about 60°F (16°C). The time for sowing depends on when you need the crop, which in turn depends on the temperature that can be maintained in the greenhouse. If you can maintain a minimum temperature of about 50°F (10°C) during the coldest weather, and the greenhouse is in a light, open position so that it benefits from all the sunshine available, you can sow in November. However, most home gardeners prefer to wait until February onwards, since maintaining the necessary warmth is then an easy matter. Even so, a November sowing should give fruit in spring, when tomatoes are expensive. With winter warmth, a late sowing in July to give pickings in December is also possible.

The seedlings should be pricked out into 3½-inch pots and grown on for a while to form sturdy plants before permanent planting. During this period, throw out any seedlings of abnormal appearance, especially those showing dwarfing or deformity of any kind, those producing numerous side shoots, and any pale, yellow or mottled specimens.

Set the young plants in the pots or rings with a distance of about 15 inches between the stems. Provide strings or canes for support and train the plants round them in a clockwise direction. Strings should be firmly anchored to a short stout stick thrust into the ground (and through the aggregate if this is used). Fasten the tops of the strings to the glazing bars or to a wire run along the greenhouse roof from end to end.

Promptly remove all side shoots that form where the leaves join the main stem. This should be a daily routine. After the fourth truss has formed begin feeding with a high potash tomato feed, of which there are several on the market. A liquid feed is preferable, and should be used according to label directions. When the first truss has yielded its fruit and ripened, remove the foliage below, thus reducing disease problems. The defoliation should not be drastic – the leaves are vital to the plant's life and functions. Defoliate upwards as the trusses crop, but if the leaves appear healthy and flourishing it is wise to leave some.

Pollination and setting of the fruit can be assisted by shaking the plants when in flower, preferably on warm, bright mornings. Spraying with a mist of water also helps. In obstinate cases try using a special hormone tomato set, available from garden shops; follow the directions on the label.

Stop the plants during August or earlier if they have reached the greenhouse roof. This directs the plants' resources to developing

194

and ripening the existing fruit. It has recently been found that watering the plants with a Cycocel solution at the time of planting reduces the length of stem between trusses. This means that more can be grown to any given height and cropping is increased. There is also evidence that you get better and more disease-resistant plants with the Cycocel treatment (see Appendix).

During summer, it is vital to keep the greenhouse temperature below about 80°F (27°C). Above this, the fruit will not ripen properly to give a good red colour and flavour. The red pigment cannot form and usually the fruit becomes blotchy or patchy. With too much sunlight 'greenback' can result, which causes the fruit tops to remain green or yellowish. In recent trials fruit has ripened well in houses lightly shaded with Coolglass. Avoid heavy shading.

Various other techniques can be used in growing tomatoes. These include grafting onto disease-resistant rootstocks, tiered-trough culture and straw-bale culture. It is doubtful whether any of these are better for the home gardener than the easy pot and ring systems given here.

It is most important to aim always at keeping tomato roots *evenly* moist, with no drastic changes from dry to wet. Failure to do this results in young fruit or flowers dropping from the 'knuckle', in the fruit cracking and splitting, and in blossom-end rot (the end of the fruit where the remains of the flower are sited goes black and rotten). Wide fluctuations in feeding and temperature will also aggravate these troubles.

TABLE SIX

Some popular tomato varieties

> *Ailsa Craig*   Old favourite for flavour, but prone to ripening troubles and other disorders.
>
> *Alicante*   Fine quality fruit of good flavour and texture. Relatively free from ripening troubles and other disorders. An excellent amateur tomato.
>
> *Big Boy* F_1 Enormous fruit, but of good flavour. Fleshy texture. Fairly easy culture. Deserves greater popularity.

Gardener's Delight   Very small fruit, but tangy flavour many
people like. Very easy to grow and relatively trouble free.

Kingley Cross F_1 Compact for the small greenhouse and a good
cropper. Relatively disease resistant.

Maascross F_1 Very early good quality fruit. Good disease
resistance. Has proved very successful among amateur
growers.

Seville Cross F_1 Fruit of fine quality, and good disease
resistance. Also has given good results among amateur
growers.

Supercross F_1 Good crops of excellent quality. Exceptionally
good disease resistance – especially to tomato mosaic virus.

Tangella   Tangerine-coloured fruit of excellent quality and
flavour. Relatively free from ripening troubles.

Ware Cross F_1 Very vigorous plants. Large fleshy fruit of good
flavour. Relatively easy and trouble-free.

Yellow Perfection   Rich yellow fruit of excellent quality and
superb flavour. Early, easy and prolific. This tomato ought to
be far better known and appreciated. Relatively disease resistant.

Cucumbers

It is usually recommended that tomatoes and cucumbers should
not be grown together because their cultural requirements differ.
Should there be pest trouble, many pesticides that can be used on
tomatoes with safety will harm cucumbers. Cucumbers also prefer
a more humid atmosphere and heavier shading. In spite of this,
numerous amateur growers do in fact manage to grow the two in the
same greenhouse and get reasonable crops, so it is evidently worth
a try. Success is more likely if one of the easier cucumber varieties
is selected. Examples include Improved Telegraph, Conqueror,
and particularly the 'all-female' types such as Femspot and Rocket
(both F_1 hybrids). The all-female cucumbers produce few or no
male flowers, which means pollination cannot occur (with cucumber,
pollination is undesirable). If ordinary varieties are grown the male
flowers must be picked off each morning; they are easily recognized
because they have no tiny cucumber attached. If you allow pollination to occur, the fruits become swollen and club-shaped, 'go to
seed' and often develop a bitter taste. The outdoor varieties (Ridge

types) will also do well under glass in company with other plants, but again the F_1 hybrids are recommended. The apple-shaped varieties are worth trying too. These are easy, delightful for salads and deserve to be better known.

General cucumber culture

To begin with, this is much the same as for tomato. The old weird and wonderful composts containing animal manures should be avoided. Use any of the modern sterilized composts or the John Innes No. 3. Both pots and rings can be used as described for tomato. However, the training is quite different. Cucumbers are best trained along wires stretched from end to end of the greenhouse, and spaced evenly along the greenhouse roof or from 6 to 8 inches apart. For the average small greenhouse about five wires will be sufficient. Stand pots on staging and train the plants up and underneath the wires; when they reach the last wire they should be stopped. In the meantime, and also after stopping, side shoots (laterals) will be produced. These must be tied to the nearest wire and trained along. The laterals usually develop at least four leaves before female flowers appear. After a fruit forms, stop the lateral two leaves further on from where the fruit is growing. From these laterals secondary laterals will develop; these should be treated similarly and so on. It is an advantage to remove tendrils and it is essential to remove all male flowers.

The plants must be kept moist at the roots at all times, but not waterlogged. Too much water may cause the young fruits to go rotten and fall prematurely. Try to maintain conditions that encourage fast development of the fruit, and do not leave the cucumbers on the plants for long after they have reached a suitable size, or they may turn bitter. For feeding, use any proprietary liquid or soluble feed according to label instructions. The greenhouse, or the part of the house where the cucumbers are grown, must be shaded with Coolglass.

It is best to grow your own cucumber plants from seed, which germinates well at about 65°F (18°C). When to sow depends on the greenhouse temperature you can maintain. Less than about 55°F (13°C) is undesirable, and about 65°F (18°C) ideal. The average greenhouse gardener will usually find April a convenient sowing time for economy in heating and for a good crop of fruit during the summer months. Sprayday (page 86) is a new safe pesticide for cucumbers and melons.

Melons

The Casaba melons are usually grown in the greenhouse. Varieties include Hero of Lockinge, Superlative, Ringleader, Emerald Gem and King George. However, you can grow the Cantaloupe type (generally much smaller) if you wish, though these give perfectly good crops in frames. Melons can be grown in a similar way to cucumbers but there are important differences. The wires should be spaced further apart, from 10 to 12 inches preferably. The house need not be shaded unless it is exceptionally hot and sunny, and when the fruit has reached full size the humidity should be lowered by increasing ventilation and reducing the watering. The best sowing time is March, to yield fruit from July onwards.

The most important difference from the growing of cucumbers is that the female flowers must be pollinated. Do this by picking a male flower, removing the petals and transferring pollen to the female flowers all at the same time. Again, the females have a tiny melon attached, and after pollination this will begin to swell quickly. Do not allow more than about three to four melons to develop on each plant. Usually the secondary laterals give the most fruit. The large fruits will need support with nets available from garden shops. Do not pick until they are absolutely ripe. Check this by pressing the end furthest from the stalk with the finger; if it is soft and resilient the fruit is ripe.

Grapes

Grape vines require little or no heat in winter but because of their culture they make difficult companions for the majority of popular greenhouse plants. For this reason they are best given a vinery of their own, and special greenhouses are available or can be built. A south-facing lean-to is ideal. Plant the vines alongside the greenhouse in a well drained border, lead the stems (called 'rods') inside through gaps in the base and train them on wires under the roof. Potted plants should be obtained from a nursery and planted in January about 4 feet apart. After planting, reduce the rods to about

$1\frac{1}{2}$ to 2 feet. The first year one leading shoot should be encouraged vertically as far as possible. If only one vine is being grown, two leading shoots can be selected and trained horizontally in opposite directions. From these, top laterals can be trained vertically and others removed. All side shoots from vertical growth should be stopped when about 2 feet long and cut back entirely in winter. Also in winter, cut back the main leading vertical shoot, or shoots (if you are growing several from a single vine), to ripe hard wood. During the second year, the side shoots should be secured to wires, as for cucumbers and melons, and you may get several bunches of grapes. Winter pruning during the second and subsequent years consists of reducing all laterals to one or two buds. In the third year there should be a good crop.

Only allow one bunch of grapes to each lateral, removing any others as early as possible. Thinning is usually necessary to give the bunch a good shape and prevent overcrowding of the berries. Do this carefully with a finely tipped pair of scissors, called vine scissors, and without touching the young bunches with the fingers.

To avoid mildew problems, always take care over ventilation. Although in winter no extra warmth is necessary, from spring onwards a congenial warmth will aid good fruiting. During flowering a minimum temperature of about 55°F (13°C) is desirable. After the fruit is gathered there is no need for warmth at all and the vines can be exposed to frost without damage. Aim at maintaining moist conditions at all times and at providing adequate moisture when the plants are growing actively. Always avoid waterlogging the roots. A limited number of grape varieties is available.

Grapes in pots

In the small home greenhouse you should grow the plants in 12-inch pots. The best varieties for this are Black Hamburgh and Royal Muscadine. Vines grown in this way can be trained up canes, but they cannot be expected to yield more than about six bunches, and their life is limited.

Pot one-year-old plants in December or January, in clay pots, and plunge them outdoors in an open position – they are perfectly hardy. During late winter bring the pots into the greenhouse and start the vines into growth at a temperature of about 50 to 55°F

(10/13°C). Thrust two 4- to 5-foot canes into each pot, one each side, and tie another across the tops to form a loop. The vine is then trained up one, across the top, and down the other, as it grows. Remove some of the laterals to leave a space of about one foot between those remaining. These in turn should be stopped two leaves beyond the place where grapes develop. The following winter, when the plant is dormant, prune it by removing half the cane formed the previous season and reducing laterals to two buds. After three years discard the plants and make a fresh start. When pruning you can use some of the laterals for propagation. The lateral should be cut up so that on each piece there is a well-formed bud with a length of stem about an inch long on either side. Press these into a cutting compost in small pots so that the bud just protrudes and root in a propagator at about 70°F (21°C). Pot on as required and plant as already described after the first year.

Vines in pots are most decorative as well as giving a useful number of grapes.

Peaches, nectarines and apricots

For worthwhile crops these are all best grown as fan-trained specimens on the rear wall of a lean-to facing south. You will need considerable space, and a well-prepared border at the wall base. It should be well drained and the ground treated as though the plants were for outdoor culture; any good general gardening book will give details. Training is also similar to that of outdoor wall-grown fruit, but more care is needed to encourage lower growth and avoid excessive height. An important difference is that under glass the flowers must be pollinated. Do this with a tuft of fluffed-up cotton wool tied to a stick, lightly dusting from flower to flower at around midday if possible.

In the greenhouse a good atmospheric humidity should be maintained but do not spray blossom or the ripening fruit with water. If a lean-to is not available the plants can often be grown up the side of an ordinary house and led along wires under the roof, espalier fashion. The selection of suitable varieties and suitably trained trees to start off with is vital to success; consult a specialist nursery. Easy peaches for the greenhouse include Duke of York and Hale's Early. For nectarines, Lord Napier and Early Rivers are recommended. The apricot Moorpark is the one generally grown. Apricots need special care: give good ventilation and avoid high temperatures during blossom formation and flowering, or the flowers may drop. Dwarf bush peaches suitable for growing in 12-inch pot s are now available.

Figs

Figs are best grown in large pots since they can become rampant if unrestricted. The variety Brown Turkey is easy. It can be fan-trained if desired. Under glass you can usually obtain good crops since fruits form on both the current and the previous year's growth. However, for quality the fruits are best restricted to about three to four per shoot. All weak and straggly wood must be cut out, and you should water generously during active growth, but reduce the amount slightly when the fruit is ripening. Plants in pots can be stood outdoors in summer to give more greenhouse space.

Strawberries

These are essentially frame and cloche crops, and the height of a greenhouse is not really necessary. However, a few pots can be grown among other plants if desired. For decorative effect, special strawberry urns can be planted up. The aroma of strawberry fruit under glass is also delightful. Buy new plants each year and grow them outside until January, when they can be brought into the greenhouse, at a temperature of 45/50°F (7/10°C) minimum, and potted in 5- to 7-inch pots. The flowers should preferably be hand pollinated. Consult a strawberry specialist for suitable varieties. The old favourite Royal Sovereign is, however, still an excellent one.

Miscellaneous fruits

Apples, pears, plums and cherries are sometimes grown under glass for early crops but because of the space they take up they are probably not worth while. However, it is now possible to get dwarf fruit trees (especially apple, pear and peach) that can be easily grown in large pots, and stood in the open garden for normal fruiting.

As curiosities, several species of physalis can be grown in small pots. They yield grape-sized fruits of very pleasant apricot flavour. One of the best is the sugar cherry, *Physalis ixocarpa*, which can be easily raised from seed as an annual.

A decorative plant producing pods useful for flavouring soups is okra, *Hibiscus esculentus*. Pot on the seedlings to 5-inch pots and pick the elongated pods before they are fully ripe, or they may become woody.

Sweet peppers

The correct name is pimiento, from the Spanish. The fruits sold in the shops are also often called capsicums, a name that leads to confusion with *Capsicum frutescens*. Sweet peppers are *C. annuum grossum* and, incidentally, are no relation to the true peppers.

Seed should be sown early, as described for the ornamental varieties (see page 116). Pot on to 5- to 7-inch pots, and keep warm and well watered. Feed as soon as the fruit starts forming. You can get as many as thirty fruits from a well grown plant, but it is best to restrict the number by thinning, so that each fruit has room to swell and develop properly. The plants need support and a well-lit position. Fruit is usually ready by July. Green fruits will turn red after picking if kept in a warm place indoors.

From November-sown plants it is possible to get crops by the following April, but only if considerable winter warmth is provided.

Aubergines (*egg plant*)

Culture is similar to pimiento in that a long season is desirable for growth and ripening. Sow not later than March, germinating at about 65°F (18°C), and pot on to a final 7-inch pot. A stout cane will be needed for support, since the fruit is large and heavy. If you wish, you can stop the plants at an early stage to encourage bushiness, or you can allow them to grow to about 3 feet. Only allow two or three fruits to develop on each plant. Water and feed well as soon as the fruit starts forming. The variety Early Purple does particularly well in pots and has a fine purple colour.

Lettuce

This is really another frame crop, but it can often be grown with other plants in the greenhouse to make the best use of space.

Obviously you want lettuce to crop when there is nothing outside, and for this you must choose your variety carefully. The following varieties are recommended (all are cabbage lettuce types):

Name	*Sow*	*Ready*
Kweik (cold greenhouse)	August	November/December
Kloek (cold greenhouse)	October	March/April
Sea Queen (cold or cool)	August/February	December/April
Emerald (cold or cool)	August/February	December/April
May Queen (cold or cool)	October/March	March/June

Note that *not all lettuce varieties are suited to culture under glass*; a number of greenhouse types are described in the seed catalogues.

The technique of sowing and pricking out is similar to that of bedding plants (see page 228). A germination temperature of about 55°F (13°C) is adequate. Although it is customary to plant in the greenhouse ground soil, excellent lettuces can be grown in pots, troughs or beds of potting compost isolated from the ground soil by polythene sheeting. The great menace to lettuce is botrytis (see page 84). Good ventilation is of the utmost importance.

Beans

Climbing French beans can be grown in the greenhouse and make good use of the height. Runner beans are rarely successful. There are a number of interesting and tasty climbing French varieties. These include Purple Podded and Violet Podded, both attractively coloured, almost stringless and of excellent flavour, Romano, which is stringless and delicious, and Coco, which has broad pods and seeds that can also be used like haricot beans.

Germinate the seed at about 65 to 70°F (18 to 21°C) and transfer first to small pots. In the home greenhouse it is best to sow in late February and plant out in March. You can plant earlier but this means maintaining the winter minimum temperature of about 55°F (13°C) for a longer period. Good light is also most important.

203

Culture is very similar to that of tomato: the plants can be set out in pots or rings. Alternatively, plant them in troughs of compost, using polythene sheeting held in place by boards or some similar arrangement. Space the plants about 15 inches apart and train them up strings. Maintain high humidity and keep the plants well watered, but on no account waterlogged. To obtain a good crop stop the laterals and secondary laterals at the third joint. For best flavour it is important to pick the beans when young and not to leave them on the plants too long. Picking starts around April or May.

Dwarf French beans can also be grown, especially in the company of cucumbers as they like a similar environment. However, in the home greenhouse it is usually convenient to sow from January to February to avoid maintaining a high temperature for so long. Set three to four plants to each 8-inch pot and give a few canes for support.

Miscellaneous vegetables

If there is space available it may be worth growing a few early radishes, carrots, turnips, and beetroots. Again the seedsmen's catalogues should be carefully consulted for varieties suitable for growing under glass and gentle forcing – though if you want these on a large scale it is best to grow them in frames. Usually there is space for mustard and cress, and the odd pot of herbs, such as mint, to meet winter requirements.

An area under the staging can often be used for forcing and/or blanching. Rhubarb can be easily forced in winter in a blacked-out space under the staging. Plant a few three-year-old roots in boxes in a temperature of about 50°F (10°C). Chicory and seakale can be similarly forced – details of varieties and the initial garden work involved will be found in any outdoor gardening book. To black out an under-the-staging area use black polythene. The blackout must be completely lightproof.

13 Specialist Greenhouse Plants

There are a few types of plant that warrant specialization because of special interest or outstanding beauty. Often it is worth devoting a greenhouse entirely to them so that any special conditions they like can be exactly fulfilled. However, this does not mean that someone with a mixed greenhouse cannot grow them very well indeed if he or she is prepared to exert a little extra effort. A number of plants already mentioned sometimes interest people so much that they devote a whole greenhouse to them. Begonias, ferns and foliage plants with various temperature requirements are examples. Some of the more popular specializations are described more fully here.

Alpines

You may think it strange that these plants, so used to adverse weather conditions, can benefit from greenhouse protection. In this country their enemy is cold coupled with wet, which can cause rotting of the roots. Many alpines are frozen and buried under snow in their native environment. The snow blanket protects the plants from excessive cold; but in the open here, they have to endure several degrees of frost when there is no protective snow. For this reason, a greenhouse kept just above freezing is an ideal environment – provided there is plenty of ventilation and light. Special alpine houses are available, designed to give the best possible growing conditions, but any well-ventilated house can be used if sited in an open position. There are also numerous alpines that will be at home in a mixed greenhouse collection.

The low-growing and dainty nature of alpines means that they look best on staging rather higher than usual, which brings their beauty nearer the eye. They are usually grown in well-drained pans or half pots. Use the normal potting composts, but add more grit for drainage and, in some cases, stone chips to give a coarser texture or limestone for those liking alkaline conditions.

Greenhouse Gardening

The great majority of alpines flower from spring to early summer. This means that there are few flowers for the rest of the year, and you can put the plants in frames if you wish. This leaves room for growing annuals in pots or similar plants that enjoy the airy, light conditions of the alpine house. Under glass many alpines will need protection from intense sunshine, so apply a weak mixture of Coolglass to the glass, unless slatted blinds are fitted.

Nearly all the rock garden plants grown outdoors are suitable for the alpine house, but there are many choice species that can be displayed to better advantage. Certain alpines can be extremely difficult to grow, and the beginner should avoid these. It is essential to get a catalogue of alpines from a specialist grower (see Appendix). There is a vast number of species and a whole book would be needed to do justice to them.

A number of other plants can be grown with alpines. The dwarf spring-flowering bulbs make a wonderful show; you can put the taller kinds at the back of the staging. The dwarf conifers are splendid evergreen foliage plants and you might like to try bonsai too. A collection of the charming *Primula auricula* varieties (show auriculas) will also thrive in alpine house conditions.

Many alpines can be grown from seed but the seed may sometimes need exposure to frost before it will germinate.

Bromeliads

These plants belong to the pineapple family and have soared to popularity in very recent years – so much so that people are beginning to collect them. However, they are very amenable and generally happy in the company of a wide range of other plants if care is taken. There is no need for a special greenhouse. The pineapple itself, *Ananas comosus*, is not really a practical proposition, since it needs more warmth and space then the amateur greenhouse can usually provide. However, pineapple tops can be rooted in summer and grown on, even producing fruit if there is sufficient warmth and humidity.

Bromeliads from warm parts of Central America grow well in the greenhouse and are little trouble. Species from the mountains of South America are usually easy, because they are resistant to wide temperature changes, typical of their home environment. There are two types of bromeliad: epiphytic and terrestrial (as with orchids). The former grow above ground in the moss or debris that collects in the forks of trees and the like. The latter root into the ground like ordinary plants. The two can be distinguished by the epiphytic smooth-edged leaves and the terrestrial barbed leaves, which look like pineapple tops. The leaves are arranged in a star or rosette shape and are often exotically marked or coloured, sometimes with dramatic effect. Many species have a cup-shaped hollow at the centre, called an 'urn', which should generally be kept topped up with water. This built-in 'reservoir' makes watering an easy matter for beginners.

Not all bromeliads have spectacular foliage. In some it is plain green. Curiously enough, these have the most flamboyant flowers; those with exotic foliage often have flowers of little interest. A bromeliad flowers only once and then forms several new plantlets around the base. These should be removed and potted. Plant the epiphytic types in moss wound around pieces of tree trunk to give a natural effect (see also page 72). A general compost recommended by T. Rochford Ltd, the famous house plant firm, has equal parts of pine needles, peat and leafmould, but when pine needles are difficult to obtain various mixtures of sterilized leafmould, peat and grit can be used. Avoid large pots. I prefer clay for these plants. Most bromeliads will be happy with a winter minimum of about 50°F (10°C) and often the temperature can fall much lower for short periods without harm, provided the plants are kept on the dry side. They need good light in winter and slight shading in summer. A moist atmosphere in summer is also desirable.

Because of their popularity as house plants there are now very many species available. To save space the reader is again recommended to get a catalogue from a specialist grower for a detailed description. Although bromeliads can be grown from seed sown in a warm propagator, their development is usually slow. It is more convenient, and quicker, to buy small plants from a nursery.

Cacti and succulents

This is another wide-ranging subject, and there are thousands of species. Many are not as particular as other plants over watering, so they are a good choice for those who cannot be in constant attendance. It is nevertheless a mistake to think that cacti and other succulents can be neglected and ill-treated. If they are given reasonable care they frequently reward you with the most beautiful flowers. It is also a common mistake to think that they need hardly any water. This may be true in winter; in summer, or when they are actively growing, water generously, but keep the compost well drained and only water when it has almost dried out.

A glass-to-ground greenhouse is ideal for cacti and succulents. It will give the good light they need and with staging and shelving a vast number can be accommodated in quite a small house. A winter minimum temperature of about 40°F (4°C) is generally sufficient, but an airy, dry atmosphere should be the aim at all times. However, many cacti and succulents are happy with other plants in a mixed greenhouse.

Most cacti and succulents are not fussy over compost provided that it is well drained. Most of the potting composts suggested in Chapter 7 (see page 90) can be used if a generous addition of grit is made to perfect drainage. Although the plants like plenty of light, the intense summer sun may cause damage under glass and slight shading with Coolglass is advisable. This group of plants is remarkably free from pests and diseases and is very easy. Once again there is such an enormous number that you should study a specialist's catalogue for plant descriptions. Many interesting species are now also sold as house plants for window-sill culture.

Epiphyllums are worthy of special mention. These are notable for exceptionally brilliant and large showy flowers, and many people make special collections of them. Numerous fine named hybrids exist. Being tall growing, these plants need a cane for support and more summer shade than other cacti.

Many cacti and succulents are easy to raise from seed sown by the normal methods (see page 106). When handling spiny plants for potting, hold them with a strip of folded newspaper to avoid discomfort.

Carnations

Although some of the garden carnations, such as the Chabaud type, can be taken up in autumn, potted and flowered in winter under glass, greenhouse carnations proper are the perpetual flowering kind – called PF for short.

A few PF carnations can be grown in pots in the mixed greenhouse, but their blooms are so pleasing and often delightfully scented that it is worth devoting a small greenhouse to growing them to perfection – particularly since flowers can be had nearly all the year round. Any glass-to-ground house will do provided there is good ventilation, but special carnation houses are available. PF carnations grow to a considerable height and they are usually quite vigorous. They must be bought from a specialist nursery (see Appendix), and are best obtained as rooted cuttings of named varieties from December to March. Pot them into $2\frac{1}{2}$-inch pots when you receive them and then pot on as required to final 7-inch pots. It is also possible to obtain plants in $2\frac{1}{2}$-inch pots that have been stopped by the nurseryman, and these should be put into 5-inch pots on arrival. Alternatively, you can buy established plants from September to November, in 5-inch pots. These will flower the following winter and can also be used for cuttings.

PF carnations like plenty of light and air and a winter minimum of about 40/45°F (4/7°C) for a good production of winter bloom. You can buy special carnation compost with a high potash content from nurseries, but the John Innes No. 2 will give good results.

Stop young plants when they have grown about ten pairs of leaves and all side shoots that subsequently develop, except for about five pairs. Stop the longest or fastest growing shoot first. Do not try to stop all shoots at the same time. The first stopping is done when the plants are about 8 inches tall, and the second stopping when the plants are in their final pots. Further stoppings can be carried out to obtain continuity of bloom. The stopping procedure depends on the variety and has to be learned by experience.

The plants will require support and, although canes and various improvisations can be used, there are proper wire carnation supports on sale. When watering, aim to maintain a nicely moist compost at all times. High potash feeds, as used for tomatoes, also work well for carnations.

To obtain fine blooms it is necessary to disbud. Remove the unwanted side buds as soon as possible, leaving only the crown bud to develop. Slight shading, preferably with Coolglass, is needed during periods of brilliant sunshine.

Do not keep old plants after two or three years. Young stock should be propagated from cuttings taken from December to February. Do not use the old plants as a source of cuttings; take them from young plants, using side shoots about 6 inches long with about six pairs of leaves. The cuttings root easily by the usual methods (see page 219), or in pearlite, at a temperature of about 65°F (18°C).

PF carnations do not make very good decorative pot plants and they should be cut. There are many exquisite varieties described in the specialists' catalogues (see Appendix). The American spray carnations which are scented and require no disbudding make better pot plants. Their culture is otherwise identical to the ordinary PF types. They are generally available only as rooted cuttings.

Chrysanthemums (see also pages 117 and 230)

These are among the most magnificent blooms worthy of specialization and easily within the scope of the home greenhouse. The later flowering types can conveniently be accommodated in a greenhouse after clearing tomatoes. Growing these chrysanthemums gives great satisfaction and the blooms are among the most long-lasting of all cut flowers.

The late-flowering chrysanthemums are grown in pots outdoors during the summer and transferred to the greenhouse for flowering from about October to December. There are a number of different types, classed according to their bloom structure as follows: Exhibition and Exhibition Incurved ('incurved' refers to petals that turn inwards to form a ball-shaped bloom); Reflexed Decorative (petals turn outwards loosely); Intermediate Decorative (some petals turn out and those near the centre turn inwards); Anemone-Flowered; Single; Pompom; Spray; Thread-Petalled; and Spidery. The Exhibition types are those bearing the enormous blooms seen at flower shows. These, the Decoratives, the Anemone-Flowered and the Singles are also divided into large- or medium-flowered forms.

General cultivation

A glass-to-ground greenhouse giving the maximum light and air is desirable. A winter minimum temperature of about 45°F (7°C) is all that is necessary. Obtain a catalogue from a leading chrysanthemum specialist (see page 241) to make your selection of varieties; new varieties and novelties appear each year and any recommended list soon becomes out of date. For a rough idea of the number needed, assume that about twenty-five will fit comfortably in a small 10 by 6 foot greenhouse and *pro rata*.

To begin with buy rooted cuttings of named varieties from a chrysanthemum specialist in February or March, and put them into $3\frac{1}{2}$-inch pots on arrival. Although the standard potting composts described in Chapter 7 can be used for chrysanthemums, the John Innes No. 2 is particularly recommended. Feed subsequently with Woolman's chrysanthemum plant food, described below, and pot as described in Chapter 7 (see page 90). After the initial potting, stand the pots on the staging and see that the temperature does not fall below about 40°F (4°C). As the plants become established, ventilate freely whenever weather permits, and keep the compost just moist.

By late March to April the plants will be ready to pot on to 5- or 6-inch pots, depending on development. Some varieties are more vigorous than others, but the plants must not be allowed to become pot bound. For this potting, and for subsequent pottings I recommend the John Innes No. 3 or a peat/grit compost, for reasons given below. From now on you will need no artificial heat except in freak weather conditions. When the plants have become established in their pots they should be transferred to a cold frame for hardening off (see page 229). Here, give them as much air as possible, but close the lights if there is night frost.

By early June the plants should be ready for transfer to their final pots, either 8- or 9-inch ones. Take particular care over drainage of the pots at this stage (see page 100) because the plants will now be standing in the open for the summer and rain can water-log badly drained pots.

The next step is to find a suitable place outdoors for standing the pots. It should be well away from trees or light obstruction, but protected from prevailing winds – this is most important. Stand the pots on a run of plastic sheeting, or any other material that will prevent worms or soil pests from entering the drainage holes of the pots and the roots from entering the ground soil. It is usual to stand the plants in rows, spacing the pots 3 to 4 inches apart from rim to rim, and leaving a space of about 4 feet between the rows. Insert a strong 5-foot cane into each pot. The John Innes composts and the peat/grit type usually give sound anchorage for the canes and, being reasonably heavy, provide a stable base for the plants. Push two stakes into the ground, one at each end of the row, run a wire between them and tie the canes to this. This is essential to prevent wind from blowing the plants over. Long rows of plants will need more stakes at intervals so that all the plants are held really well. Should there be any problem in securing the canes to the pots, use Woolman's special wire clips (see page 241).

During their standing-out period the plants will obviously need careful watering, and a trickle feed automatic system is worth considering (see page 65). No feeding should be necessary until July; at this time apply Woolman's chrysanthemum fertilizer or a top dressing of some fresh compost according to the supplier's recommendations. Avoid overfeeding. During hot spells, spray the foliage with water occasionally, after the sun has gone. Keep a constant watch for pests and take instant action if they are seen. Chrysanthemum leaf miner is a common one; its presence is betrayed by meandering lines on the foliage. Close inspection will reveal a tiny grub burrowing between the leaf surfaces, and you can kill this merely by pinching it with the fingers. Routine spraying with Hexyl Plus will deal with this and other common pests.

The time for transferring the plants to the greenhouse is generally about mid-September. Make sure that the greenhouse is thoroughly clean and cleared of all tomato debris if this crop has recently been grown there. After removal to the greenhouse the plants must be given free ventilation to get them used to greenhouse conditions. Should there be late strong sunshine the house may need slight shading with Coolglass; you can wipe this off when necessary. As the plants come into flower watch for *Botrytis cinerea* (see page 84) and take precautionary measures. Stand the pots on plastic sheeting and avoid overcrowding.

Training and stopping chrysanthemums

Left to grow naturally, a chrysanthemum first forms a solitary bud at the top of its stem, called the break bud. This will not develop, but below it a number of shoots will grow from the stem: this is called a natural break. These shoots will produce buds, called first crown buds, which will flower if left. Other breaks will occur and produce second crown buds, giving more flowers, and so on. However, if things are allowed to proceed naturally we will get inferior blooms at an inconvenient time. For this reason, both the breaks and the number of buds are controlled by stopping, securing buds and disbudding.

Stopping is done by merely removing the break bud or about half to one inch of the growing tip of a shoot. The time to carry out these operations varies considerably from variety to variety and chrysanthemum type. Arm yourself therefore with a grower's catalogue, such as Woolman's, which gives a detailed timing and stopping key for each variety, including a diagram that illustrates stopping procedure. Stopping and timing can never be exact because of variations in climate from north to south-west. The correct timing for shows can only be assessed by experience and trial and error.

Securing a bud means the opposite to stopping – the bud at the end of a shoot is left to develop and any side shoot or buds below are removed at an early stage.

Exhibition chrysanthemums For best results some varieties are flowered from the first crown buds and others from the second. Only allow one to three of the enormous flowers to develop to each plant. Buds usually begin to form on the two to three stems permitted to grow during late July and should be secured in August by removing the lower side shoots as already described. It is also possible to use the 'single stem method' – stopping the plants in early June and securing only one bud on a single stem, all other shoots being removed.

Exhibition incurved Allow three to four blooms (sometimes six) for each plant. Secure buds from late August to mid-September, removing any that appear earlier. These chrysanthemums enjoy a little shade when they are stood out during summer, and they should be fed adequately – but take special care not to overfeed.

Decorative types These are very popular. They have flowers of pleasing size, and a very wide range of lovely colours. As many as eighteen good-sized blooms can grow on each plant. Stop the plants in their $3\frac{1}{2}$-inch pots, when they are about 6 to 9 inches tall. From the resulting shoots retain only three to four to grow on. Stop these shoots again from late May to June.

Other types Treat the anemone-flowered like the decoratives. The plants are so named because of the anemone shape of the flowers. Single chrysanthemums are easy to grow, and need little stopping; they should not be stopped after early April. Do not secure buds until after the first week in September.

Other varieties grown in pots can generally be left to grow naturally. A recent introduction is the 'Mini-Mum' from the Wye College of Horticulture. This dwarf species is excellent as a flowering house plant, being only about 8 inches high. The flowers are single, sometimes with thin 'spoon-shaped' petals, and they have an attractive colour range. Buy them as rooted cuttings, pot them into $3\frac{1}{2}$-inch pots, in which they will flower, and keep them at about 45°F (7°C). From March to October the plants must be blacked out for twelve hours in every twenty-four; move them to an under-stage area blacked out with black polythene sheet. Alternatively, you can place boxes over the plants. The black-out should be provided each evening and removed each morning. Flowering usually takes place about ten to twelve weeks after potting and continues for about six weeks.

Cascade and Charm chrysanthemums are described on page 117. Dwarfing methods, using various chemicals, are described in technical literature issued by the chemical suppliers (see page 240).

Treatment of greenhouse chrysanthemums after flowering

When flowering is over, cut the plants down to about 2 feet and in January cut down further to about 3 inches. At a temperature of about 45 to 50°F (7/10°C) a good supply of new shoots should form, and these can be used for cuttings, which only need the same temperature for rooting. See also pages 219 and 230. Exhibition types are usually rooted from January to February; the latter is early enough for incurved forms. Decoratives can be rooted from February to March, and singles during March.

Orchids

You can grow several kinds of orchid in a mixed greenhouse collection. A special greenhouse is not essential, though you may want one eventually. Although there are groups of orchids to suit different temperature conditions, the cool-house types are obviously the most popular, and the easiest as far as heating is concerned. Few orchids are really difficult to grow, given the right conditions and temperature. Their culture is merely a little different from other greenhouse plants.

In general, orchids require a very open fibrous compost. Composts were at one time based on sphagnum moss, osmunda fibre (from osmunda fern), various forms of leafmould, and similar ingredients. Today, synthetic materials including forms of plastic, have been used with considerable success. It is therefore best to get your compost from the nursery supplying the plants. If possible, always try to see your plants in flower before buying if you are paying a fair sum. However, unflowered seedlings are inexpensive and fun to grow if you are prepared to wait a year or so to see results.

Undoubtedly the most popular orchids are the cymbidiums. These have showy sprays of large butterfly-like flowers which can be picked and used as buttonhole blooms. They are easily grown with a winter minimum temperature of about 45°F (7°C). The cattleyas, with their huge, richly coloured blooms, are very exotic, but they do need a congenial temperature. However, the plants are far more compact than cymbidium and you can fit a large collection into quite a small greenhouse. Laelias are similar: there are some suited to warm and some to cool conditions. Vandas also like a range of temperatures. Most odontoglossums and miltonias like cool conditions, and both are very beautiful.

Popular orchids too are the paphiopedilums (once known as cypripediums). Unlike most orchids these have no pseudobulbs (the swollen part at the base of the stems). There are two types: those with plain foliage, which like cool conditions, and those with mottled foliage, which prefer warmth. The flowers are 'slipper'-

shaped, waxy and often curiously marked, and they last a very long time.

There are thousands of orchid species and as many named hybrids, so here again the interested reader must obtain a grower's catalogue for details and descriptions. Nearly all those grown in the greenhouse are named hybrids, but there are a few species well worth adding.

General culture of cool-house orchids

Although orchids like a moist atmosphere, the air should never become stagnant: ventilate whenever the weather permits. Bottom ventilation is particularly useful, but draughts must be avoided. Temperatures below about 45°F (7°C) should also be avoided, though most plants will survive drops almost to freezing for short periods. You cannot expect to get the best results if this happens too often. Keep the temperature down in summer by shading with Coolglass. Good light is essential in winter, so keep the glass clean: but from February onwards, when many plants are coming into flower, apply shading again if the sun is intense.

Always water orchids thoroughly but do not repeat until the compost has almost dried out. Clean rainwater is best but never use filthy water; where clean rainwater is not obtainable (see page 76) it is better to use mains drinking water even if it is hard. In winter give little or no water. Orchids rarely need food; there is sufficient plant food in the compost to last until the next repotting.

Usually the best time to repot is just after flowering or in spring. The pseudobulbs are often lop-sided. When repotting, plant off-centre with the new growth and roots facing the greatest compost area and volume. Old back bulbs can usually be cut away and discarded. Push the compost down between the roots with a potting stick (see page 102). It is important to pot firmly, but not so that roots are damaged. Take special care with new, succulent-looking roots. Old shrivelled ones can be carefully cut away. Newly potted plants should not be watered for a week or so, otherwise there is risk of root rot.

The reader seriously interested in orchids, who has perhaps had success with cymbidiums, should try some of the many other exciting types. One of the best books, giving details of all the popular kinds, is *Popular Orchids* by Brian and Wilma Rittershausen (David and Charles).

Hardy orchids

The most rewarding hardy orchid, which can be grown easily in the alpine house or any cold or cool greenhouse, is *Pleione formosana*. There are several named varieties available and the flower resembles a small cattleya bloom. Pleione is best planted in a large half pot, in a compost made from equal parts of peat, loam, grit and leafmould, with a little bonemeal added. Left alone, a pseudobulb will multiply and form a clump in the pot. When the flower dies, new pseudobulbs are produced at the side of the old, and the old one shrivels. Before this happens, some tiny pseudobulbs may be formed at the apex of the old. Detach and plant these. In winter give very little water, but keep the compost moist when there is active growth. Flowering is usually in early spring.

14 *Propagation*

There are several reasons for propagating, apart from the obvious one of increasing the number of your plants. Sometimes old plants become untidy and 'leggy', or too large for convenience; they may also deteriorate and flower badly. These circumstances call for a fresh start, and often the old plant will be a rich source of propagation material – such as cuttings of various descriptions, offsets, side growths and so on.

Gardeners often want to produce more from a particularly pleasing plant. Extensive propagation may be necessary if plants are to be used for outdoor bedding, but there is little point in propagating just for the sake of sheer numbers. A greenhouse full of the same kind of plant can be very dull unless there is a good reason for it.

CHOOSING PROPAGATION MATERIAL

It is important to be very fussy about the selection of plants for propagation. Undesirable characteristics can be reproduced as well as desirable ones. You must therefore choose plants with the best habit, flower colour, flower size and quality, good foliage and so forth. The methods of propagation described here will reproduce exactly the plant's characteristics except when you are propagating from seed (see below, page 219). Do not use sickly plants of any description. Virus diseases are a great menace, since they are incurable and are easily spread by insects – and often by the mere handling of plants. They are of course passed on during propagation. Do not use plants with yellowing and particularly mottled foliage, distortion of any description or oddly shaped or abnormally striped flowers. Avoid plants that seem backward or stunted. All these are possible symptoms of virus diseases.

Plants that have wilted through lack of water or pest attack, or are suffering from chill or neglect, should not be used as propaga-

218

tion material except in dire need – for example, if you think the parent plant may die. Material from such plants may not propagate so readily. However, with a plant that has been damaged or dropped immediate propagation can restore it to your collection.

PROPAGATION FROM SEED

The majority of the choice hybrids, F_1 hybrids, named varieties and so on cannot reliably be reproduced from seed. This is true of the great majority of the plants described in Chapter 8, and the seed must be freshly bought each year. Such seed is usually produced by expert crossing, selection and pollination, often by hand and by special techniques; it is neither possible nor necessary to enter into the genetic reasons here. With pure species, however, you can sometimes collect your own seed. To be viable (that is, to be able to germinate) the seed often has to ripen and mature on the plant. Collect the seed when the plant itself is ready to shed it. If you specially want to collect a particular seed, it is often a good idea to remove all but a few flowers so that the plant can devote its energy to them. The general technique for growing from seed is described in Chapter 8 (see also page 206 for comment on the seed of alpines).

SOFTWOOD CUTTINGS

You can reproduce the great majority of greenhouse plants by removing suitable shoots, inserting them in a rooting compost, and, when roots have formed, potting in the usual way. In the greenhouse, cuttings can be taken nearly all the year round except from plants that are dormant. However, the best time to take most cuttings is when the plants are just about to begin an active period of growth. This means that spring can be a busy time. However, there are numerous popular plants that can also be propagated from cuttings taken in early autumn.

The compost used for rooting cuttings of all kinds comprises equal parts by volume of moss peat, well teased apart, and sharp washed grit. Put this into pots or seed trays, depending on the circumstances. When pots are used better rooting often occurs, strangely enough, if the cuttings are inserted around the edge and close to the side. Put a number of the cuttings – always as small as possible – in each pot.

Rooting is always quicker with a source of bottom heat (see page 57); a propagator is desirable and often essential for plants from warm countries. But many of the hardier greenhouse plants root well during the summer with no extra warmth.

For successful and fast rooting you must also reduce water loss from the foliage of the cutting. This means that the cuttings must

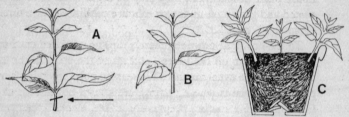

20 *Taking a Softwood Cutting*
A: shoot of plant selected. B: the shoot prepared for rooting, the final cut being made just below root node (arrowed). C: cuttings inserted around edge of pot, ready for the propagator if necessary.

be covered with transparent plastic film to keep in moisture. A modern way of preventing water loss is mist propagation (see under this heading, page 226). With hardier plants, cold frames can be used to save greenhouse space. On a larger scale, frames can also be fitted with warming cables if heat is required (see page 58).

For the occasional job of propagation, polythene bags can be used. Put a little moist cutting compost at the bottom of a bag, insert one or more cuttings, and suspend the bag in a warm place. When rooting occurs you can remove and pot the cuttings. This very simple technique is remarkably effective with many greenhouse plants.

The ease with which cuttings root varies very considerably according to the nature of the plant. Some, like nerium, tradescantia and even some fuchsias, will root merely standing in a glass of water. Some plants may take a long time to root or perhaps not root at all. To accelerate the rooting of cuttings you can use hormone powders of which there are two types; one for softwood and the other for hardwood cuttings. The latter are usually far more difficult to root, and the hormone powders are particularly useful. However, nearly all cuttings from greenhouse plants are of the softwood type; they are, as the name implies, from soft or immature growth and shoots. Semihard-wood cuttings are taken from rather more mature shoots, especially those of shrubs. Hardwood cuttings come from most trees and woody shrubs and are mostly taken when the plants are dormant. Although both semi-hardwood and hardwood cuttings are rarely used for greenhouse plant propagation, they may be taken from outdoor plants, rooted and grown on under greenhouse conditions for a time. (See Chapter 15, page 235.)

To use hormone powders, merely dip the prepared cuttings into the powder, tap off the excess, and insert the stem in the cutting compost in the usual manner. There is no point in trying hormone powders on plants whose cuttings are known not to root at all. A liquid hormone rooting preparation called Roota, recently introduced, can be used for cuttings generally, and contains a fungicide claimed to reduce the chances of rotting.

To take a cutting, choose a small, vigorous shoot and cut it cleanly from the parent plant. Carefully break off the lower leaves so as to leave foliage originating from about three nodes. Then cut cleanly through the surplus stem just below the highest node from which the foliage has been removed (see Fig. 20). Avoid taking cuttings from shoots carrying flowers or buds. If this cannot be helped, remove them cleanly. Always use a very sharp knife in taking and preparing cuttings, to avoid bruising the plant tissue. A razor blade in a holder or a surgical scalpel is useful.

Since the rooting compost contains no fertilizer, the cuttings should be potted as soon as roots form. Some growers do include fertilizer; others consider that fertilizer retards root formation. I personally do not include fertilizer.

LEAF CUTTINGS

This is another technique of special value to greenhouse gardeners. Many plants, particularly of the Begoniaceae and Gesneriaceae, can be propagated by leaf cuttings taken in various ways (see Fig. 21).

The Gesneriaceae include such plants as gloxinia, streptocarpus, saintpaulia and aeschynanthus.

Large leaves can sometimes be cut up into small pieces. The veins on the underside should be slit with a very sharp knife – but not so that the leaf is penetrated – and then the sections placed flat, vein side down, on the cutting compost already described. If

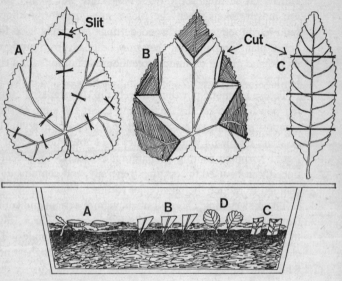

21   *Various Types of Leaf Cutting*
A: removed leaf with slits cut across leaf veins (arrowed). B: triangular pieces of leaf cut out (shaded) with leaf vein at apex. C: long leaf cut into sections. D: some leaves can be pulled off and inserted in the rooting medium directly (e.g. saintpaulia).

preferred an entire leaf, with the veins cut in several places, can be similarly treated and weighted down with small pieces of broken clay pot or the like. Many begonias can be propagated conveniently in this way, or by cutting the leaves into small triangular sections (see Fig. 21).

Plants with long leaves, for example streptocarpus, can be cut up into sections, which are inserted vertically in the cutting compost in the same way as softwood cuttings. In all these cases the roots will grow from the place where a vein is cut, and little plantlets will grow up from them. When large enough to handle they should be immediately potted in a nourishing compost.

In the case of plants with small leaves, for example saintpaulia, you must often use an entire leaf, with the small leaf stalk attached. The leaf stalk is inserted in the cutting compost vertically, so that the base of the leaf just reaches the compost surface, and a new plantlet will form at this point. All leaf cuttings must be covered to keep in moisture, as described for stem cuttings.

DIVISION

Most perennial pot plants can be easily multiplied by dividing the roots in the same way as outdoor herbaceous perennials. Do this just as the plants are expected to begin active growth. For plants that have been dormant or resting, remove most of the top growth and divide up the roots into convenient pieces. Obviously, plants that form only one stem cannot be divided satisfactorily. The best subjects are those which form a clump and have numerous growing shoots, and here you should allow one shoot at least to each piece separated. If the roots become entwined and matted, cut through them with a very sharp blade. If roots are severely disturbed, bruised or otherwise damaged they are much more liable to rot. So after potting divided plants, water cautiously at first.

Tuberous plants can be multiplied by cutting up the tubers and leaving one shoot to each piece. Start the tubers shooting before dividing by immersing them in moist peat (see page 139). Again, use a very sharp blade. Dusting the cut surface liberally with powdered charcoal will prevent loss of sap and also help to protect against disease.

OFFSETS

Many greenhouse bulbs form tiny bulblets around the side when they reach a mature size or after flowering. Separate these carefully when repotting and give each one its own pot. Although this is usually a quicker method of propagation than seed, the bulblets often take at least three years to reach flowering size.

Some tubers, rhizomes and similar storage organs reproduce themselves during the growing season. Separate and pot the new storage organs when it is time to start into growth again. Examples are achimenes, smithiantha and gloriosa.

LAYERING

This is a convenient way of training plants and climbers; upright growing species can also be layered if the stems are supple enough. Bend down a length of stem and lead it just under the surface of some potting compost contained in a separate pot. Keep the stem in place with a staple made by bending a piece of stiff wire into

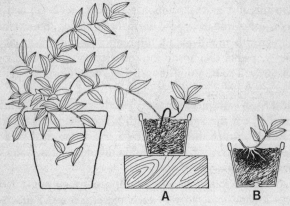

A   **B**

22   *Propagation by Layering*
A: wire staple to hold down stem (alternatively, a stone can be used). B: the rooted stem severed from its parent.

a 'U' shape. When roots have formed, sever the new plant from its parent. You will speed up rooting by removing a tiny section of the outer coating of the stem underneath the compost; alternatively, you can make a slit in the stem (see Fig. 22).

AIR LAYERING

This is particularly useful when plants growing as a single stem drop their lower leaves; a well-known example is the rubber plant,

224

Ficus elastica. Make an upward slit in the stem below the existing foliage, dust with hormone rooting powder, and wedge a small tuft of sphagnum moss into it. Then take some compost consisting of sphagnum moss, peat and grit, make it into a ball around the site of operation and hold it in place with fine florists' wire. The sphagnum moss will help to consolidate the compost. Around this you then wind polythene sheeting to retain moisture and secure

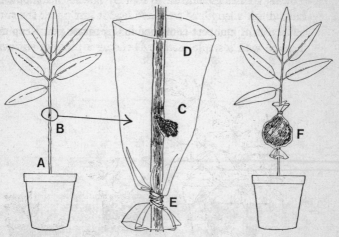

23   *Air Layering*

A: original plant from which lower leaves have fallen. B: slit in stem made in upward direction. C: wedge of peat or moss dusted with hormone rooting powder. D: thin polythene sheeting (transparent). E: secure to stem with wire or tape. F: polythene chamber filled with moist peat — when rooting has occurred it will show through the polythene.

the polythene with wire at the bottom and top of the compost ball (see Fig. 23).

When roots have formed, they can usually be seen through the polythene. For this method to be successful you often need a reasonably high temperature, so it is best done during late spring. When the roots appear cut the stem just below and pot the rooted top.

MIST PROPAGATION

All cuttings must be covered with a transparent enclosure to keep in moisture. If cuttings lose much moisture by transpiration they will of course wilt and die, since they have no roots to make good water loss. So if the foliage of the cuttings is covered with a film of moisture, there is far more chance of successful rooting (see Fig. 24). Many cuttings difficult to root by normal methods will root easily in this way.

The film of moisture is maintained by misting jets set above the

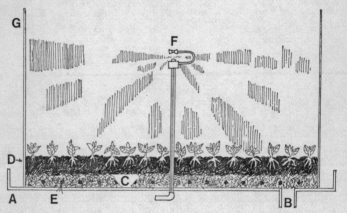

24   *Mist Propagation*
A: waterproof tray. B: drain for excess water. C: layer of sharp grit.
D: rooting medium. E: warming cable arranged as in Figure 6. F: misting jet connected to control system. G: glass or plastic screen to confine mist.

cuttings. To avoid saturation, the jets are controlled by an 'electronic leaf', which activates them when the film has evaporated. There are various types of apparatus, though recently the photoelectric method has proved far superior to the others. In this case the water jets are controlled by the light energy falling upon them, which in turn affects the rate of transpiration and water loss. Electrical control methods depending on conductivity of a film of water, or on evaporation, are liable to fail because of algae growth and lime in mains water. The photo-electric method is however independent of the water supply (see also page 66).

Although mist propagation was originally used by professional growers, small units suitable for amateur use are now available. These are easy to set up and operate and most are reasonably priced. Mist propagation is particularly effective in combination with electric warming cables to warm the rooting medium.

15 How a Greenhouse Helps the Home and Garden

A greenhouse can be so useful as an adjunct to the garden and for supplying cut flowers and house plants for the home, that it is often worth having a small separate structure especially for this purpose. A small greenhouse used in this way will cover its cost very quickly. Moreover, you can grow cheaply from seed many choice and unusual garden plants that would otherwise be difficult or expensive to buy. There are also many wonderful bedding plants not generally available from shops and nurseries, offered each year by the leading seedsmen.

BEDDING PLANTS

Obtain all the seed catalogues from the firms listed in the Appendix, and others, and make your selection as early as possible. Sowing in the greenhouse begins in January for slow-growing plants like antirrhinums and pansies, and continues until May for later flowering subjects. With the aid of the composts and techniques suggested in this book, growth in the greenhouse will be rapid and vigorous. Do not sow too early or you will have many plants far too advanced for bedding out before the weather will allow. The majority of popular bedding plants can be sown from about March or April.

For sowing, the general techniques described in Chapter 8 are applicable. However, it is usually convenient to prick out into large seed trays, 14 by 9 inches. The plastic type is best for the home gardener; the old wooden trays harbour pests and diseases and are difficult clean. Do not overcrowd the trays; with most bedding plants, allow about 24 seedlings to a tray; though you must of course take their size into account. Nursery-bought bedding plants are often very overcrowded and this results in root disturbance with growth – check when they are bedded out. Always water in the seedlings with Cheshunt compound (see page 111).

One is normally recommended to put boxes of seedlings up on shelves near the glass, rather than on the staging, so that they get more light, but there is, in fact, no need for this if the greenhouse is uncluttered. Just as much light reaches the staging in a modern greenhouse as reaches the shelves. If the seedlings are too near the glass they may suffer from chill at night.

For mass production of bedding plants, it is more economical to use soil-warming cables to keep the roots warm, with a greenhouse air temperature as low as possible – usually 35/40°F (2/4°C) is sufficient, with a root temperature of 50/55°F (10/13°C). You can make warmed benches by covering a warming cable, spread out on asbestos sheet over the staging, with an inch or so of sand. On top of this spread a layer of moist peat and in it plunge the boxes or seed trays of bedding plants. When distributing the warming cable allow about 10 watts per square foot. Temperature can be automatically controlled by thermostat. With this method strong root systems can be developed without excessive top growth – a primary aim in bedding plant production. Plants with a sound root system will grow away much faster than those with weak roots and lots of top growth.

Choice bedding plants like shrubby calceolarias (F_1 hybrids), petunias, the magnificent zinnias now available, polyanthus and so on, can be pot-grown with advantage. It is also a good idea to keep some of these under glass to fill gaps that might occur in beds and borders during the year.

All bedding plants must be hardened off before planting out. This means exposing them gradually to the rigours of the outdoor climate. The majority of bedding plants will be set back or killed completely by frost, since they are mostly half-hardy annuals. Even some of the hardier plants are best introduced gradually to outdoor conditions. Harden the plants off in frames. These need not be heated: the frame lights should be closed at first, later opened a little during the day, then closed only at night, and subsequently fully exposed all the time prior to bedding out. This process should take about two weeks, and should be timed according to your district, so that at the end of the period there is no further risk of frost.

For garden plants use special composition pots that can also be planted. The composition is usually compounded from compressed peat or similar vegetable matter so that it decomposes on contact with the soil, providing a source of humus for the roots. In this way you will avoid root disturbance and the plants will grow away very quickly after bedding out. But see that they have enough water; if conditions are too dry the composition pots may not rot down and the roots will become confined, with obvious effects on growth.

CHRYSANTHEMUMS

The greenhouse can help you grow these beautiful plants in a number of ways. The roots of outdoor varieties, called 'stools', should have their top growth cut down to about 18 inches after flowering and any new shoots should be removed. Carefully lift the roots with a fork and wash away the soil. Then 'box up' the stools by planting them in boxes of any sterilized potting compost (see page 90). Place the boxes in a frost-free greenhouse for the winter after watering to ensure that the compost is moist – not wet. Little water will be needed after this and in January the stems can be cut back again to about 5 inches. During March you should get a good supply of new shoots that can be used as cuttings. Discard the original roots. During winter, give the boxed stools a light, airy position and inspect them regularly for signs of fungi or decay. A temperature of only 45/50°F (7/10°C) is required for rooting in the cuttings.

Early-flowering Charm chrysanthemums can be sown in early February in a warm propagator and the plants grown on in pots for bedding out. Large mounds of bloom form from early autumn onwards and this type of chrysanthemum deserves to be more extensively grown. Korean chrysanthemums can be sown in the same way. They make fine cut flowers as well as decorative border plants, and grow to a height of about 2 feet.

DAHLIAS

After the top foliage has been blackened by frost it should be removed and the stem remains cut back to about 8 inches. Lift the tubers carefully, so as not to damage them, and remove as much of the soil as you can on site. Do not damage the outer skin of the tubers or disease organisms may later gain entry. Put the tubers in a greenhouse with their stems pointing downwards, thus allowing any moisture to drain away. After a few weeks gently brush away the remaining soil and cut off the old roots. Reduce the stems by about 2 inches and store the tubers immersed in dry peat or sand. The boxes can go under the staging of a frost-free greenhouse, but see that the plunge material does not get wet over winter. The tubers should be inspected from time to time for signs of disease.

During February, plant the roots in boxes of moist peat on the greenhouse staging at a minimum temperature of 45°F (7°C), but preferably higher for quick results. Shoots should soon appear and these can be used as cuttings when about 3 inches long.

Where sufficient warmth is a problem the tubers can be started during March in the same way as above. When 'eyes' begin to develop on the crowns of the tubers, divide the tubers with a sharp knife, so that each piece has an eye.

To get a very early show of blooms, pot the tubers in 10-inch pots during March or April and grow on under glass, to an advanced stage if there is room. They can then be planted out in June, when all danger of frost is past, to give a long period of bloom when dahlias are not normally seen.

ZONAL PELARGONIUMS ('geraniums')

From an early sowing of F_1 hybrids it is now possible to produce fine plants for summer-to-autumn display (see page 128). However, this is at present too expensive for large quantities of plants, though it a good way of obtaining initial stock for subsequent propagation by cuttings. Cuttings can be taken from plants in the beds in August or September. After rooting, keep the plants in the greenhouse over winter and take care not to water excessively. A winter minimum of 40/45°F (4/7°C) is desirable, and the plants should be potted on, as required, to final 5-inch pots. Harden off and bed out when all danger of frost is passed.

Plants can also be saved over winter by lifting from the beds in late autumn, just before the first frost, and either potting or planting in boxes in the greenhouse. Such plants should be kept almost dry and cut back to remove all unwieldy and straggly growth. In many cases the plants can be cut back very severely. Cut-back potted plants can be grown on for bedding out again. Alternatively, if there is a little extra warmth from January onwards, the plants can be started into growth with a slight increase in watering, and the shoots used as cuttings. The cuttings, rooted in a propagator and grown on in warmth, will yield new material for bedding out the same year.

To overwinter 'geraniums' safely in the greenhouse, take great care not to give too much water, keep out frost, and watch for botrytis (see page 84). Ventilate freely whenever possible.

SUB-TROPICAL BEDDING

With the aid of a greenhouse you can grow a number of plants that can be brought outdoors during the summer to give a sub-tropical effect to beds or borders. You can stand them in pots on a terrace or patio, or use one or two as specimen or feature plants in a lawn.

Most of the palms can be used (see pages 128 and 186), especially when they have reached a fair size. Erythrina (page 166), abutilon (page 111), grevillea (page 123), jacaranda (page 126), canna (page 143), nerium (page 171) and strelitzia (page 176) are other possibilities

An impressive plant is *Musa ensete*, which can be raised from seed sown at 80°F (27°C) during summer and grown on over winter at a minimum of about 50°F (10°C) to form sizeable plants for the following summer. (It is important to obtain fresh seed: stale seed is unlikely to germinate. Seed that floats in water is invariably useless.) The *Musa ensete* species is also known as the Abyssinian banana. It has the most handsome banana foliage and makes a fine plant for the greenhouse if there is space. You can grow good specimens in 10-inch pots. When putting this plant outdoors, choose a spot sheltered from excessive wind or the foliage may become torn.

Zea mays and *Ricinus communis* are both easy to raise from seed, and give decorative plants the first year. Select ornamental varieties of both. The first is the source of maize, but its garden forms have coloured stripe foliage and, often, decorative cobs with coloured seeds. The second is the true castor oil plant. Again there are some handsome forms, those with red foliage being especially attractive. Seed catalogues usually list several varieties. The castor oil plant will form spiky seed capsules during a warm summer and these will contain several prettily marked seeds. These should not be allowed to fall into the hands of young children, who might be attracted to them: the seeds are extremely poisonous if chewed or eaten.

The more permanent plants for sub-tropical bedding are best put out in their pots – the pots plunged. In this way they can easily be returned to the greenhouse before the frosts. Clay pots are best for such plants, since these will allow moisture to pass through. To stop worms getting in, place some coarse shingle at the bottom of the plunging hole and over the top of the pot. Worms can disturb the roots. If, on returning the pots to the greenhouse for the winter, you suspect that they have got in, you can bring them to the surface by watering with potassium permanganate solution, $\frac{1}{4}$ ounce per gallon of water. The same treatment can be given to any other greenhouse plants, such as fuchsias, that have been used for garden decoration during summer with their pots plunged.

INSTANT GARDENING WITH POT PLANTS

Very many garden plants and the more hardy greenhouse plants can be pot grown under glass to give advanced and early flowering specimens. Dahlias are one example (see page 230), but many herbaceous perennials can be treated similarly. Plants like begonias, pelargoniums, fuchsias and impatiens can also be used as bedding and border plants, as well as greenhouse pot plants. Of course, great care must be taken not to put them out too early and they should be properly hardened off. These and many other greenhouse pot plants can also be planted in pots on terraces, patios or other paved areas, or in window-boxes, to give instant effect. Always keep a few pot plants in reserve to fill any gaps that may occur in beds or borders.

CUT FLOWERS UNDER GLASS

It is probably not worth while devoting a whole greenhouse to growing flowers for cutting. However, flower arrangement is at present so popular that some devotees might like to exploit these possibilities more fully. Many greenhouse plants will of course provide some beautiful and sophisticated material. In addition, most popular cut flowers can be grown in pots to give earlier blooms, and ones of a quality rarely attainable without weather protection. But remember that outdoor flowers should not be subjected to excessively high temperatures, and conditions must be as airy, cool and light as possible.

Roses can be grown in pots for early cut flowers (see page 173). Other notable cut flowers include chrysanthemums (pages 210, 230), carnations (page 208), gerberas (page 168), spring-flowering bulbs (page 138), many annuals such as stocks, antirrhinums and so forth (page 112), and orchids (page 215). Many of the foliage plants described in Chapter 11 can be used too.

Gladioli are often worth growing for cutting and very fine blooms can be obtained under glass. Planting can begin from mid January onwards, at a temperature of 45/50°F (7/10°C). Plant in large pots or, if you need a greater quantity, in polythene-lined troughs dug in the greenhouse floor and filled with compost. As long as you supply adequate support, you need plant the corms at a depth of only 1 to 2 inches, so as to give plenty of room for the roots. If they are not well supported they may topple over.

One of the most important cut flowers is the sweet pea. This can be sown in October, so that the plants can be overwintered in a frost-free greenhouse, or in January or February. In both cases grow the plants on under glass and harden off for early planting out and early cut flowers. If the sweet peas are to be grown under glass to the flowering stage, sowing is best done during September. In this case *some care is needed in selecting suitable varieties*. The early winter-flowering types will flower under the restricted light conditions of winter and spring. The large Spencers flower well under glass but rarely bloom before April, and often the buds drop off. The Cuthbertsons are easier though smaller, and have good stems for cutting. Sweet peas need all the winter light they can get and a greenhouse at least 5 feet high. All seedlings grown under glass should be stopped; otherwise treat them as described in any general gardening book.

HOUSE PLANTS

A greenhouse with a propagator will provide an endless source of exciting house plants. Many can be raised from seed and grown on in the greenhouse until they reach the decorative stage. House plants need to be changed about frequently, so that they can 'holiday' from time to time under greenhouse conditions of light and humidity. If you want an exotic display for a special occasion, you can bring some of the permanent greenhouse plants into the house for a short while. Most of the foliage plants described in Chapter 11 make fine house plants. A list of those which are easy to grow from seed is given in Table 2, page 134.

A popular house plant especially suited to greenhouse conditions is the poinsettia, *Euphorbia pulcherrima*. This often causes disappointment because it gets chilled. A minimum temperature of about 55°F (13°C) is essential, otherwise it quickly becomes a very sorry sight. Allow purchased plants to go dry slowly, then cut back the top growth and store the pots in the greenhouse until new shoots appear around May. Take cuttings of these shoots. Rooting is easiest under a mist propagator if you have one; otherwise use a closed propagator at about 65°F (18°C). The plants are then potted on as required and stopped when about 6 inches high to promote bushiness. Keep the compost nicely moist at all times, without wide fluctuations, or the foliage may fall. Poinsettias so raised will generally be taller and mature about November. Shop-bought plants are usually artificially dwarfed (see Appendix) and controlled by artificial light.

GENERAL GARDEN PROPAGATION AND SEEDLING PRODUCTION

Innumerable garden plants can be propagated from cuttings rooted under greenhouse conditions and grown on in pots under glass for a time. Mist propagation is particularly successful (see page 226).

Many choice, rare or unusual plants – border, alpine and shrub – can be raised from seed obtained from specialists (see Appendix). This is one specially interesting and exciting aspect of the way in which the greenhouse helps the garden, and I urge the reader to explore it. Too often gardens tend to be full of plants that can be seen anywhere. The greenhouse can make yours different.

The greenhouse is also invaluable for raising vegetable seedlings. Plants like lettuce, cabbage, cauliflower and onion can be sown in the greenhouse for subsequent planting out. For exhibition results it is sometimes worth growing on vegetable seedlings in pots to quite an advanced stage before setting out in the vegetable garden. The more tender vegetables (correctly fruits), like sweet pepper and aubergine, must always be grown under glass for a time before planting out in June. Only by giving them a long season of growth will you get reasonable crops. (See also Chapter 12, page 202.)

Appendix

MAJOR SUPPLIERS IN THE U.K.

All the plants, equipment and materials described in this book are available from one or other of the following firms. In some cases several firms supply the same items and there are often many others not mentioned here – this is only a selection. Most garden shops stock common items like pesticides suitable for the greenhouse, Coolglass shading, Cheshunt compound, tomato fertilizers, tomato set (Betapal), peat, potting composts, etc., and have a selection of common equipment.

GREENHOUSES

The catalogues of the following firms illustrate all the types described in Chapter 2. Many of these firms also supply frames. Aluminium: Crittall-Hope Ltd, Braintree, Essex (also steel); Alitex Ltd, Station Road, Alton, Hants (also construct to customers' specifications); Edenlite Ltd, Hawksworth Estate, Swindon SN2 1EQ; Westdock Ltd, Manchester Street, Hull HY3 4UB (high south wall); Tropical Greenhouses, Sanderson St, Sheffield S9 2TW (plastic-coated alloy); Robinsons of Winchester Ltd, Robinson House, Winnall Industrial Estate, Winchester SO23 8LH (erection service and simple foundation design, see page 31). Timber: Alton Glasshouses Ltd, Alton Works, Bewdley, Worcs; Robert H. Hall Ltd, Paddock Wood, Tonbridge, Kent; F. Pratten & Co., Ltd, Charlton Road, Midsomer Norton, Bath BA3 3AG. Plastic: Many firms advertise in the gardening and daily press. For plastic sheeting of all kinds – Transatlantic Plastic Ltd, Garden Estate, Ventnor, Isle of Wight. Plastic greenhouses: Engsure Ltd, 36 Tooley St, London SE1 2SZ.

ELECTRICAL HEATING AND AUTOMATION

Simplex of Cambridge Ltd, Sawston, Cambridge CB2 4J (also warming cables, sterilizers, mist units, propagators, automatic watering and ventilation, artificial lighting and electrical fittings).

OIL HEATERS (WICK-TYPE)

Aladdin Industries Ltd, Kingway, Fforestfach Industrial Estate, Swansea, Glamorgan SA5 4HB (also automatic filling, see page 39); George H. Elt Ltd, Eltex Works, Worcester (also suppliers of oil-heated propagators).

OIL HEATERS (OTHER TYPES)

Fossewarmair, 1 Reservoir Road, Kidderminster DY11 7AP (burns central-heating grade oils; heat distribution by convection of warm air); Woodland Park Engineering, Benston Road, Cumnock, Ayrshire, Scotland (to fit hot water pipes; burns waste sump oil from garages).

NATURAL GAS HEATING

Bradley-Nicholson & Co., Brettenham House, Lancaster Place, Strand, London WC2E 7EN; Shilton Garden Products, 390 City Road, London EC1V 2QA; George H. Elt Ltd, Eltex Works, Worcester. Also consult local gas showroom. For local suppliers of bottled gas see Yellow Pages of telephone book (they also supply changeover valves; see page 43).

HEATING – AUTOMATIC AIDS OF ALL DESCRIPTIONS, MANY ACCESSORIES, GADGETS, ETC.

House and Garden Automation, 186 High Street, Barnet, Herts (also capillary watering matting, see page 64).

FAN HEATERS AND ELECTRICAL EQUIPMENT, MIST UNITS, ETC.

Autogrow Ltd, Quay Road, Blyth, Northumberland; Parwin Power, Holme Road, Yaxley, Peterborough, PE7 3NA (fan heaters without continuously running fan).

GENERAL GREENHOUSE EQUIPMENT OF ALL KINDS

Humex Ltd, 5 High Road, Byfleet, Surrey KT14 7QF (also instruments, thermometers and Panasand, see page 65, blinds, propagators, etc.).

HOT WATER HEATING (OIL AND SOLID FUEL)

H. E. Phillips Ltd, King William Street, Coventry, Warwicks CV1 5JH; Metallic Heaters Ltd, Bridge Works, Alfreton Road, Derby.

PHOTO-ELECTRIC IRRIGATION (see pages 66 and 226)

Wright Rain Ltd, Crow Arch Lane, Ringwood, Hants.

CAPILLARY SAND BENCH UNITS AND TRICKLE WATERING

Nethergreen Products Ltd, P.O. Box 3, Alderley Edge, Cheshire SK9 7JJ (also Algofen, see page 83).

FRAMES AND IRRIGATION EQUIPMENT

Access Frames, Yelvertoft Road, Crick, Northampton NN6 7XS. Most greenhouse manufacturers supply frames.

MOISTURE METER

(Graduated with reference tables – see page 54) J. M. A. Scientific Ltd, 152 Nelson Road, Twickenham TW2 7BX. Audio moisture and fertilizer tester (page 54) J. S. M. Marketing Ltd, 66 Carter Lane, London EC4V 5EA.

GENERAL SUNDRIES, POTS, TOOLS, FERTILIZERS, COOLGLASS SHADING, ETC.

E. J. Woodman & Son Ltd, High Street, Pinner, Middlesex.

HORTICULTURAL CHEMICALS, FERTILIZER MIXTURES FOR HOME COMPOST MAKING, PLANT HORMONES, DWARFING CHEMICALS

Chempak Products, Brewhouse Lane, Hertford SG14 1JS; Medlock Chemicals, 8 The Grove, Stubbington, Fareham, Hants. (Note: The use of Cycocel on edible crops is still experimental, and the chemical has not so far been given safety clearance for this purpose by the Ministry of Agriculture.)

PEAT, PEAT COMPOSTS, TOM BAGS, ACID AND SPECIAL COMPOSTS

Alexander Products Ltd, Burnham on Sea, Somerset.

LIQUISAFENED CHLORATE (page 49), FILLIP (page 81), SPRAYDAY (page 86), ROOTA (page 221), AND COOLGLASS (page 52).

Products of Pan Britannica Industries, supplied by most garden shops.

SEEDSMEN

Sutton & Sons Ltd, Reading, Berks (general); W. J. Unwin Ltd, Histon, Cambridge (general); Samuel Dobie & Son Ltd, Upper

Dee Mills, Llangollen, Denbighshire LL20 8SD (general and greenhouse plant seeds); Thompson & Morgan Ltd, Ipswich (general and very wide range of rare and unusual seeds, palms, succulents, alpines, etc.); M. Holtzhausen, 14 High Cross Street, St Austell, Cornwall (rare seeds and bulbs, and curiosities).

PLANTSMEN

Thomas Butcher, Shirley, Croydon, Surrey (exotics, palms, smithianthas, rare pot plants and seeds, nerines); B. Wall, 4 Selbourne Close, New Haw, Weybridge, Surrey (bromeliad and begonia species specialist, many other greenhouse pot plants); Steven Bailey Ltd, Eden Nurseries, Sway, Hants (carnation and gerbera specialist); Blackmore & Langdon Ltd, Bath, Somerset (prize begonia specialist, also cyclamen and gloxinias); Wallace & Barr Ltd, Marden, Kent (bulb specialists, rare greenhouse bulbs, nerines, lilies); Walter Blom & Son Ltd, Leavesden, Watford, Herts (general bulb specialist); W. E. Th. Ingwersen Ltd, Birch Farm Nursery, Gravetye, East Grinstead, Sussex (alpine plant specialist); Burnham Nurseries Ltd, Kingsteignton, Newton Abbot, Devon (orchid specialist); Thomas Rochford & Sons Ltd, Hoddesdon, Herts (foliage plants and exotics – their plants can be ordered from any florist. The firm does not supply direct); Holly Gate Nurseries Ltd, Billingshurst Lane, Ashington, Sussex (cacti and other succulents); Blackmore Nurseries, Liss, Hants (fruit); Treseder's Nurseries, Truro, Cornwall (camellias and half-hardy shrubs); Hillier & Sons, Winchester, Hants (choice shrubs, climbers and many half-hardy shrubs and plants including rare varieties); Nerine Nurseries, Welland, Worcestershire (nerines, named varieties and species); K. J. Townsend, 17 Valerie Close, St Albans, Herts AL1 5JD (Achimenes specialist, page 141); Efenechtyd Nurseries, Efenechtyd, Ruthin, Clwyd LL15 2PW (Streptocarpus specialist, p. 177); H. Woolman Ltd, Grange Road, Dorridge, Solihull B90 3NQ (chrysanthemum specialists, general greenhouse plants, fuchsias, pelargoniums, carnations, begonias, gloxinias, and many bulbs, tubers, etc.). Ken Muir, Weeley Heath, Clacton-on-Sea, CO16 9BJ (Strawberries).

Canadian Greenhouse Manufacturers and Suppliers of Accessories

Arnott Industries, P.O. Box 10, Grimsby, Ontario L3M 4G1; Canadian Greenhouses, P.O. Box 5000, Durham Road, Beamsville, Ontario L0R 1B0; English Aluminium Greenhouses Ltd, 1201–12 Deerford Road, Willowdale, Ontario M2J 3J3; Garden of Eden Sales, P.O. Box 405, Pickering, Ontario L1V 2R6; Lord & Burnham Co. Ltd, 325 Welland Avenue, St Catherines, Ontario; Golden West Seeds, 1108 6th Street S.E., Calgary, Alberta; Prevost Farms Ltd, 45063 South Sumar Road, R.R. #4, Sardis, British Columbia.

American Greenhouse Manufacturers and Suppliers of Accessories

Aluminium Greenhouses, Inc., 14615 Lorain Avenue, Cleveland, Ohio 44111; Garden of Eden Sales, 875 East Jericho Turnpike, Huntington Station, New York 11746; Gothic Arch Greenhouses, Box 1564, Mobile, Alabama 36601; Lord & Burnham, Irvington, New York 10533; Redfern Greenhouses, 57-P11, Mt Herman Road, Scotts Valley, California 95066; Redwood Domes, Box 666, Aptos, California 95003; Stearns Greenhouses, 98 Taylor Street, Neponset, Massachusetts 02122; StudiBuilt Manufacturing Company, 11304 S.W. Boones Ferry Road, Portland, Oregon 97219.

ACCESSORIES

Charley's Greenhouse Supplies, 1244 N.E. 124th Street, Kirkland, Washington 98033 (general); E. and W. International, 290 Sandringham Road, Rochester, New York 14610 (automatic watering devices); Sudbury Laboratory, Inc., Box 1028, Sudbury, Massachusetts 01776 (soil-testing equipment).

General Index

General Index

Plant Index

Plant Index

Plant Index

Plant Index